ANGLO-JEWRY IN CHANGING TIMES

Parkes–Wiener Series on Jewish Studies
SERIES EDITORS: DAVID CESARANI AND TONY KUSHNER

The field of Jewish Studies is one of the youngest, but fastest growing and most exciting areas of scholarship in the academic world today. Named after James Parkes and Alfred Wiener and recognising the co-operative relationship between the Parkes Centre at the University of Southampton and the Wiener Library in London, this series aims to publish new research in the field and student materials for use in the seminar room, and to re-issue classic studies which are currently out of print.

The selection of publications will reflect the international character and diversity of Jewish Studies; it will range over Jewish history from Abraham to modern Zionism, and Jewish culture from Moses to post-modernism. The series will also reflect the multi-disciplinary approach inherent in Jewish Studies and at the cutting edge of contemporary scholarship, and will provide an outlet for innovative work on the interface between Judaism and ethnicity, popular culture, gender, class, space and memory.

ANGLO-JEWRY
IN CHANGING TIMES

Studies in Diversity 1840–1914

ISRAEL FINESTEIN

VALLENTINE MITCHELL
LONDON • PORTLAND, OR

First published in 1999 in Great Britain by
VALLENTINE MITCHELL
Newbury House, 900 Eastern Avenue
London IG2 7HH

and in the United States of America by
VALLENTINE MITCHELL
c/o ISBS, 5804 N.E. Hassalo Street
Portland, Oregon 97213-3644

Website http://www.vmbooks.com

British Library Cataloguing in Publication Data

Finestein, Israel
  Anglo-Jewry in changing times: studies in diversity,
  1840–1914. – (Parkes–Wiener series)
  1. Jews – Great Britain 2. Jews – Great Britain –
  Civilization 3. Jews – Great Britain – History – 1789–1945
  I. Title
  941'.004924

            ISBN 0 85303 354 4 (cloth)
            ISBN 0 85303 355 2 (paper)
            ISSN 1368–5449

Library of Congress Cataloging-in-Publication Data

Finestein, I.
  Anglo-Jewry in changing times : studies in diversity, 1840–1914 /
  Israel Finestein.
    p.   cm. – (Parkes–Wiener series)
  Includes bibliographical references and index.
  ISBN 0-85303-354-4. – ISBN 0-85303-355-2 (pbk.)
    1. Jews–Great Britain–History–19th century.   2. Raphall, Morris
  J. (Morris Jacob) 1798–1868.   3. Adler, Hermann, 1839–1911.
  4. Great Britain–Ethnic relations.   I. Title.
  DS135.E5F45   1999
  941'.004924–dc21   98-47121
                                                                CIP

Typeset by Vitaset, Paddock Wood, Kent
Printed in Great Britain by
Bookcraft (Bath) Ltd, Midsomer Norton, Somerset

TO THE MEMORY OF
PROFESSOR MOSHE DAVIS OF JERUSALEM
1916–1996
FRIEND, COLLEAGUE, AND MENTOR

Contents

List of Illustrations

Acknowledgements

Each of these chapters is an expansion of a lecture given by the author to the following bodies respectively: Chs. 1, 4 and 6, to the Jewish Historical Society of England. Ch. 2, to the Jews' College Union Society. Ch. 3, to the conference at University College London organised by the Institute of Jewish Studies and the Oxford Centre for Postgraduate Hebrew Studies in 1985: the paper was originally published in Jonathan Frankel and Steven J. Zipperstein (eds), *Assimilation and Community: The Jews in Nineteenth-Century Europe*, Cambridge University Press, 1992. Ch. 5, to the Second International Scholars Colloquium on American-Holy Land Studies in Washington: major part published in Moshe Davis (ed.), *With Eyes Toward Zion*, Vol. 2, Praeger, New York, 1986. Ch. 7, to Leo Baeck College: part published in *The Jewish Quarterly*, London, Vol. 23, 1976. Ch. 8 is a composite and expanded form of two lectures given to the Jewish Historical Society of England and University College London (Department of Hebrew and Jewish Studies) respectively.

Thanks are expressed for permission to reprint, where appropriate.

Acknowledgement is also made to the following sources for the illustrations:

1. Grace Aguilar, from *The Universal Jewish Encyclopedia, Volume 1*, 1948.
2. Tobias Theodores, from Bill Williams, *Manchester Jewry, 1740–1875*, Manchester University Press, 1976.
3. Solomon Almosnino, from Albert M. Hyamson, *The Sephardim of England: A History of the Spanish and Portuguese Jewish Community 1492–1951*, Methuen and Co. Ltd, 1951.

   Reproduced from a portrait in possession of the Congregation
   of the Spanish and Portuguese Synagogue, London.
4. Jacob Franklin, from *The Jewish Chronicle 1841–1941*, Jewish
   Chronicle, 1949.
5. The Jews' Infant School Ball at Willis's Rooms, from Anne and
   Roger Cowen, *Victorian Jews Through British Eyes*, Oxford
   University Press for The Littman Library, 1986. Reproduced
   from an illustration by Francis Wilfred Lawson which originally
   appeared in *The Graphic*, 5 May 1872.
6. Solomon Schiller-Szinessy, from *Transactions*, Jewish Historical
   Society of Great Britain (J.H.S.E.), Vol. XXI, 1968. Reproduced from an engraving by I. Fischer. With thanks to Professor
   Raphael Loewe.
7. Moses Samuel, from Philip Ettinger, *Hope Place (Congregation) in Liverpool Jewry*, 1930.
8. Nathan Marcus Adler, from C. Roth, *History of the Great
   Synagogue 1690–1940*, Edward Goldston & Son Ltd, 1950.
9. Benjamin Artom, from Albert M. Hyamson, *The Sephardim of
   England: A History of the Spanish and Portuguese Jewish
   Community 1492–1951*, Methuen and Co. Ltd, 1951. Reproduced from a portrait in possession of the Congregation of the
   Spanish and Portuguese Synagogue, London.
10. Aaron Levy Green, from *Transactions*, J.H.S.E., Vol. XXV,
    1977. Reproduced by kind permission of the London School
    of Jewish Studies.
11. Morris Joseph, from *West London Synagogue Magazine*,
    Memorial Issue, Vol. 4, 1930.
12. David Myer Isaacs, from Philip Ettinger, *Hope Place
    (Congregation) in Liverpool Jewry*, 1930.
13. University College London, from Gerry Black, *Living Up West*,
    London Museum of Jewish Life, 1994.
14. Henry Sidgwick, from A. Sidgwick and E.M. Sidgwick, *Henry
    Sidgwick*, 1906.
15. Numa Edward Hartog, from Mabel Hartog, *P.J. Hartog*,
    Constable, 1949.
16. Marion Hartog, from Mabel Hartog, *P.J. Hartog*, Constable,
    1949.
17. Morris Jacob Raphall, from *Jerusalem Post*, 6 February 1976.
    Reproduced from an oil painting in possession of Bnai Jeshurun
    Congregation of New York.

18. David Aaron de Sola, from *Transactions*, J.H.S.E., Vol. XXI, 1968. Reproduced from a painting by N. Raphael.
19. The Birmingham Hebrew National School, from Zoe Josephs, *Birmingham Jewry 1749–1914*, Birmingham Jewish Research Group, 1980. Reproduced from an illustration from *The Birmingham Weekly Post*.
20. Matthew Arnold, from Charles H. Harvey, *Matthew Arnold: A Critic of the Victorian Period*, James Clarke & Co. Ltd, 1931.
21. Hermann Adler, from Olga Somech Phillips and Hyman A. Simons, *The History of the Bayswater Synagogue 1863–1963*, 1963.
22. Aaron Asher Green, from Rabbi Raymond Apple, *History of the Hampstead Synagogue 1892–1967*, 1967.
23. Francis Lyon Cohen, from Rabbi Raymond Apple, 'Francis Lyon Cohen', *Australian Jewish Historical Society Journal*, 1995.
24. Israel Abrahams, from E.R. Bevan and Charles Singer (eds), *The Legacy of Israel*, 1928. Reproduced from a painting by M. Cohen in possession of the Liberal Synagogue, London.
25. 'Jewish immigrants just landed' from G.A. Simms, *Living in London, Volume 1*, 1902.
26. Jacob Moser, from *Encyclopedia Judaica, Volume 12*, 1971. Reproduced from Schwadron Collection.
27. Leon Simon, from Bill Williams, *Manchester Jewry: A Pictorial History 1788–1988*, Archive Publications, 1988.
28. Selig Brodetsky, from Professor Selig Brodetsky, *Memoirs: From Ghetto to Israel*, Weidenfeld and Nicolson, 1960.

The Publisher has attempted to contact all appropriate copyright holders in respect of material used in this book. In certain cases this has not been possible and the Publisher apologises to any such copyright holders for this omission.

Introduction

This book is about changing times. More particularly it is concerned with people's differing responses. The context is almost entirely the Jewish community. Where that is not so, there is an interrelation with the Jewish theme. Much of the substance of these studies has a continuing contemporary ring.

Many factors which transformed society at large in Britain operated no less upon its Jewish constituent. These included the progress of the new sciences; the extension of industry and commerce; the expansion of population; the rise of new or hugely expanded towns, large urban concentrations, and the widening social and economic divergencies between rich and poor; the emergence of new and quicker means of transport; and the advancing political, social and religious influence of the middle classes.

Between the presentation of the first Bill in 1830 for the civil emancipation of the Jews, and the death of Hermann Adler in 1911, the Jews in Britain increased tenfold to close on 300,000. The increasingly open western society thrust forward challenges to those who remembered or who chose to cultivate outlooks of an earlier age. The rapidity of change sharpened the edge of every challenge. Meanwhile each successive generation, seeking to determine its own preferences, became itself subject to fresh nuances of thought.

The Jewish community became and remained a community of communities. Increasingly self-conscious provincial Jewish centres came into being. There arose a multiplicity of sources of lay and religious authority. The modern-style diversity of opinion, aspiration, and priority took root. In the metropolitan area, where the bulk of the community lived, changed relationships became ever more deeply marked. In varying degrees through the century, the impact of Jewish immigration was a major element in all these developments.

There could not fail to arise among the Jews as elsewhere, new styles of approach and new types of question to authority at all levels and to inherited conventions of thought and action. The ceaseless flow of change provides all these chapters with their connecting link, their historical interest and their human element.

In these chapters, dealing with a comparatively compact period and at times with interrelated themes, some minimal overlap was inescapable. It is limited to the extent required to give each chapter its own degree of completeness.

I am obliged to Professor A.N. Newman of Leicester for certain helpful suggestions. To Mr Frank Cass and his team at Vallentine Mitchell, notably Miss Hilary Hewitt and Mrs Rachel Joseph, I am grateful for the effective application to this work of their well-known publishing and editorial skills, combined with their characteristic courtesy.

My prime thanks, as ever, are to my wife, whose loving help and patience were, as only I know, crucial to this book.

Israel Finestein
London, August 1998

1

Early Victorian Anglo-Jewry: Aspirations and Reality

Civic and political emancipation was seen by those in the Jewish community who strove for it, as a recognition that the community had become or should be regarded as being a religious communion and nothing more. The Jews were, in the thinking and language of Sir David Salomons, one of the elements in the great and multi-faceted Nonconformist grouping in society, one of the religious bodies out of conformity with the Established Church. The term 'Jew' tended to replace 'Hebrew' as the Jewish self-designation; 'Jewish religion' was increasingly preferred to 'Jewish nation' to describe the context of Jewish life.

Many factors promoted such changes. Among them were the social advance and progressive Anglicisation of the Jewish middle classes; the enhanced proportion of native-born Jews following the virtual cessation of immigration during the long French wars; and some of the principles of the American and French revolutions. The 'denationalisation' of the Jews appeared natural. It was an instinctive matter, but it was also perceived as sensible public relations. The development was thought to be somehow in tune with the technological progress of the age and with the spirit of the spreading new philosophies of utilitarianism, individualism and political reform. In the newly emerging era some considered the old prejudices against Jews so plainly outdated, as likely to be socially 'outlawed'. In a coming world of improved education and heightened national prosperity, the Jews would be at ease in society.

The optimism inherent in this outlook was belied by facts but not ousted. It was shaken by periodic declarations and events which demonstrated that neither the 'spirit of the age' nor the new social studies had eroded the ancient malaise. The continued Jewish particularity, Jewish international bonds, and the undenied Jewish 'national' aspiration, inescapably encouraged that old state of mind, notwithstanding, and in part because of, the strenuously canvassed emancipation. It was not until the twentieth century that the old optimism, centring on the highly and overtly self-conscious image of the Jewish Englishman, fell away under pressure of a new and painful pragmatism which life thrust upon the genealogical and ideological heirs of the early and mid-Victorian leaders of Jewish society.

To manifest the ambition to be regarded as Jewish Englishmen, and to illustrate the justice of it and the expected benefit to society of their being so deemed, was in early Victorian England (as later) the up-to-date attitude. This was especially so among the secularly educated younger generation of the rising Jewish middle classes. It was a position held with all the fervour of new initiates.

In 1833 Francis Goldsmid published a second edition of his impressive first emancipationist pamphlet which first appeared in 1831. It was in reply to arguments levelled against the proposed abolition of Jewish civil disabilities. In the first edition he wrote: 'It is true that the Hebrews continue often to assume the denomination of a separate people which scripture in ancient times more appropriately bestowed upon them.' The implication was that such a character is less appropriate now. Two years later, in his revised version, the words 'the *Hebrews* continue *often* to assume', are changed into 'the *Jews* still *occasionally* assume'. Eloquent revision indeed. It was designed to meet more felicitously the now more favourable opinions of the new House of Commons following the Reform Act of 1832.

One of the first express repudiations of the term 'the Jewish nation' is found in the long, well-informed open letter addressed to Sir Moses Montefiore, signed 'M' in February 1844. Montefiore's enthusiasm for Jewish emancipation was not of the 'quasi-messianic' nature which so enlivened the political campaigns of his friend, Francis Goldsmid, or his kinsman by marriage, David Salomons. The writer of the letter, among many suggestions for the strengthening of communal life in matters of education, synagogue management and communal administration, voiced his concern over the continuing charge that the Jews have 'an internal

2

nationality'. The truth, he wrote, was that 'save in the slight affairs of our various congregations and the charitable provisions for our poor ... our further collective interests have been hitherto left to the keeping of the winds'. Montefiore may well have wondered whether these expressions could in any way reflect the ancient purport of many of his traditional prayers, or be at all reconciled with the collective Jewish response to the events and charges in Damascus in 1840, or relate to his own impulsion and motivation in his visits to Jerusalem. But Montefiore's 'old-world' reservations were not typical of his circle.

There were many examples of the new approach. One of the most interesting is afforded by the anniversary dinner in aid of the London Hospital in 1842. Of the 130 gentlemen who that year attended this annual event, between 30 and 40 were Jews. For reasons of history, geography and public policy, Jews regularly figured among the munificent supporters of that hospital in Whitechapel, between which and the local Jewish population there were many ties of service and memory. As was customary, the Jews at the dinner occupied a special table for the easier observation of the dietary laws. The Governor of the Bank of England presided overall, flanked by notable City and parliamentary personalities. That year was one of particular significance since in the new wing of the hospital, wards had been set aside for Jewish patients. The reasons were religious, mainly connected with the provision of kosher food and the preference of some Jewish patients for a Jewish ambience.

At all previous dinners, there had been a toast to 'the Hebrew nation'. This year, by request, it was omitted. The basis for the omission was, somewhat paradoxically, that no separate Jewish interest within the hospital wards now existed. Jewish patients had their own arrangements but this should be seen as part of the whole. Perhaps such matters should not be examined logically. The dinner was held at the height of a revived campaign in the City for emancipatory legislation. There was now a toast to the 'Trustees of the Hebrew Fund' through which the Jewish wards were largely sustained.[1] The change could not have been lost on the assembly. It touched upon sensitive issues. The dinner attracted attention in the general and Jewish press.

In her *History of the Jews in England* (published posthumously in 1847) Grace Aguilar (1816–47) wrote: 'In externals and in all

1. Grace Aguilar (1816–47), novelist and social commentator

secular thoughts and actions, the English naturalised Jew is an Englishman, and his family is reared with the education and accomplishments of other members of the community. Only in some private and personal characteristics, and in religious belief, does the Jew differ from his neighbours.' This was on her part a hope as well as an assessment of the current scene, written as much for the enlightenment of querulous gentile readers as for the encouragement of fellow-Jews. It must have occurred to her that these expressions were not in her day easily accommodated into the spirit of her many references in her other writings to Jewish national 'heroes' of the past, or the international kinship and joint aspirations of the Jews, or the religio-national content of the Jewish faith which she lauded.

In her generation it seemed self-evident to many Christians that the Jews constituted a separate and distinct nation, and that as Jews they were incapable of being Englishmen, whatever their loyalty to the Crown. The most eloquent exponent of this view outside Parliament was Dr Thomas Arnold, headmaster of Rugby and Regius Professor in Modern History at Oxford. In the House of Commons probably the longest serving and among the most vocal unswerving opponents of the admission of Jews into municipal government or Parliament was Sir Robert Inglis, for many years Gladstone's fellow-representative for Oxford University. His case rested not on any moral disparagement of the Jews who were eager to enter but on the fact that he could not consider it right to allow non-Englishmen and non-Britons, as he perceived them, into those governing assemblies.

Prominent among those Jews in Britain who expressed some

2. Professor Tobias Theodores (1808–86), Orientalist and a
founder of the Manchester Reform Congregation

acknowledgement of the fragility of the 'progressive' framework
of the new age, was Tobias Theodores (1808–86) of Manchester,
the German-born Hebrew scholar and a leading figure in the
Reform movement. The Damascus Affair and the attitudes towards
the anti-Jewish charges in sections of public opinion in the West,
alerted him. He was an effective rebutter in *The Times* in November
1840 of the 'blood libel' against the Jews. He later defended the
Talmud against its anti-Jewish detractors, without prejudice to his
sharing David Woolf Marks' detachment from the binding authority
of the oral law. He declared that it was 'the duty ... of every Jew
to ... strain every nerve ... that the cause of civilization and of
education should be everywhere promoted', in order thus to help
protect 'the moral world' against those who might seek to undo it.

Such high-minded formulation of Jewish duty was part of the
stream of Jewish opinion which was to be ever more heard in that
century under the heading of the 'Jewish mission'. Many Jews in
Britain took the idea of 'mission' all the more seriously by reason
of their belief in the perceived role of Britain as a leader in the
cultivation of the 'moral world', and the consequent special

5

obligation, as was expressed, upon her Jewish community to advance, by precept and example, the cause and the practice of good citizenship. It was a form of Jewish particularism which did nothing to disarm those critics who propounded the doctrine of the irretrievable separatism and apartness of the Jews.

Jews at the time accepted and sometimes applauded a form of two-edged advocacy which was common among Christians (and some Jewish) exponents of the cause of Jewish emancipation. It was presented in polite and respectful terms, by no one more politely or more pointedly than Alderman David Wire, later Lord Mayor, in 1848. He was a familiar supporter of all the moves in the City taken to advance that cause, a close personal friend of Montefiore, and a companion on his journey to the East in 1840. Addressing a large and widely reported public meeting convened by the Jewish Association for the Removal of Civil and Religious Disabilities, he spoke, not for the only time, of the greatness of the Jewish cultural contribution to western civilisation. He compared it favourably with that of Greece and Rome. Yet it might be said, he observed, that the Jews have since degenerated. He added: 'Admit the statement for the sake of argument. I have yet to know on what grounds those who had inflicted degradation and misery should make it an argument for the continuation of the evil ...'. Civil and political emancipation would elevate them. Jews showed some eagerness to demonstrate their gratitude for the opportunity. It was a strand in Jewish public relations which marks the age.

In 1916, Morris Joseph, then Senior Minister at the West London Synagogue of British Jews, and Marks' successor as such, wrote that 'to give ourselves more earnestly to Jewish culture, to add its fruits to the common treasury of Englishmen is to enrich England, to show ourselves capable of the very highest patriotism'. Allowing for the fact that this was written in wartime, the sentiments expressed by the Reform rabbi and the peculiar force of his language are in direct line of succession to emancipationist Anglo-Jewish thought in and around the 1840s. Indeed it was foreshadowed in David Ricardo's once famous speech in the House of Commons in 1823 in which the case for the abolition of the Jewish disabilities was first set out fully in the House. The Jewishness of the Jew, including his unfolding of his literary heritage, was viewed as part of his Englishness and marked his entitlement to the rank of Jewish

6

Englishman. It is ironic that influential lay leaders in the nineteenth century while espousing these ideas, often fell short of exercising their power or using their wealth to facilitate in practice or to encourage the scholarly pursuit in Britain of the heritage.

Anxious, as the leading families expressed themselves to be, to advance the cultural level of the Jewish community generally, the sentiment appears to have had a consistent and severely limited scope. Such scope was the provision of some means to enable the foreign Jew, the poor Jew, the hardworking 'mechanic', and the petty salesman, to become more familiar with the rudiments of general culture and more demonstrably attached to British ways, as well as, where necessary, more knowledgeable about the basic tenets of Judaism and its main practices. It was publicly declared, time without number, that this was necessary to demonstrate that Jews have interests other than the pursuit of material gain. Linked with that rationale was the earnest desire that those who led the drive for emancipation should be seen to strive for 'improvement' in terms of the Anglicisation both of the Jewish foreigner and what were often called the Jewish 'humbler classes'.

Marcus Bresslau, combatively and with some journalistic licence, looked back in the mid-50s to the early years of the century. Hebrew scholarship, he wrote, had come to be regarded as 'superfluous' or 'out of date'. The attention of Jews, he charged, had been diverted by 'the rapid advance of commerce, the spread of wealth, the refinements of luxury … in imitation of the surrounding wealthy neighbours'. Whatever might have been thought about this over-dramatic portrayal, it could not be gainsaid that the contemporary comment that 'the Jewish spirit is daily becoming fainter in the minds of our rich and middle classes' reflected reality among a large element within those segments of Jewish society.

The idea that Hebrew classics might be made available in their original language and/or in translation or that rabbinic literature or current Jewish philosophic works might be made available in translation, was considered to involve too great a cost. It was thought to border on luxury in the face of the physical requirements and elementary educational needs of the poor; or the idea was not entertained in any event at all. Associated with these perspectives was the disinclination to endow or significantly assist interested Jewish scholars (generally of recent arrival) to examine and present material from or relating to the considerable body of Hebrew manuscripts in the libraries of England. That Anglo-Jewry might have a role in the cultivation and projection of the Jewish 'new learning', sounded like a foreign-style aspiration, carrying at best a low priority. To endow Jewish higher learning for those from whatever rank in Jewish society who might wish to embark thereon, seemed in practice as much removed from communal goals as the notion of the necessity to take concerted action for the creation of an adequate system of recruitment and training for the Jewish ministry – some of which rank might indeed have emerged as significant figures in the pursuit of and teaching in Jewish higher studies.

Continental examples were of only passing interest to the generality of the communal 'elite'. It was said that in another country Morris Jacob Raphall would have been the head of a 'Jewish College', and that there was no place in Britain commensurate with his gifts and potential within the context of the European Jewish Enlightenment. There was a tendency to confuse literary patronage with charity and not to perceive it in relation to the communal system or the character of the Jewish community. Private benefactions were unaccompanied by any broad perspective of the benefit to the Jewish community of what indeed a later generation was to bemoan was lacking, namely a Jewishly learned laity.

At approximately ten-year intervals there were attempts by Jewish writers or interested laymen in London to establish a movement to promote Jewish literature. They were short-lived. The first of these efforts resulted in the struggling year-long Society for the Cultivation of Hebrew Language and Literature in 1830–31. It represented the ripples in Britain of the Mendelssohnian stir on the Continent. Among its principal figures were Raphall, David Aaron de Sola, Michael Josephs, Sampson Samuel (later Secretary of the Board of Deputies) and Leopold Neumegen (headmaster of the Jewish school in Highgate, popular among the Jewish middle classes). It was noted that for some years no Jews' Free School anniversary dinner was regarded as complete without a specially composed Hebrew ode, often by Josephs – sometimes published in full with English translation (often by Samuel) in the *Jewish Chronicle*.

In 1842, with de Sola, Abraham Benisch and Israel Lindenthal as prime movers, a plan was devised to build up a circulating library among subscribers of current Jewish works (mainly in German or Hebrew), mostly by the *Meassafim*,[2] with English translations. In significant if somewhat wishful words, the *Voice of Jacob* described the effort as 'an offspring of that spirit of progress which is now awakening in many congregations in Great Britain'. The editor of that journal, Jacob Franklin, contrasted the proposed library with the 'ancient recondite Hebrew works suited only to the profound Hebraist' in the libraries of the Ashkenazi *Beth Hamedrash* and the comparable collection in the Sephardi congregation. He added: 'No less indispensable are the modern works in other languages ... not only as necessary auxiliaries to the profounder studies of the Talmud but also essential for the qualification of a Jewish theologian of the present day.' There we have an inkling of Franklin's opinions as to the kind of Ministry required in the new age.[3]

He and Henry Faudel, a London-born merchant, were in the forefront of the public pressure for the creation of a seminary for the training of such Ministry as a fitting commemoration of Montefiore's mission to the East. By pamphlets and in the Jewish press they urged this cause.

There is in the Library of Jews' College, London, a four-page brochure which from internal evidence clearly belongs to 1841, written by one of them, entitled *What is due from the Jews on the success of the mission to the East*. It sets out the case for such an establishment with considerable eloquence and force; and the argument was further taken up in the *Voice of Jacob*.

In January 1842, in response to the strength of the argument, there was convened at the Great Synagogue a meeting of influential names, including the lay heads of the London Synagogues, presided over by Isaac Cohen, who was Montefiore's brother-in-law and the senior warden of the Great Synagogue. The meeting had been formally convened by the Chief Rabbi, Solomon Hirschell, but this frail signatory gave no lead. Franklin attended and amply reported the deliberations of the assembly in his newspaper. No concerted scheme was presented or evolved. There were powerful voices in favour of marking the mission by the presentation of an ornate silver plate gift to Montefiore. Lionel de Rothschild was prominent in the advocacy of the creation of a fund in support of such a presentation. Franklin's continued advocacy did not impress.[4] Soon

9

in that year the secessionist controversy in the community reached a new height and the movement which he had initiated waned. Hirschell's death in 1842 and the consequent public discussions over the style of, and the expectations from, a new incumbent discouraged immediate action.

Franklin abandoned his campaign on the express ground that there was a grossly inadequate appreciation of the importance of the scheme. He had envisaged the raising of a substantial sum to found a college to which parents in 'the higher classes' of Jewish society might send their sons for ministerial training. It was not a widely held parental ambition.

In August 1842 it became known that of the monies raised for the Damascus Appeal Fund there was an unexpended balance.[5] The promoters of the Fund announced their intention to return the balance to the donors at the rate of one-fifth of each of the respective contributions. Knowledge of this balance impelled Franklin to urge that the money should be used to maintain gifted Anglo-Jewish youths who might be sent to continental Jewish seminaries, pending their return to Britain as possible ministerial candidates. He regarded this as an urgent interim measure in view of the apparent current disinterest in the matter of setting up a British-based seminary, which he continued to declare was the 'most pressing want of the day'. His new plan did not deflect the promoters from their intention. Their decision may have had good legal grounds as well as reflecting their own negative appraisal of the scheme's viability and communal value. The dispatch of Anglo-Jewish young men for ministerial training abroad at a time when Anglicisation was a highly spoken-of desideratum was not an attractive policy. Yet neither, it seems, was a native establishment a compelling attraction for them.

It was against this background that Franklin campaigned with all the greater enthusiasm for support for the library promoted by de Sola and his associates. The merit of that proposal was its potential effect, even on a limited scale, in elevating the Jewish cultural level within the Jewish community.

Among the express grounds on which the *Voice of Jacob* urged support for the proposed library was 'the attention – which is fixed upon (the Jews) throughout the civilised world'. This comment was a reference to the prominence of Jewish themes in the international and domestic scenes – the Damascus Affair, the Palestine-oriented activities of the Great Powers, the intensification of the oppression of Jews in the Czarist Empire, the growing emancipation in the west, and the messianic element in much of the then thinking about Jews, notably in connection with the growing Christian conversionist efforts. The fashionable 'apologetical' nature of Franklin's thinking is clear. His message was that the Jews (and the world) should know their literary treasures (modern, medieval and ancient) and Jews should be seen to take pride in them, for they are part of the Jewish title to acceptance, uniqueness, and respect. Yet uppermost in his campaigns was his sense of the needs of the changing Jewish community. He was a communal pragmatist.

The efforts of de Sola and his colleagues, who also planned a series of scholarly public lectures, soon petered out through lack of support. The proposed publication presupposed some familiarity with Hebrew or German. Translations were expensive. Those with means lacked adequate interest. Those with interest generally lacked adequate means. Private charity was called on to meet unprecedented demands for the relief of the poor in the 'hungry forties'. Communal leadership was locked in secessionist disputes and/or in the politics of emancipation.

In 1845 came the great breakthrough on the Parliamentary front. Municipal office was opened to professing Jews. In 1847 the wider struggle for the opening of Parliament began in earnest. In the interim period there were hopes for a forward move of influential interest in the promotion of Jewish studies in Britain. It proved a largely vain hope. The *Jewish Chronicle* in October 1846 commented that the Jewish community 'appear to be sunk in lethargy, apathy and indifference to what passes around them'. In literature, added the editor, the community 'does not reach beyond a grammar and an almanack'. It was extravagant language but caught the mood of the critics of communal leadership.[6]

It was a situation which in 1845 impelled Haim Guedella (1815–1904), Montefiore's Orthodox and independent-minded nephew and prolific public letter writer, to seek at least a partial remedy by the production of a publication entitled *Sabbath Leaves* It was to be at his own expense. His object was to supply to interested parties Jewish material, especially sermons, for private study. His plan presupposed a wide Jewish reading public for the tracts. He was influenced by the model of the Christian London Tract Society. He thought that the 'poor' were in particular need of Jewish reading material. But poverty was not conducive to such response. Because of his subsidy the tracts were priced at a penny each. In all, only four numbers appeared. Not more than 50 of each number were sold. He declined to provide any further subsidy. Jewish observers at the time seem to have looked on the effort as the scheme of an over-enthusiastic public figure with time on his hands. He later called the failure 'a disgrace to our community at large'. Guedella's plan demonstrated more the desperation of a concerned personality over the communal scene in terms of culture and Jewish educational prospects.

In 1850 Henry Faudel initiated a more determined and far more advanced effort. His communal influence and personal canvass secured for his Literary and Translating Society promises of financial support from some of the leading Jewish families. The inaugural meeting was attended by about 25 men, including most of the recognised Jewish scholars then in London. Among those present were Abraham Benisch, Hirsch Edelmann, Louis Loewe, Albert Lowy, D.W. Marks, Solomon Schiller-Szinessy, D.A. de Sola and Joseph Zedner. Faudel's original plan was for the Society to commission and finance the translation of Hebrew works located in British libraries, notably the British Museum and at Oxford and Cambridge. An optimistic brochure was published in 1851 which was in effect a prospectus for a newly-planned and wider Hebrew Antiquarian Society. A striking array of continental Jewish scholars promised their aid in the selection of the texts and their translation. Their support had been recruited by Hirsch Filipowsky (1816–72), the Lithuanian-born Hebraist. They included Geiger, Jost, S.L. Rapaport and Zunz. Filipowsky became in fact the prime mover in the plans of 1851, touring the principal European centres of Jewish learning on behalf of a broadened committee, which included from England the Chief Rabbi, A.L. Green, Haim Guedella and Moses Picciotto.[7] Elaborate plans were devised to attract subscribers to the scheme and the contemplated volumes. Subscribers in Britain were fewer than expected, no endowment appeared, local interest waned, and the original Anglo-Jewish plan was not pursued.[8] The prospectus was Filipowsky's work.

The philosophy of Moses Mendelssohn (1729–86), a founder

of the German Enlightenment and a principal progenitor of the Haskalah, had much less effect in Britain than on the European continent. Such impact as he had on the Anglo-Jewish community was pragmatic rather than ideological. His emphasis on Judaism as the private creed of the citizen, his plea for the equality of all citizens, and his call for separation of Church and State, added some kind of philosophic emblem to the elemental notion, which, in any event, was natively Anglo-Jewish, that Judaism was the faith of one of the many sections of society out of conformity with the Established Church. The cultural and religio-cultural side of Mendelssohn's work attracted but limited attention within the Anglo-Jewish community. It was not a movement, but an affair of individuals, mostly foreign-born. Those who shared and sought to pursue those interests were a minority acutely aware of their isolation.

The leading emancipationist spokesmen adhered to their convictions and preferences, believing that their stand both represented a new enlightenment and met the needs of the time. Some of their critics feared that their outlook threatened Jewish attachment and particularity. An assessment by analogy may be found in Matthew Arnold's typical phrase in reference to the British aristocracy who, he wrote, have a 'natural inaccessibility ... to ideas'.[9] Perhaps the same might fairly be said about their Jewish counterparts in society and those who aspired or approximated to that Jewish echelon.

The persistent differences of outlook between principal spokesmen for the Jewish community were revealed in the public debate on the manner of marking Salomons' Lord Mayoralty in 1856. Putting aside Elias Davis's suggestion that there be erected in a 'conspicuous part' of the City of London a statue to demonstrate Jewish gratitude for his election (itself a particularly vivid sign of the prevailing spirit in the 'upper' cadres of early Victorian Anglo-Jewry), two schools of thought emerged. One opinion held that the retiring Lord Mayor, whose term of office was widely accounted as a personal, social and public success, should be presented with a lasting personal gift. The contending view held that in the contemporary scene a scholarship in his name should be founded in aid of Jewish ministerial training.

The former body of opinion was headed by the Rothschild family. The latter group was led by Henry Harris and Moses Picciotto. There was the remarkable spectacle of two virtually competing campaigns for the raising of funds, with two committees engaged in publicly advertising for funds to mark the same event. The Rothschild proposal aroused the greater support and a piece of silver plate was bought for ceremonial presentation to the past Lord Mayor – which Salomons in due course gave to the Coopers' Company in the City. Harris and Picciotto raised sufficient money with which to found a Lord Mayor's Commemorative Scholarship tenable at Jews' College.[10]

The *Jewish Chronicle* significantly commented that the foundation of that Scholarship was 'the first successful manifestation of the power of the middle classes unaided by the aristocracy'. It indicated, wrote the editor, that 'the mass of the community has come of age'. It might be more accurate to say that the episode, albeit in a particularised field, pointed to the continuing influence of the entrenched families, and at the same time demonstrated the unyielding and, in terms of public communal support, the increasing significance of the newer middle classes.

If there were many issues on which they shared a common outlook, there was nonetheless a steady decline in the communal readiness to abide by the old form of oligarchic governance. Among the newer forces there were some who went further than dissension over the communal system of government and who entertained broader thoughts on what the Jewish community's priorities in action should be. They saw a pressing need to meet the cultural and physical wants of the community's growing numbers, halt the destructive tide of disinterestedness which was in rapid motion in the widening Anglicised segments of Jewish society, and sustain the inner *esprit de corps* of a perplexingly and increasingly fractious community. The lines of division were increasingly apparent on successive issues, not only over Reform.

In the new Chief Rabbi's mind, his exercise of authority flowed naturally from the history and operation of his office, even if more assertively by him than under his predecessor. For Nathan Marcus Adler, the exercise was directed to purposes beyond the concepts of authority or attempted centralisation. He wanted to see a deepening of the Orthodox faith, a more wholesome response to the questioning coming from the secularly lettered younger generation of English Jews, a greater interest in Jewish literature, and a better educated Jewish laity. The lay leadership of the community, with whom he was in close encounter, was less moved by some of the enthusiasms which stirred him.

Soon after he took up his appointment in 1845 Adler found that he could not easily free himself from the consequences of the situation which he had inherited. The 'Caution and Declaration', issued in 1842 in the names of Hirschell, David Meldola (the head of the Sephardi Beth Din) and their respective Batei Din, pronounced in effect that any person who did not accept the authority of the oral law 'cannot be permitted to have any communion with us Israelites in any religious rite or sacred act'. This was meant to be a ban against members of the secessionist synagogue and was interpreted to exclude likewise their families. In 1846 Adler refused to sanction the marriage of a member of the Western Synagogue (which had not accepted the ban) and a bride who was the daughter of a junior official of the Reform synagogue. The subsequently published correspondence between the Goldsmids and Adler over his equivocal conduct in his handling of this episode and over some inconsistency in his operation of the ban generally, underlined his sense of predicament. His conduct satisfied neither those influential laymen around him who had been uneasy over the ban from the start nor his own Beth Din which had been among its promoters, and aroused resentment in Reform circles.

Likewise his delay in reaching a decision in 1848 over whether or not to allow the burial of Benjamin Elkin in the cemetery of the Great Synagogue, and the humiliating restrictions ultimately imposed upon that burial, reflected his consciousness of his difficult role. Leading figures in his own community were dismayed. Elkin, while attaching himself to Reform, had retained his membership of the Great Synagogue and had expressed his wish for burial by the side of his wife.

Under the terms of his appointment the Chief Rabbi (as his successors) was expressly deprived of any power to impose any such ban. The Sephardi congregation was sharply divided on that issue, a circumstance which increased Adler's turmoil. In 1849 they lifted certain penalties which had been imposed by that congregation upon the Sephardi seceders. In 1848 Adler had sought the advice of the Sephardi Beth Din on the Elkin burial issue but was informed that the dayanim thereof were 'unavoidably absent'. His attitude in the Elkin matter, especially the Jewishly unconventional delay in burial, so scandalised David Jonasshon (a long-standing member of the (Orthodox) Sunderland congregation and a coal owner in that region), as to lead him to join the Reform Synagogue in London – he was one of the four later 'rebels' of 1853. He said that he found the delay in Elkin's burial 'abhorrent', and the episode a form of 'religious persecution'.

Adler regretted the departure from the natural ranks of communal leadership of a whole section of men of Jewish attachment and western culture. He well knew that some of the changes called for by the Reformers in the first place – including English sermons, synagogal decorum, the avoidance of angelology in the services – were as much desired in his own community as by the Reformers. Many of the desired 'reformist' changes were in time introduced with his authority – even though he showed himself readier to approve of some of them in the 'Branch' (later the Central) synagogue in the West End than in the City synagogues. His published rationale did not satisfy his Orthodox critics. He stood by the binding authority of the oral law, while realising that the critics of some of its enactments were not confined to 'progressives'.

In 1850 Adler chose the 'relaxed' occasion of a Simchat Torah celebration at the Great Synagogue to describe his position as 'a difficult one'. It was a theme to which he returned on a number of occasions. He spoke of the divided opinions over the extent and speed of change in the synagogues and of his anxiety to keep a balance. The chairman, Denis Samuel, financier and himself one of the patrons of Jewish scholarship, in an unusually frank reply, stated that he had only accepted congregational office on condition that 'several salutary reforms in religious worship promised to be introduced, would be carried into effect'. Expressing himself as 'grievously disappointed' he urged their introduction without delay in order, he added, to attract the youth to the synagogues. It was a declaration of impatience directed at Adler, who was acutely aware of the needs of the day and of the painful paradox that what he deemed a vital element in the new age, namely his proposed ministerial training seminary, and the day school to be associated therewith, had not attracted support from those from whom he had expected understanding and assistance.

Adler's tenure, with the aid of the synagogal lay leaders who gave the Chief Rabbinate a more formal structure after Hirschell's death, consolidated his office. The Chief Rabbinate was strengthened organisationally, and its authority was advanced in some spheres. The union of the City Ashkenazi Synagogues was in the 1860s 'on its way' through the same historical process by which the Chief Rabbinate itself had evolved. No doubt Adler encouraged those who were thinking along the lines of the long heralded 'uniting' of the Ashkenazi Synagogues. It was not so much an original idea of his as a natural development. That an Act of Parliament (1870) should be requested in order to incorporate it, was not his idea but that of the lay leadership to which the notion of an 'establishment' had a strong appeal. Likewise the Board of Guardians (1859) was long heralded by senior lay practitioners in the welfare field, and became self-evidently desirable and prudent, in conformity with national and local models. Likewise it was 'on its way'.

The one institution which Adler created was not 'natural' to the Anglo-Jewish scene; and it was delayed by strong adverse communal opinion. Throughout its life, Jews' College (like his adjoining day school in Finsbury Square) lived on communal pittances and did not achieve Adler's hopes in intake or achievement. Despite the terms of the United Synagogue's Deed of Foundation and Trust setting forth the sole religious authority of the Chief Rabbi, the fact was that the old English and Anglo-Jewish superiority of the lay over the religious figures (together with the old Anglo-Jewish dis-interest in ideas) prevailed. There was no endowment of any institution of higher Jewish learning and there was a contentment with a Jewish educational minimalism, despite Adler's own expectations and longing.

In sum, he managed to satisfy no party entirely, and still less himself. There is a touch of tragedy about his Chief Rabbinate (from which he was happy to retire in 1880), a recovery from whose effects was to await the twentieth century. His vision was not matched by his power; his notional authority exceeded the resources which were made available for its full exercise.

A telling difference of nuance and priority came to the fore in July 1869 following Adler's public address at the Jews' Free School. Fifty years ago, he declared, 'the propriety of teaching the poor was doubted and ridiculed. Now it is admitted that education was the greatest civilizer'. Whatever may be made of the latter phrase, the essence of his message was that it 'was not enough to satisfy the

(School) Inspector. ... No one should leave (the) school unless able to translate the Pentateuch in the original, and no girl unless able to understand her daily prayers ...'. Sir Anthony de Rothschild, soon to become the first President of the United Synagogue and who chaired this meeting, demurred. He observed that 'if (this) was a wholly religious school, it would not be patronised by the community. He estimated that to meet the Chief Rabbi's wish, an additional £2,000 per year would be required.[11]

Whatever may have been the financial restraint, this public exchange exemplified the limits within which Adler exercised his authority. On that occasion, as in respect of his day school, or in regard to the ceaselessly gross inadequacy of funds provided for Jews' College,[12] or in relation to the failure[13] of his efforts to sustain the efficacy of Jewish law in English matrimonial legislation and regulation, the fact was that the personal deference accorded to him was not matched by the scale of influence which in practice was allowed him. Some further estrangement between him and a section of the lay leadership typified by Sir Anthony de Rothschild, resulted from his initial long opposition to any legislative enactment to accord the Reform synagogue the right to have its own secretary for marriages.[14]

The principal dayanim in the Ashkenazi Beth Din under Hirschell retained office long after his death. Aaron Levy (Reb Aron) served for 45 years until his death in 1876.[15] Aryeh Leib Barnett died in 1878 after holding office for nearly 50 years. These noted Talmudists, highly popular in some quarters, belonged to an earlier age which Adler understood but from which he had been able to emerge into the new age, with which they had little, if any, affinity. Like them he was aghast at the Jewish indifference which seemed to prevail within the Anglicised community and the extent of the decline in Jewish religious observance. In the mid-1850s, Marcus Bresslau, ever the hard-hitting journalist, observed that since early in the century, 'the rapid advance of commerce, the spread of wealth, the refinements of luxury in imitation of the surrounding wealthy neighbours ... (has) diverted the Jews' attention ...'. His point could not be gainsaid.

In his inaugural address in 1845 Adler had stated that he knew that some would want him 'to move too quickly' and others would wish him to 'stand entirely still'. He declared his preference for a middle course; but he never found it an easy passage. He was ever mindful that his new community was characterised by inertia in regard to that part of his task which he would describe as the cultivation of Judaism. There was, stated the *Voice of Jacob* in July 1845, an 'indifference' in the closing years of the earlier regime and indeed during the interregnum, which 'had supplanted religious feeling'. The editor's assessment was that this 'had rendered men not merely indisposed to another appointment but even ... avowedly hostile to it'. The appointment of a university-trained scholar with a ready knowledge of modern literature and an eagerness to be seen (and to be heard) in English, certainly introduced a sense of change, but his priorities and preferences did not prove infectious.

A distinct ingredient in the markedly 'Victorian' attitude of the Jewish community was the relationship of their leaders with Protestantism. It was a socio-political relationship, and did not indicate any antipathy towards Roman Catholics. Salomons, in particular, frequently spoke of the 'Protestant spirit', referring thereby to its individualistic ethos which he held to be the great English virtue and an important source of national strength.[16] Like William Gladstone, Jewish spokesmen distinguished between Roman Catholics on the one hand and the political and hierarchical claims of Pope Pius IX on the other hand. Pius had become deeply unpopular in the Anglo-Jewish community because of the oppression of Jews resident in the Papal territories. Jewish leaders did not hesitate to identify themselves in 1851 with the substantial section of British public opinion which had strong reservations against the re-establishment in England of the Roman Catholic hierarchy. The *Jewish Chronicle* expressed its fear of such a revival, a fear which had been given voice by the then Prime Minister, Lord John Russell. The prospect aroused strong feelings in Anglican circles and among Protestant Nonconformist bodies.

The reading Jewish public was aware that Protestant publicists tended to contrast the Jews favourably with the Roman Catholics. A representative Nonconformist opinion was expressed by John Mills in his widely-read survey of the British Jews in 1853. He was a Welsh Calvinist Methodist minister and an active conversionist in London and Palestine, with some residual reverence for Judaism as a parent religion. 'There is', he wrote, 'an essential difference between Judaism and Roman Catholicism'. He added: '... Popery (is) aggressive, ... ready to subvert (the) political and social order ... to ... the aggrandizement' of (the Church). Judaism, he observed 'intermeddles not with the civil rights of other creeds ... and nothing in it is inconsistent with loyalty'.

An Anglican writer, calling himself a 'Conservative' in an anonymous pamphlet in the 1840s, included in his advocacy of Jewish emancipation, the argument that 'the stake (of the Jews) in society is large' and that the subversion of existing institutions would ruin them. 'What more faithful adherents' he enquired, 'can the defenders of the Throne and altar expect to find?' 'Popery' he went on, ... 'attacks the Church of England in all ways open to it, but the Jews will be against Popery from past experience. The Jews would aid the Church if the latter would but be just towards them'. The Chartist riots of that time had sharpened public sensitivity to the possibilities of 'assaults' on 'existing institutions'. The Oxford Movement, the growing attraction of the High Church party in the Anglican Church, and the concern over conversions to Rome on the example of John Henry Newman, aroused in some Anglican minds in the 1840s and 1850s, an unrelated and vague apprehension of an 'assault' of a different kind on 'existing institutions'.

Jews became familiar with well-meant praises springing perhaps from a somewhat self-interested denominational partisanship. They did not themselves engage in comparable polemics in support of their case. They did not repudiate the laudation, but preferred their own argument to speak for itself, which was aided by a multiplicity of expressions of philo-Jewish opinion from Christian colleagues in the City and liberal Whigs in Westminster, as well as by church-men and others, some of whom were moved to back the Jewish cause by their conversionist hopes. In many provincial cities, Jews were prominent in general philanthropy and in the cultivation of local cultural enterprises for the general public. They were in regular receipt (almost always reported in the local press and sometimes in the national press) of personal tributes, often accompanied by public support for the granting to them of civic and political rights. Jews felt no need either to compare themselves favourably with other groups in society or (Disraeli's expressions of superiority notwith-standing) to present themselves as a superior people intellectually or otherwise.

An important strand in their policy was the proclamations of their denial of the frequent assertion that their entry into Parliament would tend towards the de-Christianisation of Parliament and society. At the heart of the concern of the critics who adopted this stand was the notion that the admission of Jews would imply support to those for whom the place of religion in society was a matter largely of indifference. The Church was steadily losing its privileges. The fashionableness of deism and scepticism was widening. John Keble in his long-remembered Oxford sermon of 1833 spoke of 'national apostasy'. The Church's hold on the old universities was ever more under attack, sometimes by its own incumbents. The advance of political reform, often headed by Nonconformists, weakened old assumptions concerning the place and power of authority in Church and State. Jewish entry was perceived by some opponents as tantamount to an acknowledgement that these trends mattered little, if at all; religion would not be seen as the binding cement of the social order.

Yet some Anglicans, notably Gladstone, concluded that the opposite was the case. Gladstone, who began as an eloquent opponent of Jewish emancipation, had by 1845 adopted the position that this was strategically necessary in order that it might not be said that the legislators were indifferent as to the respective merits of Anglicanism and Roman Catholicism. By acceding to the Jewish claims, it would be demonstrated that the Roman Catholics, like the Jews, were granted civic and political rights only on general libertarian principles applicable and irresistible in the nineteenth century.

Jews took seriously the contention that to accept their claims would tend towards the de-Christianisation of Parliament or society. They rejected any idea that such was their intention or that such development was likely to be conducive to such result. Repeatedly they cited examples of Jewish assistance to Christian charities and institutions (including schools) to prove their wish to sustain the Church and the religion of the land. Montefiore, Salomons and other leading Jews made well-publicised gifts to churches to illustrate their earnestness on this score. In 1853, Keeling, a donor to Christian charities, became churchwarden of a City church (provided he was not expected to attend services) and his decision was hailed in the Jewish press as further evidence.[17] At the Jews' Free School anniversary dinner in 1855, presided over by

21

Lord John Russell, Lord Denman announced that his own contribution to the appeal was a return for Lionel de Rothschild's donation at his request towards the erection of a church. It is doubtful whether such expressions and gifts by Jews had any effect on the critics. This form of Jewish response did not touch the matters which were said by the critics to arouse their anxiety.

Neither the philanthropy of Jews nor their patent loyalty nor their much paraded civic virtues would have freed Charles Lamb, the 'gentle essayist', from his distaste for the 'reciprocal endearments' between Jews and Christians, in which he detected 'something hypocritical and unnatural'. Nor was it likely to move those who looked with concern upon the new commercial and industrial age in which they tended to hold Jews to be among the principal founders and beneficiaries. Nor had any of it disabused Lord Derby of what in 1857 he described as the 'impassable gulf' between them. In the following year Derby was to head the Tory government which put through Parliament the Act which opened the House of Commons to professing Jews. It was hardly a measure which he or long-standing opponents of such a measure in either House adopted with pleasure, save to the extent that there was some political satisfaction over the settlement of an issue on which the Houses had been at odds with one another since 1833 when the House of Commons had first voted in favour (and had regularly done so thereafter). It was an act of political, even constitutional, expediency, which was inevitably acclaimed as a triumph (which in one sense it was) for 'liberalism'.

So vocal and persistent had been Jewish declarations of loyalty to Crown and State, so endemic had become the expression of many Christian supporters that the Jews had no intention to subvert or change the social order or the balance of forces in society, and so clamorous were Jewish publicists that the Jewish Relief Act of 1858 was a vindication of their reliance on British fairness and liberality, that the Act remained for many decades the main pillar of Anglo-Jewish philosophy – namely that the emancipation carried with it the special reciprocal obligation on Jews, to manifest their gratitude in the spirit of their campaigns. The pre-1858 apologetics and the Jewish self-explanations were followed by an era of yet more intense effort to demonstrate that the Jews had indeed been worthy of the bestowal or recognition of their civil rights as citizens.

22

New men, less taken up with these areas of public relations, were coming to the fore in the counsels of the Jewish community. They came from outside the old coterie of leadership. These men of talent, flair and commercial success aspired to wield greater influence in their community. The old Anglo-Jewish plutocracy dating back to the early years of the century and in some cases earlier, had by the 1840s acquired many of the traits and outward signs – knighthood and baronetcy – of an aristocracy, and enjoyed much of the instinctive deference accorded them. Now there emerged younger men of independent mind and new outlook for whom the Victorian pluto-aristocracy in early bloom held no terrors; they could not command their obeisance. Typical of this element were the three Henrys – Faudel, Harris and Keeling, and Elias Davis was a fourth.

Henry Faudel (1809–63) was a director of the Union Steam Shipping Company and of the Southampton Docks. He was a man of cultivated literary tastes and practical disposition, with an eye for detail as for the broad view. There was hardly a development of any importance in metropolitan Jewry between 1840 and 1860 in connection with which he did not make a significant contribution by word or deed. He was a skilled pamphleteer who made no assumption as to the superior wisdom or the experience of family heirs to office.

His widely noted pamphlet of 1844 in which he advocated the amalgamation of the existing Jewish charities in London was ahead of its time. It played its part in strengthening the 'uniting' spirit between the main Ashkenazi synagogues, which reached fruition a generation later. He was a creative precursor of the movement of opinion in the 1850s towards the ultimate creation of the Jewish Board of Guardians in 1859. The reorganisation of the old Jews' Hospital, as it was archaically called, and the Jews' Orphan Asylum, and their amalgamation in the 1860s (the whole being later transferred to Norwood, which geographical term the union adopted as its name – later Norwood Child Care) owed much to his advocacy and planning. He was a conscious utilitarian in his communal outlook, a firm believer in the practical value of centralised communal government, and a disciplinarian in regard to waste of communal funds and energy. His communal career served notice of the rise to communal authority of a new Jewish advanced middle class, a segment of Jewish society which at that time saw no intrinsic virtue in leadership by inheritance.

Henry Harris (1819–99) was one of London's leading solicitors. For decades he was President of the Maiden Lane Synagogue (which in 1909 was amalgamated with the Western Synagogue), and was the most resolute and consistent (if mild-mannered) upholder of Orthodoxy and of what he deemed necessary for its preservation. He was an ally of Montefiore at the Board of Deputies and elsewhere, but not uncritical and could not be taken for granted. Because of his professional standing and his impressive personality he carried much weight in debate, in which, without prejudice to principle, he generally sought to defuse and not inflame. His principal lieutenant was his fellow-warden at Maiden Lane, the industrialist Nathan Defries, who shared his sense of independence from the titled squires of the shires.

Henry Keeling (1805–80), a City jeweller, was a member of the Western Synagogue and represented the Southampton Synagogue on the Board of Deputies. He was vociferous for conciliation on all divisive issues. He was always in attendance, always in voice. His sister was Mrs Abraham Benisch, a circumstance which reinforced his influence. Benisch was himself an arch-independent in communal affairs, continuing a tradition of self-assertiveness which he inherited from his editorial predecessors and associates in more than one communal newspaper.

Elias Davis became disillusioned with the religious and lay leadership and moved over to Reform. It was as much a matter of opposition to the self-perpetuating committee which sought to rule, as a question of doctrine. This Common Councillor of the City of London was a prominent member of the Great Synagogue and a partner in a major wholesale clothing company in the City with his friend, Samuel Moses, a popular Warden of that Synagogue. Their company conducted an extensive export trade with the Antipodes. Their personal and business relationships do not appear to have suffered by reason of Davis's communal attitudes. Prior to his accession to the Reform congregation, Davis had sponsored the candidature of Dr H.S. Hirschfeld, the senior rabbi of Wollstein for the post of Chief Rabbi. Only at a late stage, when the strongly supported campaign on Adler's behalf became irresistible did many opposing votes come over so as to give Adler near unanimity. At one point, however, the Adler and Hirschfeld camps seemed dead-locked. It was then that some came out in favour of Samson Raphael Hirsch as a possibly acceptable compromise candidate, but sound-ings showed him unlikely to gain much ground. The Rothschild–Cohen identification with the Adler candidacy attracted over-whelming support for the favoured name. The Hirschfeld and Hirsch candidatures remained to the end.

One may detect three reasons which might explain Davis's robust and sustained support for Hirschfeld. First, he deplored the quasi-official sponsorship of any one candidate. It smacked of an unacceptable authoritarianism. Secondly, Hirschfeld had in 1840 and 1842 published two works in Berlin on the Bible. One of them analysed a variety of interpretations of the Bible found in the Talmud.[18] Another was a reply to attacks on the 'Old Testament' by secularists and by what were later termed 'higher critics'. Davis was antipathetic to concentration on Talmud study. Hirschfeld may well have seemed to him to be a rabbi of acknowledged scholarship whose Orthodox principles remained firm but whose fields of scholarship lay in the highways of contemporary concern. Further, he must have seemed to Davis to be more likely to heal the seces-sionist breach. The other two candidates had signed the rabbinical protest against the Brunswick Reform Assembly of 1844. His candidate had not done so, which seemed to Davis consistent with what he perceived to be Hirschfeld's personality and scholarly interests.

Davis was one of the four members of Reform who in 1853 were elected by Provincial (Orthodox) Synagogues as their representa-tives at the Board. It was a direct challenge to the leadership of Montefiore, who exerted himself unavailingly to defeat their candidatures at the respective Synagogues, including that of Norwich where Davis stood. By Montefiore's casting vote as President the four were excluded from the Board, following intense contention in debates at the Board and within the Jewish com-munity. Adler did not treat the Reformers as members of a congregation of professing Jews. Whether or not Montefiore shared that view, he certainly considered himself inhibited by the Chief Rabbi's attitude from holding the West London Synagogue of British Jews to be entitled to membership of the Board or their members individually to be entitled to attend the Board as representatives (of any Synagogue). The fact that relatives of his were members of the Reform Synagogue (including his learned maternal uncle and the notable literary patron, Moses Mocatta, who was his immediate predecessor as President of the Board when Montefiore was elected to that office in 1835) left him unmoved. His policy was strenuously opposed by Lionel de Rothschild, David Salomons and other leading members of Montefiore's family circle and close colleagues within the Orthodox 'establishment'.

The revolt of 1853, the rifts which it created or accentuated, and the vigorous and widespread presentation of their case by the four, had enduring effects. The staunchness of Montefiore's exercise of his authority, the closeness of the final voting, and the extensive publicity which the long discord attracted, could not fail to aggravate the existing tensions. In the course of the furore inside the Board and far beyond, it was inevitable that the Jewish press should claim its right (and its duty) to attend and report directly on these debates and generally on hitherto 'private' debates. Their claim could not realistically be denied. The entry of the press, with permission, into the Board marked a new stage in the changing patterns of authority within the Jewish community.

The old family structure, the traditional forms of paternalism, the old-world deference, and the 'say-so' of West End of London-based magnates, lost a degree of shine, especially in the eyes of others ambitious for influence. The establishment of a standing committee by the Board for the first time in 1854 was a measure not only of the growing complexity of communal administration but also of the desire for a curtailment of the arbitrary discretionary powers of office-holders of whatever 'eminence'. It was the fore-runner of what later became the Law, Parliamentary and General Purposes Committee. It was in its initial character a 'watching committee', mainly on pending legislation. It was a phenomenon which could not realistically have been contemplated before the dissolving impact of the battles of 1853.[19]

In 1856 the leaders of the Board decided that there was no likely prospect of success in their efforts to persuade the Registrar-General of the Government not to accord to the West London Synagogue of British Jews the right to use arrangements of its own for the registration of marriages celebrated in the Synagogue. Despite its divisions on the issue, the Board's leadership had sought in the previous session of Parliament to prevent the acceptance of the Synagogue's claim for separate recognition for the purpose. Salomons had been a vocal advocate of the statutory recognition of that Synagogue. His much-lauded term in 1855 as the first Jewish Lord Mayor of the City of London, endowed his castigation of the older arrangement with special prestige.

The new age was further marked in 1857 by the intervention of Salomons and Lionel de Rothschild with the Government in order to exclude the statutory recognition of the *get* from the pending matrimonial legislation, despite the earlier success of Adler and Montefiore in procuring a response from the Government in favour of such recognition.

Fissures in leadership reflected and encouraged a greater degree of practicality and accountability, as well as greater confidence on the part of new wielders of influence in the communal system. Notwithstanding all the differences in contexts, these changes are somewhat analogous to the passage from the age of Lord Melbourne to that of Sir Robert Peel, and the emergence to considerable political weight on the part of spokesmen of the new industrial towns and their commercial classes as distinct from the older landed interest. The four 'rebels' of 1853 betokened a middle-class revolt within the Jewish community against old styles and exponents of leadership. An incidental feature of their operations was the growing role of provincial congregations and personalities, a role which further reflected and enhanced the ever-growing self-consciousness of Jewish leadership in the Provincial communities as claimants to involvement in communal counsels.

The 20 years from Queen Victoria's accession in 1837 witnessed many changes in the communal system whose nature is further illustrated by the rise in status of the communal secretary. Simeon Oppenheim[20] at the Great Synagogue, Solomon Almosnino[21] at Bevis Marks, Israel Lindenthal[22] at the New Synagogue, and Sampson Samuel[23] at the Board of Deputies, were scholarly, prudent and influential. Less well-known were the many other members of the growing genre of communal officials called into being by the need for organisation and administrative continuity in the series of recently founded or expanded eleemosynary and educational bodies. Gone were the days when a small number of benevolent and public spirited men could effectively direct policy, administer

3. Solomon Almosnino (1792–1878)

the funds and manage the organisations. The expansion and increasing complexity of the community and its needs, thrust into being a new system of communal structure, both lay and professional.

The office of clerk, scribe or secretary was of long standing in the community. One of the early secretaries of the Sephardi congregation, Abraham de Castro, acted at the same time as secretary to the incipient Board of Deputies (as it was later popularly called) in and around 1760. In the eighteenth century the position of secretary at the Great Synagogue was in practice long vested in the Polack family. Such posts gained in prominence and effect with the new perceptions of communal requirement.

Typical of the communally less prominent but busy officials whose experienced advice was much sought was Samuel Solomon, brother of the famous educationist, Henry Solomon. Samuel served as Secretary of the Jews' Free School and for 40 years as secretary of the Jews' Hospital, as well as holding similar office in several other Jewish charities. In addition he was a leading Jewish bookseller and publisher of Judaica. In that business and as an assiduous advertiser thereof, he was almost as much in the public eye as in his capacity as a multi-faceted secretary.

The new style of secretariat involved an awareness of the value of records – not only as archives for future examination but also as aids to effective administration. This attitude differed from the older family-style administration, which was generally *ad hoc*, personal, amateur and spasmodic. From the 1830s such a 'system' of government could not sustain the weight and the necessary regularity of administration. The sense of need for a new type of official belonged to the same instinct which led to the decision of the Mahamad in 1819 that the synagogal records of the Sephardi Synagogue should henceforth be in English. That was more than a modernising change. It reflected the declining number of persons to whom Portuguese was familiar. Administration could not be left to the few who knew the language, mainly of an older school less attuned to heavier burdens involved in attention to poor relief, educational provision, congregational expansion and public relations, even if they had the time.

The need was most clearly expressed by Franklin in the first issue

4. Jacob Franklin (1809–77)

of the *Voice of Jacob* on 16 September 1841. He wrote of 'the absence of a class of functionaries upon whom the duties of supervision naturally and appropriately devolve'. He contrasted that with the current situation in which 'the direction' of the 'public institutions ... is in most instances undertaken by benevolent gentlemen whose commercial or professional avocations frequently compel them to abandon the charge for months together, to the very persons whom it is their office to superintend'.

Franklin, a former optician turned actuary and now journalist, had not forsaken his actuarial-type interest. A month later he urged in the same columns the preparation, by Jewish charities and other institutions in London, of statements of income and expenditure and other particulars concerning the growth or otherwise in their operations and requirements. Without such knowledge, he stated, any examination of schemes to improve efficiency and to meet more effectively the changing kinds and degrees of need 'must be unsatisfactory'. In this spirit he invited the organisations to send him past reports 'as far back as possible'. Under Franklin's influence there was prepared in that year a statement on the operations of the Jews' Hospital between 1807 and 1840 from past records. His aim was to avoid duplication between the organisations, rationalise their operations and avoid wastage.

His first enquiries traced nearly 60 institutions and 100 'separate trusts'. In the event Franklin, like Faudel, proved to be ahead of his time. In his day he alerted the communal bodies to the practical importance of employing experienced and suitable equipped persons to major professional office. His message in that regard accorded with an era which saw the establishment by central government of 'expert' boards (staffed by civil servants) in a variety of fields, including education and welfare, in response to the industrial age and the new 'mass' society.

In many parts of the country, especially in the capital, the sharp depression of the late 1830s and early 1840s weighed heavily on the poor. Increasing unemployment and high prices sharpened the distress. The accretions to the urban population from the country-side had added to the pressure. For many among the poor the unattractive parish workhouses offered some degree of alleviation.[24] The improved economic conditions of the late 1840s and early 1850s and the importation of foreign foodstuffs after the abolition of the Corn Laws in 1846, provided some relief, but there were set-backs in the mid-1850s. A series of harsh winters and bad harvests aggravated social conditions.

The Jewish poor suffered an accentuation of the national experience by reason of the special factors impinging upon them. These were the continuing immigration, especially after the lifting of restrictions on entry of aliens in 1836; difficulties of language; differences of habit; the requirements of religious observance; and the concentration in a limited number of trades and localities. The Jews' Free School, the Jews' Hospital, the Jews' Orphan Asylum and a number of newly created benevolent and loan societies deflected a proportion of workers into other less overcrowded trades by their apprenticeship and 'vocational' schemes, but it was a limited segment. Overcrowding continued in the traditional Jewish occupations, including the old competitive vending trades, whether of old clothes, fruit, trinkets and a variety of wares, all of which trades required capital which was hard to come by, depended much on the weather, and were unrewarding in times of depression.

The communal scene was dominated by poverty and the responses to it. Of the 20,000 Jews in London at the end of the 1840s, probably not far short of one-third received poor relief from Jewish sources. New Jewish charities sprang up to help meet the needs of the Jewish destitute. Jewish poverty heightened the Jewish self-consciousness of the better-off. The traditional practice of the 'upper classes' which was to care for the Jewish poor and discourage so far as they could their reliance on parish poor relief (whether in workhouse or through outdoor relief), was much in evidence. Those 'upper classes' treated wealth as a legitimate passport to power, eschewed ideas, and were concerned, in the perceived general Jewish interest, to be seen to bring relief to the Jewish poor. If such a course required a degree of 'uniting' between the jealously sovereign Synagogues, so be it, especially with regard to the foreign poor who were unattached synagogally. It was the attention to the relief of the poor which gave an impetus to the 'uniting' spirit of the Ashkenazi congregations and which played a significant role in the movements for the formation of the London Jewish Board of Guardians (1859) and towards synagogal union in the 1860s leading to the creation of the United Synagogue in 1870.

If poverty was endemic nationally, what especially shocked

observers was the social malady of pauperism.[25] To stem that development in the Jewish community, especially on the part of 'foreigners', was a major self-imposed task of the Jewish leadership. In the 1850s the newly formed Jewish Soup Kitchen in Fashion Street, Whitechapel (based on gentile examples) regularly supplied the basic necessities for at least 3,000 persons a year. That number may include Jewish families receiving aid from the synagogues direct and/or privately.

In December 1854 a contemporary observer described the extent of distress in the Jewish community as 'larger than ever we remember ... and without any prospect of abating'. Two months later, with peddling severely hit by the weather and with a general slackness in trade (and mounting unemployment in the stand-by trade of cigar making), he commented that 'few only can conceive ... the magnitude of the existing distress and of the numbers labouring under it'. At this time, Jewish unemployment and the pressure on communal funds were increasing through the arrival of Jewish immigrants from areas affected by the Crimean War.

The Casual Relief Society of the Jews' Free School and that of the Western (London) Jewish Free School (which initiated the schemes) were especially active. These bodies were formed under the authority of the respective School Committees to raise funds from families of children at the schools who could afford to contribute. The object was the distribution of relief by the staff under headmaster supervision to homes whose children were at the schools. Members of the committees contributed significantly to the funds. A special feature of the arrangements was that it was left largely to the teachers to detect from the gaunt or hungry appearance of children, which of them came from homes in need. In February 1855 the *Jewish Chronicle* reported that but for such aid many children could not have attended school through want of nourishment or lack of winter clothing.

In 1856 the *Jewish Chronicle* estimated that £39,000 a year was being made available by London Jewry for the relief of the Jewish poor, including £13,000 by way of private charity. On the basis of that newspaper's computations, the Jewish contribution per head of the Jewish population was about four times higher than the per head contribution in the nation at large for poor relief.[26] Beneath the drama of major communal events and disputes, the reality of threatened destitution was widespread. And while wealthy Jews agitated for the opening of Parliament, large numbers of Jews, whether in receipt of relief or not, lived with a single-minded frugality, largely unmoved by, and in many cases unknowing of, the excitement.[27]

From the 1840s, emigration to the colonies in America was encouraged and assisted in order to relieve the pressure. In 1853 a Jewish Emigration Society was formed at the instance of the Ladies Benevolent Loan and Visiting Society, to assist the process by loans and gifts. In its first annual report in 1854 the new Society, referring to the increase in congregational funds to meet the requirements of the relief of the poor was seen as a compelling factor in favour of retaining the *Mi-sheberach* in spite of the tendency for the practice to militate against devotion and decorum in Synagogue. At the Great Synagogue it was ruled in 1820 (in the face of much argument to the contrary) that 'from the manifold distresses of the poor and the consequent claims, it is inexpedient to hazard any experiment by which the revenue is likely to be diminished'. The decision to retain the practice was incorporated into, and despite later efforts to rescind that ruling, was retained in the Laws of the Synagogue.[28]

In a much publicised address at a dinner in aid of the Jews' Free School in March 1846, Salomons in carefully chosen language declared: 'We all know that a very large number of indigent foreign Jews are constantly immigrating into this country. The adults it is scarcely possible to educate but if they have children it is alike our duty and our interest to train them as intelligent and useful members of society.' Ten years later at a comparable event in support of the Western Jewish Free School, he returned to the theme, as he had often done. 'I do not know,' he said, 'why Jewish children should not be as well spoken as those of their neighbours.' He added that he had been 'agreeably surprised' at the children's manner of speech on recent visits to Jewish schools. 'There would,' he commented, 'be no occasion to recognise them from their pronunciation as Jews. The Saxon English (he was "glad" to note) was not murdered.' He concluded with the significant observation that he had always held the view that 'social progress must precede social equality', and had accordingly striven for the former. 'The first duty of the rich,' he stipulated in February 1847, 'was to educate the poor, (and) the first duty of the poor was to learn.'

This functional approach to education was a deeply embedded strand in the attitude of the emancipationist spokesmen and others in the Jewish community, to the poor and especially the foreign poor. The task of education was regarded as urgent. Quite apart from any fear of the operations of Christian missionaries (which had been an impetus early in the century towards educational provision for the poor by the Jewish community), the Jewish 'upper classes' and others looked with anxiety at the presence in their vicinity of a progressively reinforced mass of un-English and secularly uneducated poor.

The phrase 'middle class' would not be an apt description of any segment of the Jewish community. 'Middle classes' would be more accurate, ranging from small retail shopkeepers to wholesale houses and manufacturers. The lower end of this variegated stratum was in constant expansion – in the words of a contemporary, 'from beneath'. Although it was mainly from the upper reaches of this section that the new forces in the communal power structure emerged – which fact was itself at the time regarded as a democratic feature of communal life – the middle sector of the middle classes and especially those aspiring to enter that layer were a source of considerable communal initiative. These elements were at close quarters with and often sharply aware of social needs.

From them came the inception of a number of Jewish charities (some of which after initial periods of successful management came under the formal patronage of titled Jews). These included such institutions as the Hand-in-Hand Asylum for 'decayed tradesmen', founded in 1840, of which Isaac Lyon, a familiar personality in Aldgate, was President. He sold Italian fancy goods in premises in Duke Street, Aldgate; the Widows' Home, founded in 1843 which for its first decade was supported mainly by Jewish working men and women and the lower and middle sections of the middle classes; and the Jewish Lying-in Charity founded in 1945 by I.L. Cowan, a candle manufacturer. During its early years it provided its service for more than 1,000 women in childbirth.

In 1850 the *Jewish Chronicle*, in an over-generalised assertion, commented that with a few exceptions 'all our charities and institutions have originated in the circle of the middle and working classes'. The editor advised Adler, during the period of long delay in recruiting adequate support for his proposed College and School in the 1850s, to turn to those groups rather than await the interest of the 'higher' classes.

The coming into being of the Jewish press in 1841 coincided with an expansion of interest in Jewish public affairs. The Jewish press extended the ambit of communal interest, enlarged the frankness and sharpness of communal debate, and added new forums for accountability. In particular, it provided new avenues for expressing protest and public information emanating from and about new elements at divers levels of Jewish society whose opinions and actions may not hitherto have attracted attention.

When Joseph Mitchell became the owner of the *Jewish Chronicle* in 1844 he changed its title to the *Jewish Chronicle and the Working Man's Friend*. The new approach did more than reflect his own political radicalism. It acknowledged the role of newer activist elements in the Jewish community. It is noteworthy that he became honorary secretary of the Widow's Home and involved himself in charities and initiatives relating to the destitute and in association with those who promoted such efforts as represented by the Widows' Home.

The Jewish National Friendly Association for the Manufacture and Sale of Passover Bread, of which Mitchell was a Patron, illustrates the growing enthusiasm for self-help. It was set up in Coulston Street, Whitechapel in 1841 and was later transferred to a larger store in Great Prescott Street in the same area. Its object was to supply matzo at the cheapest price to its members – soon extending its service to non-members – instead of their having to seek it by way of charity from the synagogues. The rising price of flour plus the tax imposed on the manufacturers by the City Synagogues (including the Sephardim) jointly, increased the cost to purchasers. The tax went towards the general relief of Jewish poor, which included matzo distributed at the synagogues. The Association claimed that its operation, which included bulk buying, reduced the retail cost generally and advocated the abolition of the tax which, they said, penalised the industrious poor who preferred to buy their own matzo. When from time to time the Synagogues reduced the tax on the matzo flour, the Association claimed that this was due to their own operation and pressure. The Association survived the creation of the United Synagogue, which retained the matzo flour tax.

There was much talk among more affluent Jews in and around the 1840s about the worthwhileness of educational missions to the Jewish poor. It was a time when, as among Christians, it became fashionable in London and elsewhere for Jewish ladies to visit the Jewish poor. Some 'ladies visiting societies' in the Provinces in areas of marked immigration and poverty had as Patrons Jewish women of high social rank in London. In the capital, the Jewish Ladies Benevolent and Loan Society, founded in 1844 and aiming to encourage self-help and reduce any pauperising trend, engaged in forms of investigation into actual needs in given cases and were in some instances able to provide from the Society gifts or loans selectively. It was to these visiting ladies that some optimists turned for assistance in the distribution among the poor of moralistic Jewish literature and the encouragement of those for whom it was intended to read this material.

This latter effort was part of what from the 1830s attracted the description, adopted from Christian terminology and example, of the 'diffusion' of Jewish knowledge. It was a well-intentioned but ill-organised effort of limited, if any, efficacy. The kind of scene which more particularly troubled some concerned Jewish observers was portrayed in a graphic editorial in the *Jewish Chronicle* in December 1849. On Friday nights, wrote the editor, many Jews, including 'Jews of the poorer classes' attended 'theatres' and 'ill-reputed saloons of Whitechapel and Mile End' … and 'the public houses in the vicinity of Sussex Hall on Friday nights thronged with Jews'.[29] The term 'poorer classes' had a wide meaning, not confined to those in receipt of relief and the unemployed. It was sometimes used to include hawkers and small street dealers at market stalls or otherwise.

In 1845 one Jewish observer, seemingly well-informed about the communal scene, urged that the Jewish school in Birmingham was worthy of emulation. Such schools were a good method of 'improving … the station' of the Jewish community. In stating that the example should be followed throughout the Provinces, he added: 'Not till then will a grand and decisive change be perceived in their moral state. … Until the lower classes are completely metamorphosed (*sic*), the progress of the Jewish nation must necessarily be much constrained.' By 'lower classes' he meant not only the poor who might be in receipt of relief but also those Jews deemed to be at a certain low level of social and economic rank. It was a term of class distinction which came readily to those habitually spoken of as middle class or upper class. The language and sentiment were Victorian and not confined to Jews, even if sections of the Jewish community had their own conscious or subconscious reasons for their avid adoption of these ideas. Neither wisdom nor virtue was a guaranteed preserve of their own station in society.

There was a pervading sense, as in society at large, of the fixity of class. The term 'the humbler classes' was both a euphemism for a wider range of poverty (not limited to recipients of poor relief) and connoted an expectation or recognition of a certain demeanour and attitude. The Jewish 'humbler classes' met the affluent always in circumstances which evidenced and reinforced the sharp class distinction. The habit of deference was deep-rooted. Some held that education should not be advanced too far lest class distinctions be thereby blurred. Some thought that it was unnecessary and 'inexpedient' to provide more than the rudiments of elementary education to the poor.[30] The Chief Rabbi and the *Jewish Chronicle* were prominent in the repudiation of these opinions.

The proliferation of public receptions and dinners in support of Jewish charities was a stimulus to the development of the kosher catering business. For the public festive fund-raising occasions the 'outside caterer' became common. The names of Myers, Lipman and Barnett became familiar. Sometimes competition between charities, notably the smaller ones (especially as some secretaries were the organising officers of several charities at the same time), meant that a charity would miss its anniversary celebration for a given year. The broad regularity of these events from and including the 1840s expanded the catering trade. In some instances, the caterer was already well-known as proprietor of a kosher 'eating house' in the City of London or its environs. The venues for these events were halls in then fashionable 'rooms' such as Willis's in St James', Aldgate, or the London Tavern in Bishopsgate.

These 'anniversary dinners', both in name and as a means of high-profile fund-raising for charities (welfare and/or educational) followed gentile models. The practice was virtually universal among Jewish charities save for the smallest. They provided a platform for speeches by leading public figures – politicians, churchmen, municipal leaders, philanthropists, men of letters – and were always

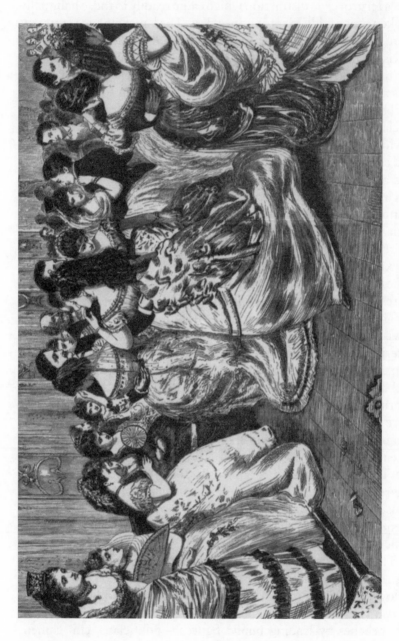

5. Ball at Willis's in aid of the Jews' Infant School, 1872

reported extensively in the Jewish press and sometimes in the national press. Similar events became regular in the Jewish communities of the larger provincial cities, where the proceedings were invariably reported in the local press, often lengthily. In London and elsewhere, these events were significant exercises in public relations, particularly in connection with major public issues affecting Jews. In all cases leading figures in the Jewish community responded, usually in terms much noted within and beyond the Jewish community. The importance of these 'dinners', often attended by gentile friends and benefactors to Jewish causes, as well as by Jews, went beyond the fund-raising objective. They were a form of open public or communal debate on live questions by and in the presence of opinion-makers in politics and society.[31]

A graphic element in the changing scene of the Jewish community was the growth of the kosher restaurant as a fixed institution in the City of London and the Jewish areas immediately to its east. This development sprang from the need for such amenities on the part of Jews who had moved from the older centres of residence to 'suburban' localities. Most Jews continued to live in the regions of Aldgate and Whitechapel. From the 1830s many of the affluent migrated to the Finsbury Square area on the northern edge of the old complex of Jewish streets, and some further afield to the west central areas of London and the West End, or southward to Vauxhall and the Kennington region. From these more fashionable and salubrious addresses, came those whose business took them into the inner area. The Jewish migration and the rise of the Jewish 'eating-house' followed gentile examples and models. Some of these kosher establishments became household names within the Jewish community, and their advertisements were a regular feature in the Jewish newspapers.

There was a kosher 'eating house' in the City in 1830, located near the Royal Exchange. It is reasonable to assume that its opening at that time was encouraged by the decision of the City Corporation in 1830 to change its long-established rule and permit professing Jews to open retail shops in the City. The need for such establishments thereafter grew, especially following the arrival of the train as a means of locomotion between the 'suburbs' and the City. A member of the Myers family announced in June 1843 that he had opened a suite of rooms in Cornhill opposite the Exchange.

He declared that 'very many of our leading commercial men and provincial visitors ... have undertaken' to afford him every encouragement. The family was already well known in the catering business. Among the widening numbers of Jewish 'restaurateurs' in the City there appeared in 1846 a new name which was long to remain communally familiar. Morris Barnett announced that he had opened an eating house next door to Sussex Hall in Leadenhall Street near the Bank where 'kosher chops and steaks' were available 'at any hour of the day', as well as 'kosher sandwiches ... and wines and spirits of superior quality'.

The expansion of the Jewish middle classes was a factor in the proliferation of private Jewish schools in the 1840s and 1850s. These proprietary schools varied greatly in the quality of teaching, but generally had a social attraction for better-off families which the 'charity schools' could not emulate. Some were small in-house family establishments for a limited number of boarding pupils. For parents who did not send their children to the prestigious and expensive 'public' day schools such as the City of London School[32] and University College School (or who could not gain entry), the high-quality private schools such as Neumegen's in Highgate (later at Kew) and Henry Solomon's in Edmonton, had great appeal. The founder of what became Neumegen's had been Hyman Hurwitz who became the first Professor of Hebrew at University College, London. Not only did these schools combine fashion and high standards, but also had the advantage for many parents in any event of providing a Jewish as well as a general education.[33]

Parents were eager to secure for their children a good general and commercially useful education in an age of increasing opportunities in business. Prospectuses and advertisements abounded in the Jewish press concerning schools in London and beyond, with many notices of the extension of existing school premises. There was a growing number of schools for girls. This reflected the general middle-class fashion of the age and was also in line with Adler's frequently repeated warning against neglect of girls' education.[34] In 1856 at Kew, Neumegen's opened an adjoining separate establishment as a girls' school under Mrs Neumegen's superintendence.

In the increasingly fashionable area of Bayswater–Hammersmith, the Misses Benjamin conducted a girls' school for 15 years from

1840, whereafter it was continued under new Jewish management. It was significantly announced that the locality was connected with the City in that an 'omnibus' left the City for the area every quarter of an hour.[35]

Among the more notable Jewish schools outside London was that of Dr Louis Loewe in Brighton (later in Broadstairs). He later became the first Principal of Jews' College. He announced that in his school there was 'no distinction of social classes' among the pupils, all of whom 'are treated alike as gentlemen'. In addition to an extensive general curriculum, Loewe's school taught 'Jewish religion and Hebrew language and literature'. Raphael Isaac Cohen at Dover let it be known that his own school's 'course of studies will be entirely under the direction of the Chief Rabbi'. The school which was opened in Ramsgate in the 1840s by Isaac Henry Myers, chaplain to Montefiore, took in a few Christian boarders, as well as Jews. It was virtually inevitable in that age that this circumstance should be hailed by the *Jewish Chronicle* (in 1849) as 'bearing testimony to Jewish talent in education, (reflecting) credit upon our nation, and one of the strongest proofs of the growing liberality of the age'.[36]

Between 1837 and 1860 the number of provincial Jewish communities stood at about 40. There had been a decline in the size of some of the communities and a rise or expansion of others.[37] Size varied from some hundreds to six or ten families. The newer and larger communities were in the North and Midlands, formed in the wake of urban growth during the commercial and industrial expansion. The principal ports of arrival from the continent were London and Hull. The congregations outside London had almost in all cases sprung from the long-established synagogues in the City of London, with which (especially the Great Synagogue) many of the founders of provincial congregations had retained their personal link. The Chief Rabbi was acknowledged as the religious authority of the provincial communities. In the early 1850s two-fifths of the Anglo-Jewish community lived outside London.

In many of the settled communities there continued to be old-established Jewish businesses – silversmiths, jewellers, tailors, furniture makers and the occasional optician, dentist and chiropodist – many originally engaged in various forms of petty trade as peddlers and hawkers. In some localities immigration swelled numbers

אולי , ין חקין מזני זקין היעים האלינ מורי הירן זנו הלס לעיבה ,

6. Solomon Schiller-Szinessy (1820–29), Minister of Manchester
Reform Congregation and later, Reader in Rabbinics at Cambridge

greatly. The proportion of peddlers, hawkers, the poor and the
unemployed steadily grew.

In Hull, the strains between the old English Jewish community
(dating at least from the 1770s) and the new arrivals became an
ever more marked feature of communal life. In the early 1850s the
old synagogue (erected in 1826 and itself the combined effort of
the two former rival congregations) was rendered entirely inadequate. The cost of the extended building, together with the
mounting necessary expenditure on poor relief, imposed a long-
term burden on the congregation. In all these particulars the Hull
community was typical of many other provincial congregations,
especially in the North and Midlands. Personal and 'doctrinal'
differences resulted in a temporary secession in the 1850s. For a
time the seceders affiliated themselves to the newly-formed Reform
synagogue in Manchester headed by Schiller-Szinessy,[38] notwith-

standing that they were mainly 'foreign' Jews who were not thought likely to adopt the ideas represented by Reform.

The burden of congregational funds in Liverpool by reason of the considerable number of resident poor and the temporarily resident transmigrant Jews, was especially heavy. The radical moves taken or attempted in Liverpool to limit duplication and 'waste' in the administration of Jewish poor relief, were followed in London and elsewhere. The Jewish schools in Birmingham, Hull, Liverpool and Manchester, set up by the local congregations, were cited as examples, notably that of Birmingham where fee-paying for tuition was not obligatory. In fact discretion to dispense with fee-paying in given cases, applied in the other schools. The practice of regular English sermons was initiated in Liverpool and Manchester. The somewhat more malleable structure and protocol away from the City of London was more conducive to experimentation and innovation.

The issues which agitated the local communities were predominantly local. In Portsmouth in the 1840s it was the need to find new premises (ultimately purchased in Queen Street) to replace the eighteenth-century synagogue in White's Row – once a 'quiet and respectable' locality and now an area 'of immoral character', a street of 'brothels and drinking houses'. It was announced that the Mayor and other Christian townsfolk had contributed to the appeal for funds to meet the overall outlay. In Canterbury anxiety sprang from the acquisition by the South East Railway Company in 1846 of statutory rights for railway development over the land on which the synagogue had stood for 80 years. The congregation was eventually obliged to rebuild elsewhere. In Southampton the congregation of 24 synagogal members was rent in twain in 1846 by the use locally of an unauthorised shochet. It required Adler's visit and his personal enquiry and mediation to reunite the two factions. On some occasions wider concerns impinged upon the communities. In particular, those of Chatham, Norwich, Portsmouth and Sunderland were sharply divided over the local candidatures of members of Reform to the Board of Deputies.

The communities, especially the larger ones, were jealous of their lay independence. They did not accept uncritically the opinions of the lay leadership in London. If the numbers of provincial communities who were represented at the Board had risen, that was not intended to limit their independence but to preserve and enhance

7. Moses Samuel of Liverpool (1795–1860)

it. The number of provincial communities who were content to be represented at the Board by London residents declined.

In the 1840s and 1850s a series of local personalities became prominent figures and vocal spokesmen in the wider Jewish community – Bethel Jacobs of Hull, Joel Fox of Norwich, the Magnus family in Kent, the Franklins in Manchester, the Ezekiels in Portsmouth and others. These personalities were leading characters in the municipal and cultural life of their cities, as well as often promoters of Jewish literary effort in their local Jewish communities. In 1846, Moses Samuel, the scholarly silversmith of Liverpool, founded and edited *The Cup of Salvation*: a serious Jewish literary magazine and communal commentary. Although it lasted less than a year, its existence reflected the cultural level and aspiration of a section of the local Jewish community and yet, at the same time, the inadequacy of funding for such projects.[39] His collaborator was David Meyer Isaacs, the preacher, who in the same spirit had founded in Liverpool a Literary Hebraic Society in 1844. The creation of the Jewish Literary Club in London in 1869 – the progenitor of the extensive Jewish literary society movement towards the end of the century – followed the fashion of the latter years of Sussex Hall and of provincial Jewish communities.

The era of early Victorian Anglo-Jewry may be said to have come to an end around 1860. The House of Commons was now open to professing Jews. An increasing number of Jewish students were entering the Universities. A distinctive form of communal structure was emerging, together with the beginning (with all its limitations) of a distinctive Anglo-Jewish ministry. The acerbities which had clouded the closing years of Hirschell's tenure appeared to have entered upon a period of quiescence. Ashkenazi and Sephardim shared a common self-conscious Anglicisation. Serious social problems remained, as did pressing educational issues. If intermarriage and indifferentism were features of communal life, so too was a striking degree of Jewish public religiosity. Within 20 years everything was to begin to change, with the transformation of the Jewish community through the new and vast immigration. Placidity was to be shaken. The turbulence of the early Victorian period was to return in a more intense form, in which old issues were more sharply defined, new issues were bound up with the old, and the shade and light of the twentieth century begin to be discerned.

NOTES

1. The Hebrew Fund had been instituted in the 1830s following the winding up of a Jewish Sick Society, which itself was created after an abortive effort in that decade to found a Jewish Hospital in the Jewish quarter of London. A leading figure in that movement was Zadok Jessel. Its main opponents were Nathan Mayer Rothschild and David Salomons. The London Hospital set aside two wards for Jews (principally at the instance of Rothschild) to which the Hebrew Fund contributed. The suggestion for a Jewish hospital long met with consistent opposition from leading figures within the Jewish community: see Israel Finestein, *Jewish Society in Victorian England* (1993) p. 51; *Hebrew Review*, Vol. III, 11 September 1835; *Jewish Chronicle*, 16 April, 23 April and 7 May 1869. The 'most recent example' of statutory reference to Jews as 'persons of the Jewish nation' appears to be in s.11 of the Charitable Donations Registration Act, 1812, repealed by the Charities Act 1960 as obsolete: Anthony Lester and Geoffrey Bindman, *Race and Law*, 1972, pp. 156–7.

2. Contributors to *Hameassaf* (The Gatherer), the influential Hebrew periodic journal in the late eighteenth century in Germany; they were followers of Moses Mendelssohn. The articles and poems in the journal were original and contemporary (including writings by Wessely) or were translations of or reproductions from Hebrew classical literature.

3. Franklin contended, *inter alia*, that the existence of a 'regular Jewish Ministry' and the Ministers' educational impact on the congregations could operate towards the decline of gentile prejudice as well as encourage greater unity among Jews.

4. The grandiose silver monument stands over a yard high and portrays, *inter alia*, David conquering the lion and rescuing the lamb. It was ordered from Messrs Mortimer & Hunt of Bond Street at the price of £1,500 and designed by Sir George Hayter. The presentation was deferred until the completion of the mourning for Hirschell. The gift was shown to the Queen and Prince Albert at Windsor before it was presented to Montefiore at his London home. The Jewish press reported that they had expressed a wish to see it after the makers had sent them a copy of the design.

5. In total £9,000 had been raised, of which Montefiore and his wife had contributed £2,200, as well as, it seems, paying their own expenses and those of their retinue: per correspondent in *Voice of Jacob*, 19 August 1842. The Affair is described in that issue as having been 'like a thunderclap ... from an apparently cloudless sky', arousing Jews from 'the slumber of security' into which the progress of toleration and civilisation had lulled them. For the latest work on the Affair, see Jonathan Frankel, *The Damascus Affair*, 1997.

6. There were some significant works of translation, albeit functionally related to topical interests. Among such were Louis Loewe's translation of Haham David Nieto's *Mateh Dan* (first published in 1714) in defence of the Oral Law, which appeared in 1842 and of which a second edition was published in 1845; and Moses Mocatta's translation of Isaac Ben Abraham Troki's sixteenth-century work, *Chizzuk Emunah* in 1851, concerned to refute Christian interpretations of the Bible. That work perhaps had added appeal to the translator, a prominent adherent of the Reform synagogue, by reason of Troki's Karaite conception of the primacy and authority of the Bible as against the binding character of rabbinic authority enshrined in the Oral Law. The translation of the Mishna by Raphall and David Aaron de Sola (and its unauthorised publication by Benjamin Elkin) likewise served a topical functional purpose, namely to expose to the Jewish reading public the basis of the Oral Law at a time when its binding authority was in dispute. For biographical notes on scholars in Anglo-Jewry, see Vivian D. Lipman, 'The Age of Emancipation', in Vivian D. Lipman (ed.), *Three Centuries of Anglo-Jewry History*, 1961, pp. 69–106, esp. pp. 101–5.

7. For Moses Picciotto (1806–79), merchant, man of letters and forward-looking communal activist, see prologue to this author's edition of his son James Picciotto's *Sketches of Anglo-Jewish History* (1895), 1956, pp. xvii–xx.

8. Filipowsky, a remarkably extensive linguist, proceeded with some success in the plan of his own. Faudel had contemplated an Anglo-Jewish enterprise. Filipowsky, in contact with many Jewish scholars on the continent of Europe and exploring European libraries in search of Jewish manuscripts, had wider horizons. In 1851, he became the prime mover in the formation of the Hebrew Antiquarian Society. By courtesy of the late Walter Schwab of London, I examined the prospectus of that year. Filipowsky, who had arrived in London in 1839, practised for many years as an actuary in Edinburgh. The object of his Society was to facilitate the publication of medieval Hebrew texts. Among those in Britain who gave public support to the effort were the Chief Rabbi, Schiller-Szinessy, A.L. Green and D.M. Isaacs; the only lay figures from Britain

who were members of the committee were Moses Picciotto and Haim Guedalla. Among the 'ordinary members' were Lindenthal, Sampson Samuel and Henry Solomon (Adler's son-in-law). If Filipowsky's plan was less concerned with the Hebrew manuscripts in British libraries than Faudel's, and if his range of scholar-collaborators was far more extensive and far more widely continental-based than Faudel had contemplated, it is clear that his scheme sprang from the original initiative of Faudel. On 9 December 1859 the *Jewish Chronicle* adopted the proposal made in its columns in previous weeks for the creation of an 'Anglo-Jewish Historical Society'. Its purpose would have been the publication of Anglo-Jewish historical documents to assist in historical study. Nothing seems to have come of it. The editor, Abraham Benisch, did not receive much response save that his historical interests were continued in that newspaper. In the late 1860s the then editor, Michael Henry, commissioned James Picciotto's well-known work.

9. *Culture and Anarchy* (1869), Ch. 111.

10. According to Guedalla, 'few' contributed to both appeals. £700 was raised for the plate from the public appeal, and £1,000 was raised by the appeal for the Jews' College scholarship in Salomons's name.

11. *Jewish Chronicle*, 30 July 1869. Rothschild declared that the school had been founded 'for the poorest class of children, then running wild and selling fruit in the streets ...'.

12. The need for ministerial training facilities was among the earliest and most consistent of Adler's public themes. There were reports in December 1845 that he had assembled delegates of the metropolitan synagogues and presented to them his proposal for the creation and maintenance of a 'college for the training of Ministers'. The views expressed were 'many and various': *Voice of Jacob* 19 December 1945. In his Shevuoth sermon at the Great Synagogue in 1846, he expressed the hope that 'the resources, high standing and influence of the English Jews' would soon 'roll away the reproaches that there was not yet adequate provision for training Ministers'.

13. A particular source of sharp disagreement was the attitude to be adopted to the Bill of 1857 directed to the creation for the first time of a civil court of divorce in England. The Attorney General and the Home Secretary assured Adler and Montefiore that existing Jewish rights (namely in this instance the presumed efficacy of the Jewish divorce to dissolve a Jewish marriage in English law) would be preserved in the Bill. At Adler's request the Board of Deputies in that spirit petitioned the Government to introduce a clause which would expressly exempt Jews from the operation of the new Act. This was moved by the Lord Chancellor and accepted by the Lords without opposition on the Report stage. Approaches to the Government by Salomons and Lionel de Rothschild succeeded in procuring the deletion of the clause. The Bill was passed into law without the clause, in spite of efforts by Adler to secure the restoration of the exemption. For a fuller account of this episode and its implications, see this author's article thereon in *Jewish Chronicle*, 19 April 1957.

14. A.J. Kershen and J. Romain, *Tradition and Change: A History of British Reform*

Judaism 1840–1994, 1995, *passim*; *Jewish Society in Victorian England*, ibid., pp. 71–2, and ch. 2; and H.S.Q. Henriques, *Jewish Marriages and the English Law*, 1909.

15. The *Jewish Chronicle* on 25 August 1876 described him as 'the idol of the poor'. In his prime, he regularly attended the *Beth Hamidrash* at 5 a.m. to engage in Talmud study with many pupils. He was well known in his day as a scribe of distinction.

16. A certain attitude was revealed in 1853 by Lionel de Rothschild during the debates at the Board of Deputies on whether to admit members of Reform. He declared that he 'would not be led blindly by the Beth Din like some are led by a Catholic priest. They may well ask what the law is but have no right to inquire into our conduct.'

17. One Christian parishioner informed the Jewish community via the *Jewish Chronicle* that his election was 'a reward' for Keeling having helped to resolve a disagreement within the Church concerning repairs to the fabric, and for his firm having contributed to the expense thereof. The editor commented: 'We doubt whether the Church will have a firmer supporter in the parish than the Jewish Churchwarden': *Jewish Chronicle*, 6 May 1853. There was some Jewish public criticism of Keeling's action, but he was not deterred and was elected to like office at another Church in 1855, on the same terms as to conscience.

18. In its review of Hirschfeld's *Halachische Exegese* in November 1842, the *Voice of Jacob* described it as 'the first investigation of the Talmudical interpretations of the Bible in all its extent and bearings, as an independent aim, and the primary object of profound and extensive study'. The author's objective, added the reviewer, was 'a reformation of the method of instruction in higher Jewish theology'. In November 1844, the *Jewish Chronicle* under Mitchell's editorship reviewed both books, commending Hirschfeld for his work in a 'neglected field', namely the history of Jewish intellectual development and of 'Jewish theology'. The books, commented the editor, will have a 'salutary influence in directing the theological studies of young rabbis. ... (Hirschfeld) possesses that dignity and strength of character ... indispensable to the due discharge of the functions of the Chief Rabbi'. Mitchell observed (perhaps to some extent by way of expressing his own preference) that there was reason to hope he would be elected by a large majority. Franklin regarded Mitchell as tending towards support for Reform.

19. See *Jewish Society in Victorian England*, ibid., ch. 9.

20. (1798–1874). Oppenheim served as Secretary of the Great Synagogue from 1843 to 1866, having formerly served as Treasurer, a circumstance which measures the significance attached to the office of Secretary, which Cecil Roth described as 'the hub of the Anglo-Jewish community' at the time: Cecil Roth, *History of the Great Synagogue*, 1950, p. 275. See also pp. 193–4.

21. (1792–1878). Almosnino retired in 1875 after serving as Secretary for 54 years, prior to which appointment he was assistant secretary: A.M. Hyamson, *The Sephardim of England*, 1951, pp. 194, 367.

22. (1796–1883). Lindenthal was a member of the intellectual circle of which

Morris Raphall and David Aaron de Sola were members. He frequently acted as *chazan*, occasionally preached, was confidant of and in some instances spokesman for the lay heads of the New Synagogue, and enjoyed some added prestige through the association of the Salomons family with that Synagogue.

23. (1806–68). He was a solicitor and was appointed Secretary to the Board in 1838, the first to hold such office there. His appointment opened a new epoch in the Board's history in terms of continuity and effect. An illustration of the consequences of the absence of such office was the Board's failure to know or take heed of the passage of Lord Lyndhurst's Marriage Act of 1835 which was later thought to have a possible bearing on the law in relation to Jewish marriages. The Board's minutes show that the Board met three times that year, all the meetings being at Montefiore's London home. Two of them were mainly concerned with the pending presentation of a draft new constitution. Hirschell attended one of the meetings, when the main item concerned his jurisdiction. During the years of division within the Board and challenges to the leadership, Samuel's stabilising role was crucial. He was loyal to Montefiore, while encouraging the younger aspirants to be heard. For responses to the Act of 1835 see *Jewish Society in Victorian England*, ibid., pp. 58–64.

24. For communal attitudes on proposals for a Jewish workhouse, see A.M. Jacob, *Transactions* (*Trans.*), Jewish Historical Society of England (J.H.S.E.), Vol. 25, p. 104, and *Jewish Society in Victorian England*, ibid., pp. 47–8.

25. The practice or effort to encourage self-help was applied in provincial communities affected by depression and increased immigration, as in London. In July 1845 the two synagogues in Liverpool set up a joint 'relieving committee' whose aim was 'the suppression of mendicancy'. In language typical of the times, the announcement in the Jewish newspapers was that the committee would, by loans and advice, place before the applicants for relief 'such powerful inducements as may lead the habitually idle and vicious to abjure those practices which now impair their energies' so that they might become 'useful members of society' and earn their own living.

26. *Jewish Chronicle*, 8 August and 5 September 1856.

27. Many Jewish working men followed the emancipationists' campaigns with genuine interest. From time to time, especially after 1847, members of that section of Jewish society initiated public meetings to arouse support, sometimes complaining of the lack of 'adhesion' to such effort on the part of men 'of wealth and talent' – described by one such initiator as 'the English characteristic of perfect success': *Jewish Chronicle*, 8 July 1853. Mitchell of the *Jewish Chronicle* encouraged these efforts, seeing in them more counter-weight in communal life as distinct from the wealthy and titled. Among the interested working men active in this field were those who aspired to or had reached the ranks of the self-employed in their trades. Among their prominent spokesmen was Isaac Lyon.

28. For the policy of the Board of Guardians and communal practice regarding emigration, see V.D. Lipman, *A Century of Social Service 1859–1959*, 1959. For the *misheberach* at the Great Synagogue, see Roth, p. 252.

29. Sussex Hall was the name given to the recently founded Jews' and General Literary and Scientific Institution in honour of the late Duke of Sussex (a patron of Jewish causes and the collector of a considerable library of Judaica). It stood on the site of the original New Synagogue (established in 1760) before its relocation in Great St Helen's, Bishopsgate, in 1838. It was described by Arthur Barnett as the 'first venture in (adult) popular Jewish education', and by Lucien Wolf as 'a kind of Jewish Birkbeck College'. For its growth and demise, see Arthur Barnett, 'Sussex Hall', *Trans., J.H.S.E.*, 1960, Vol. 19, pp. 65–79. Friday evening lectures were a regular feature at Sussex Hall. The particular reference in the *Jewish Chronicle* to Friday nights would have been seen as a telling irony. For the rise and impact of 'Mechanics' Institutes' from the 1820s (on which models Jewish Mechanics' Institutes were formed) see Thomas Kelly, *George Birkbeck: Pioneer of Adult Education*, 1957. Sussex Hall was an advanced form of Mechanics' Institute in terms of the quality and diversity of the mainly Jewish educational programme; attendance (for which fees were generally charged) was not confined to working people, nor to Jews – who were preponderant in numbers. It is of interest that Michael Henry (1830–75), a former staff member on the *Mechanics' Magazine* and editor of the *Jewish Chronicle* from 1868 until his death, assumed the management of the *Magazine* from 1857 until his death. His active interest in adult education in all levels of the Jewish community (and beyond) was a consistent theme in the *Jewish Chronicle* during the period under review.

30. Frederick Hyman Lewis of Euston Square, who had attracted some fame as a chess-master, describing himself as an 'intense advocate for the education of the Jews' wrote that he would be sorry 'to see them all receiving an equally excellent education, for the distinction of class which must to a certain extent be kept up would immediately vanish'. He noted, it would seem with regret, that 'the distinction between classes is being gradually broken up', in proportion to the approximation in education: *Jewish Chronicle*, 26 October and 9 November 1855. At the general meeting of subscribers to the Orphan Asylum in 1856, some declared their opposition to the provision of more than the rudiments of elementary education to the poor. In a long, reasoned editorial on 12 December 1856 the *Jewish Chronicle* rejected this approach, declaring that it was wrong to withhold a 'liberal education' from the 'masses'. There was a time, declared Adler, 'when the East End of London, the seat of learning, and the West End, the seat of fashion, were repellent to each other. That time was happily gone by ... and now (there is) no antagonism between them ... only a noble rivalry': *Jewish Chronicle*, 30 May 1856. 'Some mutual incomprehension' might have been a better description. In one of his periodic references to the kind of view expressed by Lewis, Adler in the presence of 'nearly the whole élite of the Jewish community' at the anniversary dinner of the Jews' Free School in 1855, declared that 'the time was gone by ... when the education of the poor was not only considered superfluous but by some even dangerous'. The opinion which he disowned had prevailed in some sectors of the wider society (save for a mainly religious education) and had not been entirely discarded. One facet of that opinion was that knowledge

created 'discontent'. In a public address at Sussex Hall in November 1850 Adler expressly rejected the suggestion, acknowledging that he preferred 'education' to 'knowledge', adding that 'religion' is 'the prime wisdom'.

31. Upon the completion of the meal and the formal parts of the occasion, there would often be a 'ball'. A typical instance was reported in the *Jewish Chronicle* in April 1853, from where we learn that at this 'anniversary' event at Willis's in support of the Jews' Infant School, attended by 250 people, 'dancing was kept up with great spirit till nearly 4 a.m. to the enlivening and fashionable music of Coote & Tinney's band'. The refreshments were described as 'of a more *recherché* kind than usual'. The word 'fashionable' and the French term were commonly used, each perhaps expressive of a conscious modernity free from the grim experience in a world outside – in which, one should perhaps add, some joyously present might have been involved in the provision of succour.

32. In 1851 Joseph Mitchell reported that of the 600 boys at the City of London School, 17 were Jews. He found that of the 16 prizes awarded on the basis of the latest public examination at the School, nine were won by Jews: *Jewish Chronicle* 15, August 1831. Similar proportions were noted at University College School: e.g. see *Hebrew Observer*, 22 September 1854. The fact that private Jewish education of some kind might have been provided at home or elsewhere for Jewish pupils of this and other schools, including some of the proprietary schools, did not inhibit criticism over the attendance at schools where no Jewish religious education was provided. In reverse, there was occasional public criticism to the effect that some parents sent their children to the Jewish 'charity schools', funded by the Jewish community, who could afford fee-paying schools and, where necessary, private Jewish education. For Jews' Free School, see S.S. Levin, 'The origins …', *Trans.*, J.H.S.E., Vol. 9, 1960, pp. 97–114; and Dr Gerry Black's *History of the Jews' Free School* (1997). For the charity schools generally see V.D. Lipman, *Social History of the Jews in England 1850–1950*, 1954.

33. In the 1860s Bernard Spiers, later a dayan of the London Beth Din, opened a 'collegiate day and boarding school' in Russell Square, Bloomsbury. By advertisement he tellingly invited Jewish pupils at University College School (then in that vicinity) to consider boarding at his school where he would provide Jewish religious and Hebrew education while they continued as day scholars at University College School.

34. In his first pastoral letter (August 1845) Adler urged the importance of education for girls as well as for boys. In the degree of reorganisation carried out at the Jews' Free School upon his direction, the curriculum for girls was extended. In April 1846 as a result of his request the governors of the Western Jewish Free School in the Soho area of London opened a school for girls in the locality of that school. Those events were one facet of a somewhat growing communal interest in the Jewish education of women, young and less young, an interest encouraged by women themselves. In 1852 Bresslau published a work specially directed to Jewish women, explaining the liturgy and commenting upon the scriptures. In the same year a book with like purpose

by Raphall went on sale in England. In the early 1850s a number of Sabbath and Sunday classes sprang up for Jewish women and girls, including one in Soho. The latter, financed by Lady Anthony de Rothschild, was directed by A.L. Green, whose main assistant was the headmistress of the girls' department of the Jews' Free School.

35 In general for the structure of London Jewry in the mid-century, see V.D. Lipman under that title in H.J. Zimmels and others (eds), *Essays Presented to Chief Rabbi Israel Brodie*, 1967, Vol. 1, pp. 253–73, and 'Rise of Jewish Suburbia' in *Trans.*, J.H.S.E., Vol. 21, 1968, pp. 78–103.

36. There was regular criticism of standards in many of the private schools. Lack of teacher training and an amateur discharge of the duties of school administration, militated against effective instruction. A special target of criticism was the inadequate attention to Jewish education by some schools, 'The elements of *Jewish* education,' commented the *Jewish Chronicle* on 17 August 1849, 'have always been step-motherly treated by the proprietors of Jewish boarding schools.' If that object is not attained, Jewish parents 'cannot (be) blamed' for choosing those (private) schools 'where the other elements of education ... are taught at cheaper rate, and have their children taught Hebrew at home'. Another light was cast on the overall situation by Marcus Bresslau's observation in that journal in September 1856 when, pointedly charging some Jewish boarding schools with neglect of Hebrew, added: '... it is not too much favoured – parents are said not to want it'. Some parents chose schools abroad for their children, among which was that of Dr Julius Furst, whose agent was the Hull merchant and a former pupil, Bethel Jacobs, and among whose 'references' was Adler.

37. Cecil Roth, *The Rise of Provincial Jewry*, 1950; Aubrey N. Newman (ed.), *Provincial Jewry in Victorian Britain*, 1975.

38. Raphael Loewe, 'Solomon Marcus Schiller-Szinessy 1820–90, *Trans.*, J.H.S.E., Vol. 21, 1968, pp. 148–89; Bill Williams, *The Making of Manchester Jewry 1740–1875*, 1976, pp. 242–6, and *passim*.

39. B.L. Benas, *The Evolution of Literary Efforts in Liverpool Jewry*, 1906; B.B. Benas, 'Survey of the Jewish Institutional History of Liverpool and District', *Trans.*, J.H.S.E., Vol. 17, 1953, pp. 23–37. Professor B. Wasserstein's paper to J.H.S.E. (May 1998) on Moses Samuel is, as yet, unpublished.

2

The Anglo-Jewish Pastorate (1840–90)

The distinctive Anglo-Jewish Ministry is traceable to the early nineteenth century.[1] Its central feature was the emergence in the synagogue of the vocation of the English preacher. Whatever further congregational, communal or general pastoral tasks might engage the preacher, the English sermon became the pivot of his operations. From his regular occupancy of the pulpit on Sabbaths and Festivals, he would propound what he deemed the essentials of Judaism, expound the biblical portion of the day, and/or recount and comment upon selected Jewish historical experiences. His addresses were directed to the edification and moral enlightenment of his congregation in terms capable of appeal to the secularly educated English Jew, without detracting from his own sense of duty to retain the simultaneous interest of the Jews of an older outlook. In few areas of communal enterprise is there revealed more clearly the character of modern Anglo-Jewish history and communal life and attitudes than in the evolution of the rank and office of Minister during the nineteenth century.[2]

The sermon has a history dating back to ancient times. It differs in form and substance from the *derasha* in that it is bereft of close *halachic* argument, and is also likely to be free from the extent of rabbinic *aggadic* material which might infuse the *derasha*. Nor did the sermon, or 'discourse', generally partake of the dramatic or the emotional substance and presentation associated with the *maggid* of old.

In 1825 a committee of Elders of the Sephardi community were invited by their colleagues to consider how best to improve the tone of their synagogue services. The sermon had not yet become a marked characteristic of Anglo-Jewish life. The committee's recommendation in favour of a resort to the practice of sermons, proved a significant stage in the history of the Ministry. The practice had already been set in motion in Liverpool and at the Westminster Synagogue. Some saw it as a positive requirement of the changing times, and it steadily became increasingly so seen. In Liverpool there was at first 'an unaccountable superstitious prejudice against the English language being used in the Synagogue ...', reminisced Moses Samuel in 1844.[3] That sentiment was not confined to Liverpool.

The absence of adequate provision for ministerial training, and the insufficiency of potential incumbents, became serious topics for persistent communal debate. Some preachers were self-taught. Some emerged out of the *chazanut* class of the Jews' Free School in London, combining the roles of *chazan* and preacher. The coming into being of an Anglo-Jewish press provided a considerable stimulus to the discussion. In that connection, the *Voice of Jacob* (1841–48), the *Jewish Chronicle* from 1841 and the *Hebrew Observer* (1853–55), were more than forums for nation-wide advertisements for synagogal appointments. They were also, editorially and otherwise, important channels of communication about the many issues involved in the delay in meeting acknowledged needs. The practical value of 'English discourses', and the communal damage suffered from the neglect of training, were virtually ceaseless themes in their columns.

In December 1840 a brochure was widely circulated in London and the larger provincial Jewish communities setting out some pressing reasons for urgency in remedying this condition. The publication was signed 'F'; the author was either Jacob Franklin or Henry Faudel. Their views were largely identical. In particular, the writer referred to the 'lamentable dearth of spiritual information and ... indifference and laxity of observance'.[4] He called for the establishment of 'a college ... to train young men of the higher classes for the Ministry. ... With a few honourable but partial exceptions the gentlemen styled reverend by courtesy, are selected for their vocal capabilities exclusively'. He asked: 'Can it be wondered at that our places of worship are deserted when the service is so conducted?'

A few months later a pamphlet was published by an equally well-informed anonymous polemicist which developed F's case further.

He contrasted the enlightened minds of 'our munificent brethren' with 'the negligence with which so excellent an undertaking (namely, the establishment of a college for the training of a "regular Jewish Ministry") has long been allowed to lie dormant'. Among other reasons for meeting this need, he cited the desirability of restoring 'unity' within the Jewish community after the Reform secession of 1840. He considered that more dignified religious services and regular English addresses could help heal the breach or limit the extent of the secession. He also related his plea to the importance of producing 'advocates' within the Jewish community to meet the 'menace' of conversionism, and who would also be able in the wider society to 'attack' the 'Gentile decryers of Judaism'.

On the High Festivals in 1842, Franklin reported that his journal had heard of only three congregations where sermons had been delivered. They were in Liverpool (David Meyer Isaacs), Birmingham (Morris Jacob Raphall) and Westminster (Henry Abraham Henry). There was an increasing awareness of the growing number of secularly educated laymen, especially in the younger age groups, and of an advancing interest in the new sciences and philosophies. There were frequent public expressions of concern over the apparent indifference of many congregants to the meaning of the synagogue service. The absence of any vernacular exposition of Judaism or of Jewish history seemed to close observers to constitute a major indictment of communal leaders. If their best energies were directed to the pursuit of civil emancipation, it was becoming clear even to them, that the improvement of the synagogue services, including the introduction of the much vaunted English discourses, would, by enhancing the 'English', 'western' and 'enlightened' character of the synagogues, add strength to the emancipationists' case.

Thus it was that the pulpit became an important element, from many angles, in communal thinking; at least among those whose own best energies were not taken up with making a bare living or finding their feet in their new country.

The patronising and sometimes painfully frank attitude to *chazanim* who ventured into the pulpit was often demonstrated, not least in the *Jewish Chronicle* under the editorship of Joseph Mitchell. This native-born activist in the emancipationist campaigns was of independent mind and robust temperament. He showed particular interest in Hermann Holzel, the Hungarian-born *chazan* of Hamburg who in 1845 was appointed to such office at the Hambro Synagogue in London. It was stipulated on his appointment that periodically he should be ready to preach. In 1850 that is what the lay heads of the congregation invited him to do for the High Holydays. It was a significant term in his contract, and the invitation was in line with the now more widely-used practice of Sabbath and Festival discourses. In an editorial note on 11 October 1850 hopes were expressed that Holzel's first attempt in the pulpit would be 'given the indulgence which it is the characteristic of Englishmen to give to every foreigner, however defective is (his) pronunciation and mode of elocution ... when he essays to convey his thoughts in their language'.

Holzel overcame these words of kindness. He had mastered English and soon acquired a reputation for trenchant addresses. On 18 July 1851 the same journal observed that his sermons 'are always pleasing to us and ... to most of his congregation'. Mitchell's limitation was significant. 'We live,' he added, 'in a thinking age, where every human mind considers itself privileged and entitled to think ... and to ponder upon everything it conceives, ... (so that) ... it is useless to stifle enquiry.' Judaism, he observed, courts investigation. It was thought to be in Holzel's favour that he came to the pulpit 'prepared' for the 'querist ... the sceptic ... and the indifferent'. In effect the editor now presented Holzel as something of a model. If the preacher wants to rivet the congregation's attention and 'dispel the doubts of the rationalist and convince the sceptic', he 'must anticipate the questions'. Holzel was described as rejecting the notion that sermons should be non-controversial.

Holzel's style of address was often what the laudatory editor termed 'argumentative', by which he meant that the preacher presented an argued case, as distinct from adopting a dogmatic approach. How far Mitchell's comments reflected his own predilection towards the argument of the Reformers for greater freedom of enquiry, is not clear. He was quick to point out that there were many who did not welcome the new style. The non-controversial was more comfortable. The old and new styles had their respective eloquent exemplars then and later.

Holzel attracted favourable comment in some quarters, but unease in others. His adoption of an 'argumentative' style did not indicate any lessening of his attachment to traditional teachings. Nor is it clear that Mitchell, as a protagonist of emancipation, would have supported Holzel's brand of messianism. Holzel would also at times combine rabbinic lore with candid castigation of features in the current Anglo-Jewish scene. On 31 July 1852 he declared that the messianic redemption is 'within our power to cause ... even in our days'. If all Jews 'as one body would think and act as Jews in the strictest sense of the word ... and would have no other object than to speed the restoration of Jerusalem ... (and if the same) 'holy zeal' (and) 'national spirit' were now among all the Jews as in the days of Ezra and Nehemiah, then 'the Lord would decidedly listen with favour to such a sincere and genuine application'.

Possible implications arising from these expressions, from the point of view of some of the prominent Jewish advocates of the emancipationist cause, were not left undrawn by the outspoken preacher. The Jew, he went on, 'who is satisfied with the present state of religious affairs' and does not hope for the (national Jewish) Restoration, does not know 'how to value the dignity of a real free man'. He boldly attributed to such Jews a lack of feeling for Jews in lands of oppression, commenting that they do not see that 'their personal liberties' are 'a boon ... at the hands of fellow-creatures' who will expect 'gratitude in return'. He added: 'They do not know what delight the words "independent nation" imparts ... they know nothing of our prerogatives, nothing of the genealogical table of our nobility ...'.

This widely noted address was in some respects less than fair to the emancipationists. Many were far from insensitive to the condition of the Jews under oppression or threat, nor was the disavowal of the Restorationist hope as stark as Holzel portrayed. Yet his general delineation was too near reality for comfort. The lengthy campaign for the opening of Parliament to professing Jews was at an especially sensitive stage in the years 1851–53. The publication of Holzel's Restorationist rhetoric was embarrassing to some.

The airings of proto-Zionism in his day in the Jewish press (notably in the *Hebrew Observer*, edited in turn in the 1850s by the Zionistic enthusiasts, Marcus Bresslau and Abraham Benisch, who was formerly at the *Voice of Jacob* and later proprietor and editor of the *Jewish Chronicle*) were familiar to Holzel. Added spirit was given to exchanges concerning the wisdom and propriety of advancing the Jewish national claims to Palestine, by the arrival in England in 1852 of Judah Alkalai, Rabbi of the Sephardi community of Semlin, then in Hungary. Alkalai's call to Jews to rally to Zion by a return to greater Jewish personal piety had attracted attention in the Jewish world. The call, based on biblical and mystical grounds, met with tentative favourable interest in some limited quarters in London, notably in a section of the Sephardi community. The divisions of opinion on the subject found expression in the Anglo-Jewish press in mid-1852. In that year an English version of one of Alkalai's Hebrew Zionistic pamphlets was published in London. Its dramatic title was: *Harbinger of Good Tidings: An Address to the Jewish Nation on the Prospects of Organising an Association to Promote the Regaining of their Fatherland*. There were unmistakable similarities in ideology and expression between Alkalai and Holzel.

Alkalai's philosophy and his call were opposed by some Orthodox spokesmen in Europe, as well as meeting with the disfavour of those in the leadership of Anglo-Jewry who were made aware of them. Further, Alkalai's suggestions of complacency in the face of Jewish need, echoed by Holzel, would have been likely to arouse adverse reactions. From his pulpit at the Hambro, Holzel expressed disapproval of life-styles of luxury, excessive finery of dress and what he perceived to be the accompanying weakening of Jewish attachment, the neglect of Jewish study and the inadequate provision for it. He deplored what he considered an exaggerated emphasis on the modes and virtues of integration into the wider society in everyday life.

In 1853 Holzel left England for a rabbinic post in Hobart, Tasmania, under the Chief Rabbi's authority. An organised Jewish community had come into being in Hobart in 1843, with the opening of the first synagogue there. Holzel had long ago received rabbinic ordination from prominent rabbis in Hungary. There is no indication that in London he had any occasion to exercise the rabbinic authority of deciding questions of Jewish law.

How far his outspokenness and the responses to it played a part in his decision to venture to the distant colony, one cannot assess but only speculate. His rabbinic authority was later extended to the Australian mainland. There were frequent departures of rabbis and ministers from the United Kingdom to posts overseas. His departure would not have been unwelcome in some sections of Jewish life in London. His career in England demonstrated, albeit in a somewhat special form, a certain gulf between continental yeshiva-trained rabbis (not all of whom shared his 'Zionism') and the men and women by whom the *mores* in the affluent Anglo-Jewish social circles were seen as natural, sensibly conventional and desirably English. To the developing pastorate, his brand of critique was too forward and more adventurous than prudence dictated. Rabbinic qualification was no guarantee of influence or of acceptance when the Preacher, least of all the Reader-turned-Preacher, cut too sharply across the habits of mind and the acknowledged aspirations of the 'laity'.

Ministerial migration to the colonies was regarded as being in part the discharge by Anglo-Jewry of a duty to the distant English-speaking world. Colonial communities were regarded by the Chief Rabbi and the metropolitan lay leadership as daughter congregations. The colonials saw themselves in the same light. On his assuming office as Chief Rabbi in 1845, Nathan Marcus Adler included the colonial communities in his enquiries about the state of congregational life and Jewish education. They received from him thereafter his regulations for the conduct of their religious and educational affairs. In the more personal sense, the migration was the response by individual ministers (or advanced aspirants to that vocation) to hoped-for rewards, materially and in status. They would leave behind the constraining culture of deference as well as face the bracing challenges of a new world.

Notable among those who went overseas were Abraham de Sola (1825–82), son of the Chief Minister of the London Sephardi community, who migrated to Canada in 1847, where his distinction as Orientalist and Hebrew scholar was allied to skills as a preacher, notably in the rabbinic exposition of Orthodoxy; Henry Abraham Henry (1806–79), Minister of the Western Synagogue in London (formerly headmaster of the Jews' Free School), who left for the United States in 1849 and was eventually appointed to rabbinic office in San Francisco; Morris Jacob Raphall (1798–1868), who retired from the Birmingham Hebrew Congregation in 1849 and was appointed rabbi of the Jeshurun Synagogue in New York; Sabato Morais (1823–97) who, after five years in a senior teaching post in the London Sephardi community, left for Philadelphia in 1851, where his fame as Hebrew scholar outmatched his life-long career as *chazan*, becoming a principal founder of the Jewish Theological Seminary of New York in 1887; and Joel Rabinowitz (1828–1902) who left a junior synagogal position in Birmingham in 1859 for the role of Senior Minister in Cape Town. Raphall, in particular, gave incisive public expression to disenchantment with the general disinterest in Anglo-Jewry in the promotion of Jewish studies.

Adler was mindful of this disinterest. He believed that an English-trained ministry, educated in rabbinics, bible, and general Hebrew literary and secular courses, could make a significant difference to the intellectual climate in the Jewish community. He did not overcome his disappointment at the general attitude towards the relevance and value of rabbinic study and higher Jewish learning. He had frequently delivered sermons in the vernacular when he served as Rabbi in Oldenburg and later in Hanover. Nor did he underrate the value of secular studies in the modern age. He had combined intense rabbinic learning with university studies in classics and modern languages, and gained his doctorate at Erlangen University at the age of 25.

The leaders of the Jewish community, Sephardi and Ashkenazi, were acutely aware of the case for the founding of training facilities for a native or 'native'-educated Jewish Ministry. They appreciated the value of such a development to the further Anglicisation of the community, including the immigrants, and to the progress of efforts towards emancipation.[5] Yet there was considerable hesitation and delay in acceding to the series of demands in the 1840s and 1850s for the creation of the desired college. The delay and the reasons for the inhibition had a bearing on the distinctive character of the Victorian Jewish pastorate.

There was limited appreciation on the part of the aged and sick Solomon Hirschell (1762–1842), the outgoing Chief Rabbi, both of the changing intellectual styles and the nature and extent of Anglicisation in the Jewish community. The bounds of his scholarly interests were largely encompassed within the *Beth Hamedrash*.[6] No initiative or effective response was truly expected from him.[7]

Adler had applied his mind to the issue of the college as a matter of immediate priority on his settling into office. He envisaged a

Jewish day school as a 'feeder' for his proposed college, which he regarded as of the highest importance to the success of his tenure. David Salomons led a body of influential opinion to whom the idea of the new Jewish day school was most unwelcome. To them it was a form of unnecessary and easily misinterpreted segregation.[8]

In 1857 widespread regret was expressed that among the applicants for the post of Second Reader at the Great Synagogue in London there was 'not a single Englishman'. That post was recently vacated by the English-born Aaron Levy Green whose calibre as scholar, preacher and counsellor had given the post a high profile. The successful candidate was Moses Keiser, previously of the Hague. For the next 25 years Keiser set professional standards in every field of pastoral care, thereby enhancing the office of *chazan* during a period when vocal talent on its own was subject to stern criticism. Green emerged paramountly as a preacher and was to gain added influence by his regular articles (under the name of *Nemo*) in the *Jewish Chronicle*, often of current practical interest, and at times highly controversial.

The demand for English preachers, with their moralistic sermons, was accompanied by an impatience with cantorial presentations by whomsoever except when their art might occasionally be a genuine high-grade attraction in itself. The institution of the choir was considered an aid to such presentation and to the imposition of elegance and decorum, which qualities acquired the attributes of a moral virtue in themselves in the context of the self-consciously Anglo-Jewish synagogal service.

Such assessment of the choir was not universal. One skilled pamphleteer in his survey of the communal scene questioned whether there was or could be 'real devotion' where 'the attention of the congregation is captivated by the sweet notes of the choir in new and fanciful tunes, not seldom taken from fashionable operas' and also while opinions were being exchanged during the service 'about the performance of the Reader'.[9] He looked to the new Chief Rabbi to introduce remedies to stir 'devotion'. Those who shared these concerns set their faith in the hoped-for institution of an expanded Ministry with adequate measures for recruitment and training. In his letter to all congregations upon his appointment, Adler included among his objectives the inculcation of the necessary 'quiet and decorum, dignity and solemnity' during the service. He does not appear to have regarded the choir as militating against such achievement. He considered it incumbent upon the Ministers and lay heads to secure that elusive condition, assisted by the choir.

The caution which tinged the innovatory spirit regarding the choir, was expressed by Franklin in the *Voice of Jacob* in December 1846. 'We may consider' its introduction into the service 'as an offspring of transitory circumstances.' He acknowledged that the 'duly constituted religious authorities' must exercise their power 'according to the notions of the age, to the desire and even the convenience of the community'. But the choir, 'designed only for an ornamental appendage', must not 'supersede the congregation', nor 'assume the appearance of a performance'. Its task is 'to assist (the congregation's) devotion'. For Franklin the educational effect of the preacher should precede in importance the cantorial or choral elements of the service, useful though they might be to devotion and decorum. In 1847 Adler published his 23-page 'Laws and Regulations for all the Synagogues in the British Empire'. The guidance for the conduct of the service was directed to achieving the solemnity of the proceedings, aided by an 'expressly trained' choir, by which 'performance' (in Franklin's sense) or supersession was excluded or clearly discouraged.

At Adler's installation in the Great Synagogue in July 1845, the choir of that congregation (formally established in 1841), whose director was the celebrated Julius Mombach, combined with that of the New Synagogue for the occasion. The choral element in the service may have attracted less attention on the part of some than the novel use of an orchestra (called a 'temporary orchestra'). But the prominence and quality of the choir added greatly to the fashionability both of the use of choral aid for the services and the practice of giving more serious training to choirs. Much reference was from time to time made to the fact that choirs ought not to be viewed (as some continued to regard them) as an imitation of church practice, but as in harmony with the biblical precedents for instrumental accompaniments to worship. They were increasingly viewed as beautifiers of the service and therefore commendable on religious principle. At the very least it was argued that the choir was an improvement upon an old-style unmusical Reader, with or without his untrained assistant chanters.

The effect of the increasingly widespread use of choirs on the

Ministry was twofold. First, the choir heightened the degree of cantorial expertise expected of Readers. This helped to differentiate that category from the preachers. Secondly, and by contrast, there was an inbuilt tension between preacher and choir regarding the respective lengths of sermon and chant. At the Great Synagogue, where the Chief Rabbi did not preach more than once monthly, such tension was not marked – and in any event was unlikely in that arena. Where the desire was for weekly sermons the inbuilt tension was a factor which inclined preachers to express reservations about excessive musical display. Adler's warning against choral 'supersession' and choral 'performance' raised sharp issues which were widely and popularly debated.

The old highly personalised and subjective forms of religious expression involved 'unmodern' definitions of decorum. The forms of solemnity of one age were the unacceptable manifestations of the indecorous in another. In June 1869 a Sephardi correspondent in the *Jewish Chronicle*, describing himself as an Orthodox Jew, observed that 'an English Minister should be an educated English gentleman'. He spoke the mind of large elements within the Jewish middle classes. It might not have occurred to him that the new 'Anglicised' forms of sophistication would seek to make do without the degrees of enthusiasm of an earlier age, which the new aids for enhancing the tone of public worship might not be able to replace and the sometimes negative effect of whose absence they might indeed magnify. In an earlier age decorum in a later sense would have seemed the antithesis of devotion.

The fact was that in the new age there were new questions, new aspirations and new standards. In the new age the preacher sought to be or was expected to seek to become the projector of the new within mainly traditional canons of thought and expression. Lay inertia, some confusion of purpose and contrived frugality, impeded the growth of the requisite cadre.

The case for the 'modern' Ministry had been starkly put by Benisch in the *Jewish Chronicle* on 17 August 1855. Earlier in the century the 'foreigner' who officiated 'was perfectly well understood'. He added: 'His manners and habits were quite akin to the taste' of the congregation, but in a new generation 'there was no congeniality between pastor and flock ... they were in language, habits and tastes ... widely separated ....' (The need arose for) 'ministers, combining the scholar with the man, theological knowledge with classical lore, Jewish piety with Gentile urbanity, Hebrew learning with English tastes and feelings ...'. Benisch heralded the opening of Jews' College in 1855 with the comment that 'with ... (its) establishment the emancipation of English Judaism from continental Judaism begins'. He had already declared the public launching of the scheme as 'the most important meeting ever held by the Jews of England'.[10]

As a long-standing protagonist of the idea of the College, Benisch may be forgiven his robust optimism. The reality was that the school and the College failed to attract significant numbers or adequate material support. Support for it had the character of a pittance. The hope, indeed the expectation in some quarters, that the 'higher classes' might send their children to the College was not realised. The College was also envisaged by its protagonists as a place of higher Jewish study for young adults who would not necessarily be minded to enter the Ministry. That remained largely a forlorn idea.

Not only had 'the ultra-liberal party' shown 'manifest hostility' to the idea of the College but the 'ultra-orthodox party' had displayed 'caution in its dealings with the College' and distanced itself from it.[11] Some clearly thought that Adler's concessions to Salomons had gone too far. 'School, pulpit and religion,' wrote Dr Mensor, rabbi in Dublin, 'stand at a very low ebb ... (in Anglo-Jewry). Israel wants proper rabbis but not merely English lecturers.'[12] The 'English lecturers' had their defenders. One such 'lecturer' wrote that their object was 'to improve the hearts of our auditors ... more to enlighten than to mystify (their) minds'.[13] Adler's institutions remained caught between conflicting emphases in a society undergoing transformation.

At the celebratory opening in November 1855, Adler, in referring to '... numerous difficulties' experienced over the realisation of his scheme, lamented that 'some regard it (the College) as unnecessary, nay injurious to the purpose of the community'. He had 'at times despaired' of its attainment. He added, defensively: 'We require only a very small number of students ... so that the supply might not be greater than the demand.' If by 'demand' he meant 'need', this ill-defined statement must have seemed to some to be more a plaintive cry for support than an actual assessment.

He was to contend with long-term insufficiency of support.

Typical of the response was the situation revealed in the College's tenth annual report in 1866. In an explanatory comment upon the deficit between income and expenditure, the report observed that the students were 'almost invariably' from those 'classes' which cannot afford the expense. Reflecting Adler's already expressed wishes, the report urged congregations to pay for students selected by them for training with a view to their becoming their Ministers. Only one synagogue had so far done this. Despite the need and this demand, it did not become an adopted course.

The 'preacher' was often at first regarded as assistant to the Reader. The latter, usually known as the *chazan*, conducted the Sabbath and Festival synagogue services or the major parts thereof. In some cases the Reader would occasionally preach. That would depend on his inclination and talent and on the request or permission of the lay heads of his congregation. Some later preachers of distinction began their careers as *chazan* or as *baal tephilah* (conductor of synagogue services but without the cantorial virtuosity or the aspiration thereto which a *chazan* might be expected to demonstrate). The preacher would generally be called Second Reader, thus marking the higher category of office held by the Reader.

Synagogal preaching in England was a slowly developing practice. For some Jews there remained about the practice a touch of 'church' flavour. It was an unprescribed interruption in the sequence of the statutory prayers, and a somewhat strange introduction of English into the recital of the Hebrew prayers set out in the time-honoured *siddur* (prayer-book). But the spirit of the emancipation and the widening Anglicisation of the Jewish population (including in due course the succession of immigrants following the removal of restrictions on free entry into Britain in 1836) progressively gave preaching (by whichever 'cleric') extra prestige and fashionableness. What had been new, alien and curious, came to be largely taken for granted.

Nathan Marcus Adler's monthly English sermons at the Great Synagogue in London and occasionally elsewhere in London and beyond (sometimes reported fully in the Jewish press), heightened the sense of fashion, as did the addresses of the Sephardi rabbinate. It is ironic that the grade of Second Reader was in time transmuted into the rank of Minister, taking precedence over that of Reader.

8. Dr Nathan Marcus Adler (1803–90), Chief Rabbi (1845–90)

9. Benjamin Artom (1835–79)

The process was distinctively English. The title and role were likewise distinctively Anglo-Jewish. To say that the Jewish pastorate was an Anglo-Jewish invention would be wrong, but only because that would suggest a policy decision. The reality is that it evolved and emerged out of the Anglo-Jewish scene and its English context, as did the Chief Rabbinate itself. In 1866 Benjamin Artom (1835–75), the Italian-born rabbinic scholar and gifted preacher, was installed as *Haham* of the Sephardi community. His induction address was tellingly entitled 'The Jewish Pastor in the Present Age'. Twenty-five years later, Hermann Adler was installed as Chief Rabbi in succession to his father. He chose with equal significance, as the title of his address, 'The Ideal Jewish Pastor'.

The title 'Pastor' was more than a matter of Victorian language. It betokened a moralising preacher who would not necessarily be intellectually demanding; usually high-minded; manifestly patriotic; consolatory, hortatory and somewhat Anglican in garb, in the cadences of his speech and in his designation as 'Reverend'. He may sometimes have acted as *baal tephilah* and may often have read the stipulated weekly biblical portions for the congregation, but it was as the Preacher that he became the standard-bearer of the Synagogue; and because of his training, level of learning and presumed influence, he became the acknowledged religious spokesman of his community to the wider society, as well as accordingly senior in rank and usually in salary to the Reader.

The similarities in style between the 'Jewish clergy', as the Ministers were often called, and their Christian colleagues of the cloth, satisfied the preferences of the self-consciously Anglicised lay leaders of the Jewish community and those of the broader Jewish middle classes who followed their example. The sense of need for a vernacular exposition of the Bible and of the principal tenets of Judaism sprang from and was ever more sharpened by the growing desire to present the Synagogue in Britain in a modern light as the campaign for civic and political emancipation grew in intensity. These considerations vested in the pulpit a centrality in synagogal life which had long before been occupied by the old-style rabbi and had sometimes been shared to some extent by the *chazan*. The sermon tended to become the distinguishing feature of the synagogue service.

From the 1840s, if not earlier, British birth was at a high premium in the appointment of congregational officiants of all kinds. The word 'foreigner' was not used necessarily as a term of personal depreciation, but it tended to denote a possibly disabling factor in appointments. Its, allegedly, disabling effect could well be eroded by long residence and personality. Hermann Adler himself was of Hanoverian birth. He was deemed a Jewish Englishman. That was a category of person who was perceived by those who set the governing communal fashions as likely to be possessed of acceptable ways and outlook and to be more suitable, almost by definition, for the holding of office. This view was partly conditioned by the need for spoken English, and partly by the related concern to further by every means the visible Anglicisation of the Jewish community.

In addition to an ingrained disinclination to endow Jewish higher learning, there was among the upper middle classes an equally deep preference for the non-segregated education of their teenage children. They were thought by Adler to be the likely source of recruits for the ministry. Events belied his optimism. It is paradoxical that the Anglicisation (and efforts to extend that process) which lay behind the movement to create the Anglo-Jewish seminary, should itself have been part of the motivation for seeking to narrow and impede Adler's plan.

When in 1853 Adler attended a Jewish public occasion in Birmingham, the event elicited much publicity in the Jewish and local press. It fell to Alderman David Salomons, soon to become the first Jewish Lord Mayor of London, to propose the toast to him. Adler had by then presented his scheme for the seminary with the controversial Jewish day school attached and in association with the *Beth Hamedrash*. Salomons' aversion to the involvement of the *Beth Hamedrash* rested on his anxiety lest an emphasis on talmudic study might arise therefrom; he did not think such study was necessary in the training of a modern Anglo-Jewish Ministry. His publicly known reservations about the scheme added to the piquancy of the commendatory tone of his remarks about Adler, which went even beyond any customary forms of tribute.

While Salomons deplored that many congregations and communities were without ministers and while he acknowledged the gravity of this failing, he urged the importance of procuring incumbents possessed of 'thorough English feelings'. He condescendingly expressed pleasure that the Chief Rabbi had the required combination of possessing such 'feelings' as well as being 'thoroughly orthodox'. The message was clear. In 'thorough English feelings' he would have included moderation, accessibility, wide culture (especially familiarity with English literature), and manifest and unquestionable patriotism. He did not exclude rabbinic learning but it was not of the essence. The community had the Chief Rabbi and the *Haham* for the resolution of any halachic issues. The habit of minimalism in Jewish education ran deep. It was not limited to ministerial training.

Adler reluctantly abandoned that part of his plan which related to the *Beth Hamedrash*. In 1855 Adler's school was opened in Finsbury Square; this was in effect the initiation of Jews' College. The school closed 25 years later, through lack of support. This was also in part the result of the steady movement of Jewish families from the inner areas to the central and western regions of London.

The debates and events of the 1840s and 1850s affected both the expectations of the Jewish community and the general aspirations of the Ministers themselves. There was no rabbinical diploma course at the College until the end of the century. There was an emphasis on homiletics and pastoral care – important areas of ministerial responsibility but far removed from the levels of attainment aimed at in the rabbinic and ministerial colleges on the Continent. The term 'Reverend', adopted from Christian usage, became the fixed undifferentiating prefix to Preachers and Readers, sometimes to the incomprehension or derision of the less sophisticated or the unassimilated Jews throughout the century, especially in the newer immigrant sections of the community.

Advertisements in the 1850s would sometimes call for Englishmen only, or in some other way indicate that preference. When the College was at last opened (albeit at first in the form of the day school), the *Jewish Chronicle* reverted to Salomons' language and tone. Our future ministers, declared the editor, 'will be men of thorough English feelings and views', adding characteristically, 'and as conversant with the classics of their own language as with those of the sacred tongue ...'. Benisch, now proprietor and editor of that newspaper, again reflected in this field the tastes and the social and intellectual needs of the middle classes of the Jewish community.

To present Judaism to the outside world was deemed no less

important than teaching Jews the tenets of their faith. The object was to relieve potential critics of their inherited picture of the Jew as un-English and Judaism as irretrievably foreign. Such responsibilities were expected to be exercised in a recognisably English style, bereft of undue reliance on talmudic argument, and free from flights of higher Jewish learning. Yeshiva study was perceived as neither English in nature nor relevant to then current purposes. In 1881 at the inauguration of Jews' College's new premises in Tavistock Square in Bloomsbury, Arthur Cohen, Vice-President of the College and President of the Board of Deputies, caught the mood well in his formulation of the tasks of the Ministry. In addition to being educated to present their religion worthily to Christians, they must be educated so as to be able to show 'that those who revile the Jewish people might see that they were in the wrong'. In addition, at a time when the Jews have become 'better educated', there was need for 'a cultured clergy'.[14]

New freedoms for Jews in the West had brought opportunities and inclinations for the pursuit of general interests in history, languages, science and philosophy. Such pursuit may well be wrapped within a religiously defined Jewish society and may well coincide with the retention of regard for family traditions. Jews' College was one of the training establishments created in the new era of the Emancipation and the Enlightenment; their general aim was to provide Jewish communities with 'spiritual guides' imbued with standards and interpretations serviceable in the new Jewish historical experience. However, the community which gave birth to Jews' College not only lacked enthusiasm for higher Jewish learning but in its upper reaches deemed such aspirations to be foreign in inspiration, unrelated to the policy and objectives of sound administration, and (at least within the Ashkenazi community) extraneous to what seemed to them the priorities of their fathers and to the requirements of 'religion'.

It came to be a common assertion that a principal reason why the Ministry often failed to acquire a 'superior position in the Synagogue' was that Ministers did not have a sufficient measure of modern academic attainment. The Jewish press, especially from the 1860s, regularly urged that steps should be adopted to raise the status of the Ministry in the life of the synagogues, and related this requirement to the advancement of their intellectual pursuits.

Michael Henry, editor of the *Jewish Chronicle* from 1869 to 1875, himself a son of a scholarly family with his own personal aspiration as a man of letters even if in a somewhat minor key, long called for provision for serious ministerial study of modern Jewish history. Benisch in his periods as editor of that newspaper (1854–69 and 1875–78) frequently related the standing of Ministers (including their own degree of professional and even personal self-esteem) to their levels of general education.

The scheme introduced in 1879 whereby facilities were to be provided for students of Jews' College to pursue degrees at London University, was hailed as one of great significance. The new editor of the *Jewish Chronicle*, Asher Myers, while welcoming the plans, declared that 'the community must make up its mind to modify somewhat considerably the position held at present by our Ministers 'in the Synagogues'. He roundly berated the congregations who 'persist in their tacit refusal to give (the Ministers) that superior position in the synagogue which they must occupy if their talents and training are not to a great extent to be wasted'. He hoped the scheme of 1879 would help rectify a situation where the Minister is treated 'as such an underling'. He thought it was especially unhelpful for the Preacher to serve at the same time as Reader or synagogue secretary.

The multi-purpose officiant long remained a common feature. This was sought to be justified on grounds of economy. The practice was also the product of the assumption that the dominant office in the synagogue was that of the lay heads, who deemed themselves as ultimately, if not also on a day-to-day basis, entitled (even obliged) to give instructions to all in the employ of the synagogue, including officiants at all levels. This outlook sprang from the long-standing lay paternalism (operated in the upper echelons of Jewish society in the spirit of *noblesse oblige*) which expected a one-sided 'reciprocal' obedience.[15] In the Reform community the weekly sermon was a distinctive feature from its inception. The status of the religious head was higher than that of his counterpart in many Orthodox congregations. Their long-serving Preacher, David Woolf Marks, was the founding minister of their Synagogue, a preacher of great power and eloquence, and in his early days in Liverpool one of the pioneers of the English sermon. Volumes of his popular and learned discourses were published during his tenure at the West

71

London Synagogue of British Jews, where he was the central personality for two generations.

In his installation speech as *Haham* in 1866, Artom defined preaching as 'religious instruction'. He used the occasion to express his concern over the growing scepticism of the age and the indifference to Judaism. The 'pastor', he stated, was under a duty 'to resist and check the threatened danger, the tendency which menaces with ruin our national literature, national sentiments and national bond'. By 'national', Artom referred to the religio-national character of Judaism. His Ashkenazi colleagues would probably have used language more redolent of a specifically religious definition than that adopted by their new Italian fellow-preacher, without their departing any less than he from belief in the ultimate national restoration under divine providence.

They were also at one with him in attaching importance within the pastor's agenda to the search for ways to conserve and strengthen self-conscious Jewish identity in the open society of the West. They all exercised that responsibility as men who by training and habit (and the expectation of those to whom they might be accountable) tended to view decorum, protocol and the preaching of virtue as prominent in the interface between pulpit and congregation. It was not an unfailing recipe for the condition of which Artom spoke, but its advocacy enjoyed the hearty approval of the laity.

The Ministers, including the 'pure preachers' (as those engaged to preach and were not Readers were sometimes called) were but too well aware of the dominant role of the lay readers in their respective congregations. To most of the Ministers this did not seem unnatural, nor a cause for resentment. Yet personality tells. Given a vivid or persuasive personality, and with tact and independence of mind, it was open to the preacher or Reader-preacher, to exert substantial personal influence on congregational or wider communal policy in education, social welfare, public relations and even administration. In some instances, the bonds with the lay heads became ones of high mutual respect and close friendship in which the Minister's counsel, generally in private, would be sought on major contentious issues. Ultimate control, like the purse strings, remained with laymen. Deference was expected from 'the clergy'.

The discussions between the lay leaders of the main Ashkenazi congregations in London, which led to the foundation of the United

Synagogue in 1870, took place with the awareness of the growth of an Anglo-Jewish preacher vocation, whether or not the preacher also acted as Reader, or as was usually the case, much engaged in pastoral care. The category in London included some preachers of distinction – Hermann Adler at the Bayswater Synagogue, Samuel Marcus Gollancz at the Hambro, Aaron Levy Green at the Central, Simeon Singer at the Borough Synagogue (later of the New West End Synagogue) and Morris Joseph at the North London Synagogue (later Senior Minister at the West London Synagogue of British Jews in succession to Marks). In the Provinces the category of distinction included George Joseph Emanuel (Birmingham) and David Meyer Isaacs (now in Manchester).

By 1880 residual inhibitions about sermons had waned into remote memory or distant paternal hearsay. The use of the vernacular in congregational addresses was no longer looked on askance as an alleged imitation of Church practice or as a sign of incipient Reform among the Orthodox. The introduction of a fixed pulpit in the synagogue as distinct from the old-style moveable wooden lectern, was not now any cause of unease. Nor was the English sermon at the fixed pulpit considered inconsistent with the occasional delivery thereat of an old-style *derasha* on particular occasions, notably *Shabbat Hagadol* and *Shabbat Shuva*. The early restiveness over what used to be seen as an unwonted interruption was a thing of the past. Nor was it assumed, as was formerly sometimes the case, that a pulpit address in English was in practice somehow likely to instil forms of secular wisdom antipathetic to 'proper Jewish learning'.

If some felt nostalgia for the old regular *derasha*, it was retained as nostalgia rather than as a case for its return. Fashionable preachers were progressively less shy of indicating their familiarity with the works of the great English Christian exponents of the art of preaching, still less with English and European literary classics.

But such trends and choices did not extend to Jews of more recent arrival or to those who had stood apart from that Westernisation and Anglicisation which the Anglo-Jewish leadership had endeavoured to cultivate. Whatever might be in the long run the extent of Anglicisation among the descendants of the less assimilated Jews, the pastorate, to the latter, somehow belonged to a different class. The pastors, whatever their own origins, could not

10. Aaron Levy Green (1821–83)

11. Morris Joseph (1848–1930)

escape their English patronising air in their relations with the ladies and gentlemen of the usually Yiddish-speaking small synagogues or conventicles, or even with the younger generations of those sections of the community. Generally that attitude came to them unreflectingly. It was an attitude which sometimes inclined spokesmen of the intended recipients of pastoral care in whatever form to hold themselves and their colleagues and families aloof from.

The pastor's clerical dress gave an added dimension to 'religious' differences as well as to the marked mutual sense of class difference. The facilities agreed in 1879 between Jews' College and London University were of little interest to such groups (if they knew about them) or to their rabbinic or lay leaders. To them such arrangements served only to confirm or indeed sharpen their suspicions over the halachic authenticity of the Judaism of the English Jewish 'ecclesiastical' system – even though (and perhaps, ironically, especially because) the subjects studied at the University under those arrangements would be related to the mishnaic background in Jewish history, the language of the Talmud, the thinking of philosopher rabbis, or other Judaic-connected topics.

Differences of opinion concerning ministerial training and qualifications, reflected the diverse character of the Jewish community.

12. David Myer Isaacs (1810–79), *c*.1850

They endured far into the next century, and were indeed accentuated in the widening intellectual and religious 'pluralism' of that new era.[16]

A constant and telling feature of the pastorate, notably in the provinces, was the limited salary scale of the incumbents. In part this resulted from the limited income of some of the congregations, and the pressing need in some communities to provide for the relief of the Jewish poor. It also in part reflected the widely prevailing modest level of status accorded to the 'clergy' within individual synagogues and the Jewish community. Comparisons with the limited remuneration of Christian clergy did not alleviate either the distress sometimes caused to incumbents and their families or the concern felt by some observers who, among other considerations, deemed that the Jewish minister's influence was in turn likely to be adversely affected by his apparent acceptance of his attributed standing, reflected and confirmed by the limited remuneration. His standing was not likely to be enhanced by private gifts from congregants, nor, especially in the smaller provincial congregations, was such a 'source of income' likely, if it existed, to prove significant.

There were frequent references in communal discussion and in the Jewish press about, in particular, the financial plight of incumbents during illness or in retirement, as well as of their dependents. Advertisements appeared in the press from time to time by or on behalf of retired or sick *chazanim* and preachers for financial aid. Some congregations had adopted the practice of requiring officiants, as a term of appointment, to insure their lives in the long-term interests of their wives and families. Some of them found the insurance premiums burdensome in the light of their income. In 1856, after some public debate about possible ways of meeting the problem, Michael Hart Simonson, the Manchester shochet, Jewish littérateur and communal activist, proposed the creation of a 'benefit society' by congregational officiants from whose annual contributions of £1 each it was hoped that a standing fund for individual aid might be established. Following his invitation,[17] officiants of 13 provincial congregations soon joined the society, which grew and of which the elder Adler became President. They included those of Glasgow, Edinburgh, Dublin, Norwich and Hull.

In May 1884 a Provincial Jewish Ministers' Fund was created. It followed a significant public letter from the Chief Rabbi calling for such a fund, in support of which a financial appeal by lay sponsors[18] appeared in the *Jewish Chronicle*. Adler's letter was more than a call for adequate funding for the provincial ministry. It was a grim assessment of standards and conditions in many provincial communities 40 years after he had first urged the setting up of a training seminary. 'A generation is now growing up,' he wrote, 'ignorant of the sublime significance of Judaism (and) of the meaning of its precepts and consequently indifferent as to their observance ... ignorant and therefore careless of the high morality it inculcates.' He referred in particular, as a cause of this situation, to officials with slender knowledge of English. 'The utmost they succeed in accomplishing is to teach their pupils the reading of Hebrew and to convey to them a hazy and indistinct conception of the meaning of parts of the liturgy and scripture.' The Fund would supplement salaries of candidates competent to be Ministers and teachers and able to converse in grammatical English fluently. It is likely that the language is that of Hermann Adler, then his father's deputy.

If improved standards were thereafter noted and attributed to the Fund, this was in part because candidates of quality might not have been deterred, as formerly, from seeking positions in provincial communities. Among such were Aaron Asher Green who served the communities of Sheffield and Sunderland, aided by the Fund, until his election at the new synagogue in Hampstead in 1892; and Moses Hyamson (later a dayan of the London Beth Din) at Swansea. The absence of an adequate or any communal system for the recruitment, training and remuneration of teachers, remained among the factors which sustained in practice minimalist educational standards in broad areas of the Jewish community.

NOTES

1. For the early history of the English 'Sabbath discourse' see Cecil Roth, *History of the Great Synagogue, London 1690–1940*, 1950, pp. 158–69; Arthur Barnett, *The Western Synagogue 1761–1961*, 1961, pp. 48–51 and 148–51; B.B. Benas, 'Survey of the Jewish Institutional History of Liverpool and District', *Trans.*, J.H.S.E., 1953, Vol. 17, 1953, pp. 23–7; Albert M. Hyamson, *Jews' College London 1855–1955*, pp. 13–17 and *The Sephardim of England*, 1957, pp. 220–61; Anne Kershen and Jonathan Romain, *Tradition and Change: A History of Reform Judaism in Britain 1840–1995*, 1995, especially in relation to the career of David Woolf Marks, formerly of the Seel Street Synagogue, Liverpool and the first Rabbi of the West London Synagogue of British Jews. For early Preachers, including Reader-Preachers, see C.K. Salaman, *Jews as They Are*, 1882; lists and notes thereon in Isidore Harris, *Jews' College Jubilee Volume*, 1906; and V.D. Lipman, 'The Age of Emancipation' in *Three Centuries of Anglo-Jewish History*, (ed.) V.D. Lipman, 1961. For the new trends in preaching, see Alexander Altmann, 'The New Style of Preaching in Nineteenth Century Germany', in *Studies in Nineteenth*

Century Jewish Intellectual History, (ed.) Alexander Altmann, 1964, pp. 65–116.

2. See generally Israel Finestein, 'Anglo-Jewish Opinion during the Struggle for Emancipation 1828–58' in his *Jewish Society in Victorian England*, 1993, pp. 1–53; 'J.F. Stern 1865–1934: Aspects of a Gifted Anomaly', ibid., pp. 327–49 and A.M. Jacob, 'Aaron Levy Green 1821–83', *Trans.*, J.H.S.E., Vol. 25, 1977, pp. 87–206.

3. *An Address on the Position of the Jews in Britain ...*, Liverpool, 1844.

4. For the state of observance, see Steven Singer, 'Jewish Religious Observance in Early Victorian London, 1840–60', *Jewish Journal of Sociology*, Vol. 28, No. 2, 1986, pp. 117–37.

5. In the 1840s and 1850s a frequent theme adverted to in advocacy (by pamphlet, press and public debate) for serious ministerial training was that an effective Ministry would help to set bounds to the attraction of religious indifferentism on the part of those who found no comfort in the old ways. This requirement was regularly asserted to be especially urgent among the children of the affluent, whose Jewish education was equally regularly declared to be flawed: 'Public instruction in pulpit and school' became linked as an interdependent and combined desideratum, typically and sharply propounded in a lengthy and characteristic editorial in the *Jewish Chronicle* on 2 November 1849. The contrast between the care for synagogue structure and neglect while the spirit within 'withered' struck home. Yet the ever-mounting campaigns over the educational and ministerial inadequacies of Anglo-Jewry – including abundant contrasts with conditions in some continental countries–did not appear to imbue the generality of the communal leadership with any sense of urgency or apprehension.

6. 'House of Study', a resort in the City of London for rabbinic study, much frequented by Hirschell, towards the end of whose life the House was considered a suitable seminary for prospective rabbis and ministers. The acquisition, for the House, of Hirschell's rabbinic library after his death was perceived as a likely encouragement towards that end. It continued as a venue for talmudic study. The new Chief Rabbi frequently conducted Talmud sessions there for those interested, but it did not gain ground as a professional or vocational seminary. See Philip Ornstein, *Historical Sketch of Beth Hamedrash*, 1905; and Rabbi Dr H. Rabinowicz, 'The Beth Hamedrash Library, London', in *A.J.A. Quarterly*, June 1962.

7. The closing years of Hirschell witnessed a spate of petitions or 'memorials' (and counter-memorials) from members of the main metropolitan synagogues to 'wardens and vestries' and to the religious heads of the Ashkenazi and Sephardi communities. The memorialists urged a variety of changes which 'shall tend to remove imperfections and to promote religious knowledge'. They were not limited to the initiators of the Reform movement. The call for 'English discourses' was prominent throughout. The memorialists acknowledged that there was 'some difficulty' in finding people of the right character and attainment, but considered that if a policy of making appointments were adopted and announced, appropriate candidates might emerge. Age, outlook,

infirmity and hostility to the Reform movement inhibited Hirschell from giving guidance to the lay leadership, thereby encouraging a 'policy' of inaction.

8. I am grateful to Rabbi Raymond Apple of the Great Synagogue in Sydney for the information that on 12 November 1841 Montefiore in a letter to Adler on other matters added: 'I would feel most anxious to obtain a copy of your sermons. ... It would be presumptuous in me to express how greatly they would prove serviceable to our brethren in England.' It is remarkable that Montefiore, who well knew of the growing desire and need for English sermons and the relevance thereof to the movement for the creation of a training college, should have allowed the lengthy delay in its foundation, in spite of his close friendship with Adler following the latter's election as Chief Rabbi. It was a term of Adler's appointment that he should be able to deliver sermons in English within two years. He was able to do so within the first year.

9. *A Few Words ... to the Committee for the Election of a Chief Rabbi ... and the Electors at Large*, by 'A Friend of Truth', 1844, pp. 9–10.

10. *Jewish Chronicle*, 9 January 1854.

11. Ibid., 23 November 1855.

12. Ibid., 15 February 1856.

13. Ibid., 22 February 1856.

14. Isidore Harris, *Jews' College Jubilee Volume*, 1906, p. lxvi.

15. See Todd M. Endelman, *The Jews of Georgian England (1714–1830)*, 1979, esp. pp. 142–9, regarding the decline of the authority of rabbi. See also, Michael Goulston, 'The Status of the Anglo-Jewish Rabbinate 1840–1914' in *Jewish Journal of Sociology*, Vol. 10, No. 1, 1968, pp. 55–82 and Todd M. Endelman, *supra*, Chapter 3, 'Native Jews in the Victorian Age'.

16. In July 1923 the Chief Rabbi, Dr J.H. Hertz, addressing the fourth Anglo-Jewish Preachers' Conference, described the Ministry as 'a very young institution in this country'. He added: 'The community has not yet become used to its own creation and does not yet quite understand its relation to it.' The community, he observed, is 'educating itself to it'. What lay behind his striking words was the contrast between the almost ubiquitous 'Reverends' of his day and the older-style rabbis, some of which category still served in a number of congregations. The first Conference of Anglo-Jewish Preachers had been convened in 1908 by Hermann Adler, whose tenure as deputy for his father from 1880 and then as Chief Rabbi from 1891, coincided with the period in which the new-style Victorian Ministry had become a deep-rooted characteristic of the Jewish community, side by side with the survival in some quarters of the old rabbinic tradition. The latter segment was reinforced by the inflow of yeshiva-trained continental rabbis in the Eastern European Jewish immigration from 1881. The ambience of the Federation of Synagogues and the Union of Orthodox Hebrew Congregations was more congenial to them than the Congregations of the United Synagogue. Adler was at home with the Anglo-Jewish 'type', of which he was a prime cultivator. Hertz, who encouraged higher Jewish studies in many fields, including rabbinic study,

sought to bridge the diverse 'types'.

Hertz was sharply critical of what he called the communal 'neglect' of scholarship. Jews' College, he declared was 'still starved and beggared and without bursaries', and the Ministry was 'miserably underpaid'. He decried what he regarded as the limited opportunities afforded to Ministers for serious study. 'Scholarship,' he commented, 'is the very soul of the Ministry. Without it (the) Minister can never hope to meet the religious perplexities that agitate both pastor and people at a time of religious and social unrest as the present ... Only scholarship will enable him to justify our progressive conservatism – the synthesis of the best citizenship and broadest humanitarianism with the warmth and colour, the depth and discipline, of the olden Jewish life, in the eyes of our people.' If Hertz's oratory was not always sufficiently particularised, one detects therein some disillusionment with Victorian-style priorities, including the idea and the practice of the Minister as a synagogal functionary. If he expressed his broad vision in Victorian language, it was nonetheless the eloquence of revolt. He did not regard rabbinic scholarship as a luxury or a dispensable extra, nor higher Jewish studies as an encumbrance, nor ministerial independence of mind as an eccentricity. Nor did he view political Zionism as dangerous or as not fit to be welcomed in the synagogue. He represented and helped to mould new categories of fashion. The Victorian pastorate, with some exceptions, had had its day.

17. See *Jewish Chronicle*, 23 May and 21 November 1856. The inaugural meeting of what was called the Congregational Officials Association, presided over by the Chief Rabbi, was convened by a circular letter which was published in the *Jewish Chronicle*. It stated that an added purpose of the association could be to act as 'a centre of intercommunication between its clerical members' and that it would 'naturally lead to the exchange of ideas on the spiritual wants of the community. The circular must have had Adler's prior authority. It was among the earliest intimations of the creation of a conference of Anglo-Jewish ministers, which under his successor took genuine shape, marking an advance in the ministerial *esprit de corps* within, at first, an Adlerian mould.

18. The President of the Fund and principal signatory was Samuel Montagu (later Lord Swaythling). Isaac Livingstone quotes Hermann Adler as reporting in 1884 that, in one town, 'an efficient Minister', with wife and seven children, received the wage of £80, paid irregularly: see Isaac Livingstone, *The Provincial Jewish Ministers' Fund* (1935) p. 5.

3

Jewish Emancipationists in Victorian England: Self-imposed Limits to Assimilation

Acculturation is not the same as absorption. The former consists of increasing the levels of similarity in the way of life between individuals (or a group) on the one hand and the larger body within which they live on the other hand. It is a mood as well as a process. It has its own momentum, whether by design or by the sheer impact of fashion.

Similarity in speech, dress and public behaviour may be the instant objective, which itself will be directed towards fuller and easier acceptance into the wider society. But the immediately aimed-at similarities can in time come to reflect and induce deeper inner changes in outlook and inspiration. The fuller the acceptance, the more pervasive and more effective those changes.

The long-term results may endanger the remains of any distinctiveness, subject only to the impact of any outside hostility or some dramatic resurgence of ethnic interest or historical pride. In the Victorian era the conventional wisdom was that for the most part hostility would wither with the expansion of education and improved social conditions. Nor did Victorian Jewry experience any dramatic resurgence of ethnic self-consciousness.

Meanwhile, those who consciously advocated a high degree of integration were often acutely concerned not to be acculturated to the point of total absorption, by which I mean the loss of transmissible distinctiveness. The leading Jewish emancipationists assumed that the wider society was both ready for Jewish assimilation and would, on the whole, not misconstrue the setting of limits to that process. Their campaign for Jewish civic and political equality was conducted within this framework.

Jewish separateness was presented by Jews as a religious requirement. Historical recollections and inherited mores inevitably intertwined with and strengthened the social effects of religious difference. There were special features of the Anglo-Jewish experience which constituted a strong moving force towards the cultivation at one and the same time of pride in being English and of pride in Jewishness.

Among the most important of those features was the growing social emancipation of the Jews since the late seventeenth century. The retention of a distinct Jewishness was part of a continuing style of living amidst a surrounding public which seemed to expect it. The influence of the Bible on English life and thought made that distinctiveness seem the more natural to Christian as well as to Jew. It had the character of a long-standing convention. Furthermore, the highly personalised form of Jewish communal government, associated with habits of centralisation and lay power, encouraged the leadership to treat the measure of difference as a matter of family pride and public duty.

These considerations, some conscious, some instinctive, were reinforced by the nature of the 30-year public debate in the nineteenth century on the case for and against Jewish civil emancipation. It was a debate in depth, conducted largely between Christians of whom many, whatever their opinions on the particular issue of Jewish emancipation, were unalterably and favourably impressed by Jewish survival, and by the role of Jews and Judaism in the world. There was also on the Jewish side of the debate a universal conviction as to the virtues of Britain's hegemony and British procedures.

There was a strong attachment among Jewish emancipationists to the institutions which embodied Jewish separateness – the synagogues, the schools, the welfare agencies and family cohesion. It went beyond nostalgia. They were eager to sustain, and to be seen to sustain, the nature of the Jewish community as a community of faith. It was axiomatic that it was as a religious community that the Jews were presented as worthy of the full rights of citizenship.

The pervasiveness of religion in the public life of Victorian England gave Judaism (whether in its Orthodox, that is normative, style, or in its Reformist model) the character of an emblem of self-conscious patriotism and normality.

If the English Jews took on the colour of their environment, they did so even in the very fashioning, conscious and subconscious, of their own responses to the danger of absorption. The combination of their leaders' attachment to the institutional life of the Jewish community with a high degree of proud and articulate assimilation, became and long remained a distinctive feature of Anglo-Jewish life, and was an example widely followed in the community.

The Victorians would have been at a loss to grasp any assumption concerning the availability of a secular Jewishness. As far as they entertained the Jewish national idea, it had wholly different connotations. For them Jewish continuity was worthwhile in so far as it was rooted in, and defined by, reference to religion. If religious faith, for historical reasons, gave expression to certain national ideas, they regarded this as either a subject for rabbinic eschatological exposition or as essentially an anachronism. What a remote future might be thought to have in store would be, if anything, a matter not only for Jews but for the whole world, even if there were some current philosophies related to an inscrutable particular role for the Children of Israel within the supposed eventual universal transformation.

The concern of the emancipationists for the transmissibility of their distinctive qualities as Jews, was no less real for being in many cases an offshoot of family commitment. There was room, within their own world outlook, for an anxiety to preserve points of Jewish difference. The far-reaching acculturation of their households, and of those who followed their examples, was relied on initially to justify the claim for emancipation and once that was attained, to evidence its propriety and good sense. The envied accolade was the acceptance of Jews as Englishmen. As long as full civic rights had been withheld, that title, so it was felt, had been visibly, hurtfully and in defiance of reality, denied to them. These sentiments were shared by Jewish middle-class families in the provincial cities, many of whose members were prominent in municipal life and in local literary and philanthropic activity.

The extent of British power and wealth and the strength of Britain's liberal image were such that, to the Jews of Britain, it seemed that fortune had smiled upon them in the distribution of the Jews in the world. These considerations heightened the sense of an Anglo-Jewish duty to intercede on behalf of less fortunately placed Jews abroad. Any such intercession was a reflex of Jewish self-esteem. It was both a counterpart to Jewish acculturation and a parallel to the Whig-and Liberal-related popular British policy of public sympathy (and sometimes diplomatic and other practical support) for liberationist movements abroad. Anglo-Jewish leaders responded both as Englishmen and as Jews.

The Jewish pride in their capacity as Englishmen likewise sharpened the Jewish desire to have what was called 'a native ministry'. The needs of the day – Anglicisation of the broad Jewish community, improved standards and techniques in Jewish education, a more Westernised and sophisticated synagogal service, regular addresses in English to the increasingly integrated congregations – pointed to the imperative nature of the call for Englishmen to occupy the pulpits and for the creation of a modern pastorate. It was an internal Jewish desideratum, a postulate of being English and an earnest of the sincerity of Jewish emancipationist polemics. These motivations were seen as one. Long-standing social emancipation and the pragmatic habits of English public life gave the Jews not only an assured sense of liberty but also, so to speak, a sense of unpressured timelessness. In this condition they lacked the spur needed to invest real effort in higher Jewish learning or intense Jewish study.

The outward religiosity of English domestic life – largely Bible-based and Evangelically inspired – was reflected in the fashionable religiosity of the more prominent Jewish communal leaders. In such matters genuine sentiment was allied to pubic prudence and social convention.

It was believed that the Anglo-Jewish community had attained a beneficent balance. This was viewed as a goal, which either under divine providence or through historical evolution awaited other Jewish communities. Time, effort and patience would be required. The British example was considered important in the unfolding of this dispensation. England was held to be in the van of what was regarded as the rapidly advancing moral and cultural regeneration of the Western world. Even the Tsarist Empire was not regarded as permanently immune to relevant changes.

Anglo-Jewry experienced no radical break with the past. For them, historical perceptions, common sense and contemporary Jewish needs combined to warrant their integration and to require and justify their attempted limitations upon it. Their leaders (unlike those of French Jewry under Napoleon) at no time felt called upon by public events to declare the precise principles of their civic creed. Nor were there sudden changes – now towards liberalism and now towards autocracy – by which public policy and Jewish responses were pulled hither and thither, as in Central Europe. Nor was there that particular sense of utopia achieved, which deeply affected and affects American Jewish reactions. It was always far easier for an American Jew to declare 'Philadelphia is my Jerusalem' than for a Jew in England to announce 'London is my Jerusalem'.

The Jews in England did not feel it incumbent upon themselves to evince their modernity by a public rejection of the distinguishing attributes of Judaism and Jews. Their circumstances and often their inward faith told against their so doing. The place of the Bible in English thought and sentiment would in any event have made it difficult and artificial for the Jews to repudiate expressly their characteristics as a people with a special and an awaited providential role. The founders of Reform Judaism in England did not in principle reject the authority of the Mosaic law. They challenged the obligatory authority of its interpretation and development in the Oral Law. Nor did they disown the Jewish Messianic hope.[1] They shared with the generality of Jewish spokesmen a preference for allowing it to be classified, by way of a public intellectual analogy, with a Christian's belief in the Second Coming.

The long-term influence of Puritanism as an outward religious discipline and as a factor in the advancement of economic individualism and industrial expansion was a major element in British public life. With that influence were involved assumptions concerning chosenness, grace, divine favour and personal moral accountability. The Old Testament was a living influence on Christian life and thought, affecting attitudes to the Jewish people. Among the implications for Jews was that their own degree of separateness was the more readily perceived by Anglicans (notably the Evangelicals) and especially by the Nonconformists as divinely ordained. St Paul had proclaimed (whatever else he may have said) that the old promises had not been overturned. For whatever

86

purposes, their one-time chosenness was widely taken for granted. There remained a residue of speciality about the Jews not only in the public mind at large but also in the Jewish mind. However assiduously their uniqueness might be defined in terms of utterly remote eventualities, it was by its nature and by its widespread acknowledgement a limitation upon easy, absorptive assimilation. It reflected and seemed to give a meaning and even a sense of pride to differences.

Jewish publicists carefully avoided associating themselves with Disraeli's doctrine of Jewish superiority. But this did not prevent them from giving expression to their sense of the Western world's indebtedness to the moral teachings of the Jews. It fell to them from time to time to rebut attacks upon the moral standards of the Talmud. Morris Raphall, the *maskil* who was the Minister of the Birmingham Hebrew Congregation in the 1840s, was in his day the main and self-appointed defender of the rabbinic tradition against such detractors.[2] Jewish apologetics in the middle of the century rested upon assumptions and contentions as to the moral and practical value of Jewish distinctiveness from the point of view of the societies in which they lived.

One Jewish writer in the *Voice of Jacob* (edited by Jacob Franklin) on 28 April 1843 reflected a Jewish mood of unconscious irony. He urged the need for a Jewish movement not only to press for advances in the civil status of the Jews but also to advance their moral standing in the public mind. He presupposed that the latter advance needed to be made and that it would be conducive to the success of the movement for emancipation. His concern was that the Jews should demonstrate to the public their readiness for the high role expected of them in society. 'England', he commented, 'religious England is perhaps the only country which would afford us free scope' for a movement directed to these ends. While preaching the virtues of emancipation and the value of measures directed to its attainment, there was characteristically purveyed an inbuilt particularist philosophy.

No clerical party arose, as in France, to disturb Jewish equanimity. No *Volk*-type xenophobic romanticism, as in Germany, stirred their peace of mind. Their self-esteem was satisfied by their evidence of good citizenship, their care for their own poor and their acknowledgement through practical measures of the international Jewish kinship. Such insignia were taken seriously. An active respect for them was inculcated into the succeeding generation.

Ideological debate was as little Anglo-Jewish as it was English, but the sound administration of communal institutional life was as important to the communal leadership as was the sensible administration of the new Victorian public Boards to the rising caste of bureaucrats. The cessation of immigration during the long French wars had greatly increased the native element within Anglo-Jewry. The Jewish community was as much affected by a kind of insular pride as were the self-made men of Christian faith in the emerging middle classes. As Todd Endelman has observed, 'the transformation of Anglo-Jewry at all levels ... took place largely in terms of new patterns of behaviour rather than new lines of thought'.[3]

A behaviourist acculturation, largely concerned with a search for indistinguishability out of doors and in club and market-place, did not alter the fact that inner traditions died hard. There was no sense of haste for inner change. If it was to come, the pace could be left to whatever emancipation might reasonably require or induce.

In 1830 the unreformed House of Commons rejected a Bill which would have placed the Jews on a par in law with the Roman Catholics. It would have included their admissibility to Parliament, a reform not achieved until the Jewish Relief Act of 1858. In his influential emancipationist pamphlet in 1831, Francis Goldsmid referred to the Jewish dismay at the rejection of the Bill. His language of surprise has the ring of truth. There was, he wrote, 'so little' in the measure that seemed likely to alarm the staunchest opponent of change. 'Parliament'; he added,

> had so solemnly sanctioned the principles of religious liberty [by the Acts of 1828 and 1829 relating to Protestant Dissenters and Roman Catholics respectively] that – any very serious opposition – was regarded as an impossibility.

Goldsmid's essential point is clear. The Jews submitted their claim as a religious communion, one of the Dissenting bodies, even though Jewish distinctiveness raised special questions concerning the nature of the Jews as a body and the purposes of their retained identity. Goldsmid rested his case on the broadest principles of religious liberty, as did the Whig and Radical supporters of the

Jewish cause. They were presented as entitled to civil rights in spite of, as well as because of, their faith and qualities.

In his survey of the Jewish community entitled *The British Jews* (1853), John Mills, the Welsh Calvinist preacher, observed: 'Just as many [Englishmen] attribute the prosperity and happiness of this country to its Saxon blood and pride themselves upon it, so do the Jews in the same spirit pride themselves upon being still the chosen people of Heaven.' No representative Jew would have challenged the proposition. When Mills averred that 'the Jew's faith and his nation are synonymous', he was expressing a widespread belief, shared by Jews. It was not in its day held to be a pejorative formulation.[4]

When in the next generation Goldwin Smith, the historian and Liberal polemicist who was deeply averse to the policies and style of Disraeli, presented to the reading public a renewal of the equation between Jewish faith and nation, it was hotly resented. Jews were no longer aspirants but highly self-conscious *arrivistes*, alert to the implication of the growing anti-Jewish movement on the continent and watchful of the effects of the expanding Eastern European Jewish immigration into Britain. Smith contrasted the reality of Jewish inwardness and cohesion, on the one hand, with the outward conventionality of Jews and their public influence on the other. For all the differences in motivation between the philanthropic and conversionist-minded Mills and the antisemitic Smith (who propounded a Zionist remedy for 'the Jewish question'), there was some degree of common ground between them, if unwittingly.

During the decades leading up to 1858, the special suffering of the Jews over the ages was prayed in aid as imposing upon Christian society a liability to make redress by the granting of civil rights. It was a point made more by Christian supporters than by Jews, who none the less welcomed the notion. Allied to that argument was the assertion made, in this case by Jews, that by reason of their history they were especially conscious of the value of religious freedom unfettered by penalties. In his election address to the voters of Reading in 1860, Francis Goldsmid described himself as 'descended from a race and belonging to a religious community which for centuries was the object of persecution'. He went on to attribute to that fact his own attachment 'by feeling and conviction to the great value of religious freedom' for all in society.[5]

Goldsmid's words were typical of the age. Not only did he thereby add a personal element to his electoral praise of liberty, but he also thus used his Jewishness and the special history of his people (he makes no reference to 'nation') to further his candidature, which was successful.

In the 1860s Francis Goldsmid again and again raised in the House of Commons the treatment of Jews abroad, especially the denial of fundamental rights in Romania, despite the undertakings of authoritative Romanian spokesmen. His successor as the Jewish 'representative' in the House in the 1870s was his fellow-founder of the Reform congregation, Sir John Simon. Like Goldsmid, Simon was a prominent member of the Liberal party. He actively supported many progressive reforms in Parliament and was among Gladstone's most forceful lieutenants in the House. On the issue of the Jews overseas, he was at public odds with his leader. He upbraided Gladstone for seeming to ignore the plight of Eastern European Jewry, notably in the Tsarist Empire, in pursuit of his pro-Russian policy and in the context of his protracted attack on Disraeli's pro-Turkish foreign policy. Simon publicly warned Gladstone that, while the safety of the Christian communities within the Ottoman Empire was a laudable and necessary objective, he risked the loss of some Jewish support for the party because of his apparent indifference to the condition of the Jews under the Tsar.

It was in connection with these issues that in December 1879 an extensive correspondence appeared in *The Times* on the motivations of the Jews in politics. Letters from leading Jewish figures demonstrated their concern to equate their attachment to the cause of Britain and her honour with their advocacy of Jewish interests.

However, the crucial public debate over the ideology of Jewish emancipation had taken place in the 1840s. Once the municipalities were opened to professing Jews by the Act of 1845, the way to Parliament was clear, save for a rearguard action by inveterate opponents and the gambits of politics. This was fully appreciated by most people on all sides of the argument.

In those circumstances the Jewish responses to the Act of 1845 are of considerable interest. No Jewish statement was more indicative than that of the *Voice of Jacob* on 1 August 1845. 'We Jews', commented the editor, who claim first rank for our nation as the chosen one before God, may well afford to be indulgent towards Christian prelates, peers and other legislators whose preconceptions would have been revolted and whose sensitivities would have been wounded by any broad proposition that religious profession is not a needful qualification for offices of trust and authority.

This bland and practical approach was not entirely in accord with the more robust ideas on which the Goldsmids had acted. They consistently protested on principle against any Jewish exclusion from full civil rights; but it was the attitude expressed by Franklin which prevailed within the Jewish community – supported as it was by Peel and Lyndhurst who, as Prime Minister and Lord Chancellor respectively, adopted in the form of the Act of 1845 a pragmatic stage-by-stage approach. Admission to Parliament would take its course.

The above editorial pronouncement related to much more than tactics. Jews were reluctant to press their claim on the basis that religion did not matter for public office, despite the eminent sponsorship by Macaulay and others of that very doctrine. Jews had no wish to face the charge of encouraging the transformation of society by advancing the cause of its secularisation.

What in the end won the day for the campaign for admission to Parliament, as earlier to the municipalities, was the recognition of the impracticability of exclusion, the political nuisance of seeking to sustain it, the shifting of the burden of proof to its opponents and the persistent demonstration of services to state and society by Jews. The Jewish case had to be presented on practical grounds relating to practical grievances, unjust anomalies, party considerations and public needs.

When Christian opponents of Jewish emancipation argued that the Jews in London had more in common with Jews in the continental capitals than with their local Christian neighbours, there were respects in which the claim was true. When they spoke of Jewish international links, they were referring to what the editor of the *Jewish Chronicle*, on the occasion of the Queen's Jubilee in 1887, called 'Jewish solidarity'. This was a solidarity which the emancipationists were not minded to deny. Hermann Adler described the links as being those which tie together people who have a common history and a common hope. If he were thus concerned to depoliticise the character and the appearance of such linkage, his expressions nevertheless enhanced to the ears of Jew and gentile the sense of bonding. On the lips of gentile critics, solidarity was a pejorative term. To Jews it represented a self-evident virtue and responsibility.

Typical of the inward-lookingness of the Jews – even when no less concerned to procure civil emancipation – was the discussion in the *Voice of Jacob* in 1843 of the idea of a Jewish 'conclave'. Abraham Benisch was an enthusiast for the proposed scheme, which had the encouragement of Franklin. The phrase was presumably adopted from Vatican practice and certainly implied that such an assembly should enjoy a degree of international authority within Jewry. The proposed body was discussed as possibly exercising 'spiritual authority' over the Jewish people. One motive mooted for such a convocation was to stem Reform. Another was that, speaking for Jewish communities from many lands, it might be able to exercise a proper persuasion on governments to improve the Jewish lot.

The suggestion was also related to the fact that in some countries 'representative' Jewish assemblies were growing in self-confidence. It seemed appropriate that they should consult together on common interests. On 14 March 1843, Franklin referred to the effect of the Jewish press on both sides of the Atlantic on the increasingly organised and cohesive Jewish communities in the West.

An important feature throughout these discussions was the Damascus Affair of 1840. The suddenness of that episode, the resurgence of the ritual murder charge and the apparent credence given to it in high places in the capitals of Europe, were in stark contrast to the rationality and libertarianism which the eighteenth century was thought to have bequeathed. The cross-frontier co-operation in reaction to the events in Damascus, together with the related and influential public meetings of protest in major capitals in the West in which Christians were as prominent as Jews, encouraged both the notion and the practice of international Jewish consultation and, when necessary, co-ordinated action.

The Jewish avowal of a mutual Jewish responsibility was a distinctive particularist phenomenon. To describe this phenomenon simply in terms of 'spiritual authority' within Jewry would be misleading, for it had a quasi-political quality in defence of Jewish rights. Before the creation of the Alliance Israélite Universelle in 1860, there were many calls for, and much discussion in Jewish counsels on the need for, such machinery. The Anglo-Jewish press was a regular forum for discussion of this type. Benisch was in the forefront of the debate.

If the leaders of the Board of Deputies of British Jews preferred to act independently, that was not inconsistent with the co-ordination of efforts. Their preference was related to their own sense of *noblesse oblige*, the pre-eminence of British power, the comparative antiquity of the Board and perhaps its deliberative procedures, a sense of British insularity and the personality of Sir Moses Montefiore. In so far as the Jewish leaders regarded themselves as acting as Englishmen as well as in their capacity as Jews, one may therein detect some response by them to the ever-recurring strictures by critics of the Jews both before and after their admission to Parliament on the score of Jewish internationalism.

The Anglo-Jewish Association, of which Benisch was the principal founder in 1871, came into being (with the declining power of the Alliance following the defeat of France) in order to sustain international Jewish consultation and action, especially in the face of what was considered to be the slow operation of the Board. Many of the most prominent emancipationist activists became leading members of the Association from the start. Just as the Damascus Affair led to the marshalling by Jews of sympathetic gentile opinion in Western capitals and precipitated the creation of international Jewish co-ordinated action, so too in the 1870s and later, such action was undertaken in response to the plight of Romanian and Russian Jewries.

Anglo-Jewish leadership had evolved out of a group of families with a highly cultivated sense of responsibility for a community whose members they had long tended to regard in the last resort as dependants. It represented the psychology of patron and retainer, and owed much to English class-consciousness. It was reinforced by a sense of religious duty, compassion, habit and enlightened self-interest. No one can read, for example, the memoirs and journals of the Cohen and Rothschild ladies without being struck by the strength of personal and family commitment arising from such attitudes and instincts, including those who married out of the faith.[6] A somewhat formal relationship with Judaism, even in some instances a marked and conscious attenuation of attachment to its forms, was combined at times with strenuous involvement in communal administration.

Directly and indirectly, such states of mind gave to a large array of ruling families, as well as to those who adopted their kinds of communal action, a strong sense of pride in being involved in the sustaining of Jewish institutional life. There having been no ghetto, there was none of the continental drive to demonstrate that they had left the ghetto, even though a high priority was accorded to the nurture of Anglicisation. The process of Westernisation was gentler in Britain.

The existence and the entrenched privileges of the Established Church encouraged establishmentarianism within the Jewish community. It was seen as a bolster to tradition, a force for moderation, and an 'in-fashion' device for control. The creation of the United Synagogue in 1870 through the union of the main Ashkenazi congregations in London, provided the founders of the organisation with an English-style instrument against deviation from received ritual and liturgy. The union rested on the principle of rationalised mutual support between the synagogues. In practice it also rested upon the personal influence and communal power of the lay heads of the parent congregation, the Great Synagogue, notably Sir Anthony de Rothschild (who became the first President of the United Synagogue) and more especially his kinsman, Lionel Louis Cohen who had led the way towards union and who personified the outlook of the Jewish emancipationists and their immediate successors.[7]

The formation of the union by Act of Parliament which was passed upon the initiative of those men, was a remarkable event. They had prided themselves upon the voluntary nature of their religious community and upon the 'Nonconformist' character of Anglo-Judaism within the pattern of religions in the kingdom; yet they hinged their institution to statute, and expressly provided in its deed of foundation that the religious administration was to be under the sole control of the Chief Rabbi. No less striking was the provision that the synagogues were to follow the German and Polish ritual. That requirement retains its especially striking character in the historical context, even when one allows for the importance of the wish of the founders to exclude Reformism and even when one takes account of their respect for the example of their senior and prestigious sister community, which was known as the 'Spanish and Portuguese' congregation.

Each one of the above provisions ran counter in one way or another to the public case defended by the emancipationists. They become more intelligible when set within the totality of communal thinking. It was always an inherent part of their public campaign that the Jews should be free to cultivate those elements in Jewish life which were deemed necessary to ensure their distinctive survival – and in particular to do so free from the anxiety that such an approach might come to be looked upon by themselves or by others as constituting or implying some unacceptable self-isolation. The success of the campaign for emancipation was taken as an indication that their acceptance in society as Englishmen arose in spite of their necessary exclusivity.

The principal founder of the United Synagogue was the banker, Lionel Louis Cohen, prominent in the Great Synagogue and the Central Synagogue. In January 1885, Cohen, a vice-president of the United Synagogue, addressed the Council of that body on the subject of foreign Jews in London. His words expressed attitudes which had long been prevalent in his school of thought. 'It is a mistake', he declared,

> to suppose that a radical difference exists between persons coming from Eastern Europe and the English Jews. Differences do exist, but they are less than formerly, and are rubbed off by the responsibility which comes when persons ... are brought into contact with each other.

This practical, if also patronising, approach lay behind the efforts of the United Synagogue and related organisations to exert an English and West End influence over the expanding immigrant Jewish community after 1881. Such control was particularly difficult to impose in the decades of rapidly increasing immigration, but it had not been an easy task even in the 1870s when the independent-minded Jewish congregations in and around the East End, although still relatively small, were often imbued with their own distinctive enthusiasms and a brittle pride.

However much Cohen's policy was motivated by the desire to Anglicise the newcomers (and later to help stem anti-immigration agitation), his stance strongly reinforced the general image of Anglo-Jewry as a closely knit community, within which newer and older elements influenced each other and which could retain its character as Jewishly traditional, English in style and mutually supportive.

Long before he succeeded his father as Chief Rabbi in 1891, Hermann Adler was the senior exponent of the views of the Anglo-Jewish leadership. He came to be so regarded from the 1860s in the early course of his long tenure as Minister of the Bayswater Synagogue. To that Synagogue were attached many of the leading families in the hierarchy of communal leadership. Hermann Adler is often portrayed as the epitome of the Anglicised Victorian Jewish pastor. Until near the close of his career, he failed to promote study for the rabbinic diploma among the pastorate of which he was the head.[8] He was a frequent public advocate in effusive terms of pride in England and all things English. It was both a form of self-conscious patriotism and a part of the Westernising process in which religious and lay leaders were consistently engaged. His regular public discouragement of Yiddish had the eager support of Lord Rothschild. It was held to be a needlessly separatist jargon, even though many of those who spoke it were likely to regard the language as semi-hallowed by time and by its usage in religious study. Adler was the major public advocate of Jewish attendance at the Local Authority Schools newly established under the Education Act of 1870.

At the same time he consistently upheld rabbinic Judaism. His public identification with the Jewish cause was equally eloquent and consistent. He frequently gave expression to the official disapproval of the growing practice in the older families of exogamous marriage. He was an influential advocate of the creation of Jewish Houses at the public schools attended by the children of the Jewish upper middle classes. He publicly argued again and again that separateness was necessary to ensure that the Jews could continue to serve mankind by their dedication to an ideal of moral duty.[9] He publicly deplored any falling away in the readiness of adequate numbers in the Jewish 'upper classes' to succeed to positions of leadership in Jewish institutional life.

Whatever divergencies there may have been between the religious principles which the Chief Rabbinate sought to uphold, and the outlook and practices in some sections of the lay leadership with whom he worked, there was thought by all to be communal benefit and public desirability in retaining an 'official orthodoxy'. That term came readily from the lips of critics of the system, on the religious 'right' as well as on the religious 'left'; but its implications were not disowned by those against whom the criticisms were levelled. The point was often made that the Chief Rabbinate was highly suited to the temperament of British Jewry, especially in respect of the principles and attitudes evinced from the 1860s by Hermann Adler. What was meant was the preference for the practical, a contentment with the public forms of piety and the non-ideological spirit of their performance, an ultimate moderation in contentious debate, deference to established authority and the assumption as to the value of comprehensiveness and union.

Adler discerned no contradictions in his policies. This devout ecclesiastic was devoted to the task of assisting the integration of the Jewish community into the life of the nation while retaining as its ethos the principles of traditional Judaism and seeking to sustain its transmissibility.

The Jewish community could not be immune to influences affecting the whole of society. In his *The Secularization of the European Mind in the Nineteenth Century*, Professor Owen Chadwick wrote of the 'elusive shift in the European mind' which gained momentum in the 1860s.[10] It was a long-maturing shift away from beliefs and outlook resting upon metahistorical inter-pretations of history. Since Anglo-Jewry prided itself upon its denominational character and since the image of the Jews as a nation was increasingly shunned, the consequences of the advance in the secularised outlook gave particular pause to those who looked ahead. Thus, the sophisticated leaders of the Jewish community remained religionists. For many it was a matter of conviction. Where it was not, or where the issues were encased in inward personal debate, few were ready to make a conscious withdrawal from the religious system by which the community was defined and within which it operated.

The growing respectability of secular philosophies was not the only erosive factor impinging upon the Jewish community. There were ever more opportunities for public service outside that com-munity. Furthermore, the advancing social fraternisation between the Jewish and gentile middle classes, especially in the upper echelons, tended to broaden the gulf between the cadres from which Jewish leadership had traditionally come and the expanding base of the Jewish community. However, communal policy required that the gulf be bridged and this perception in many instances encouraged the privileged to retain communal responsibilities and personal communal involvement regardless of social distance and ideological divergence.

In 1852 the City of London School, following the example of University College School in Hampstead, opened its doors to all, subject to fees, regardless of religion. On 6 August the *Jewish Chronicle* in classic Victorian terms welcomed this liberalisation. 'Our surest hope', wrote the editor,

> of enlisting the future sympathies of our educated fellow-citizens is to make ourselves more worthy of their friendship and respect by raising up in the next generation a body of Jewish gentlemen who shall be equal to their Christian fellows in intelligence and mental acquirements no less than in pecuniary means.

The enlisting of the 'sympathies of our educated fellow-citizens' continued to be an important objective and in its own way required that the above-mentioned gulf be bridged.

The comparison between Henry Keeling and Samuel Montagu is picturesque and instructive. The former was a jeweller in the City of London and a vocal member of the Western Synagogue and the Board of Deputies. His easy manner and charitableness made him a popular figure among Jews and Christians. In 1853 he allowed himself to be elected Churchwarden of St George's in the City, stipulating only that he should be excused from taking part in the religious services. His condition was accepted. His election, which was unanimous, was hailed as evidence of the folly of the scare that the admission of Jews to Parliament would 'unchristianise' the legislature.

Keeling was also among the leading Jewish spokesmen against opportunities for excessive fraternisation between Jewish and Christian children in the schools. In the *Jewish Chronicle* on 23 July 1869 he sternly warned against the risks of Christian influence at school. Asserting his own liberal outlook ('I have always been liberal in my ideas'), Keeling added,

I have always considered the prime purpose in the struggle to attain civil and religious liberty was to secure the Jewish community in its exclusive right of upholding our institutions distinct from those of other creeds.

Sir Samuel Montagu (later the first Lord Swaythling), the banker who in 1887 founded the Federation of Synagogues out of the intensely Orthodox bethels (or *shtiblekh*) of the East End, was from the 1870s the most resolute layman in metropolitan Jewry in defence of firm Orthodoxy. He was also among the most outspoken critics of Jewish day schools, save for the children of the immigrant poor. For the latter, they would be a valuable Anglicising factor. For the children of the Jewish middle classes, Jewish schools would, he stated, cause narrow-mindedness and foster inhibitions in the relationships between the Jews and their fellow-citizens of the Christian faith in later life.

Throughout the nineteenth century, Anglo-Jewish opinion retained the paradoxes involved in the non-merging of the Westernised Jews. Those paradoxes are the stuff of which modern Jewish life is made. Many issues which were debated in the middle decades of the century remained in the public consciousness – the nature and purpose of Jewish identity, the meaning of the Jewish national idea, the character of the Jewish kinship, the forms and extent of Jewish integration. Such issues became more highly charged around the turn of the century. However, if in the twentieth century the mid-Victorian scene takes on the remote air of distant familiarity, it is familiarity none the less.[11]

NOTES

1. Prior to Claude Montefiore, the most vocal Anglo-Jewish advocate of the kind of advanced Reform well known in Germany was Alfred Henriques. On 7 August 1906, the *Jewish Chronicle*, in its obituary notice which was in personal terms sympathetic, rightly observed that 'his ideas were not palatable to many members of the community'. While the implications of the Reform Synod convened in Leipzig in 1869 were much discussed in Anglo-Jewry, it was noted that the Reform congregation in Britain was not represented there. See D.W. Marks, Consecration Discourse at West London Synagogue of British Jews, 1842, in *Collected Sermons* (London, 1851), p. 132; D.W. Marks, *The Jews of Modern Times* (two lectures London, 1871); and D.W. Marks and A. Lowy, *Memoir of Sir F.H. Goldsmid*, 2nd edn (London, 1882).

2. See in particular the correspondence between M. Raphall and Charles N. Newdegate, MP, in M. Raphall, *Jewish Dogmas* (London, 1849).
3. T.M. Endelman, *The Jews in Georgian England 1714–1830: Tradition and Change in a Liberal Society* (Philadelphia, 1979), p. 9.
4. The emancipationist spokesmen, regardless of their differing opinions on the proper pace of emancipation and integration, were aware that, on the whole (the optimistic hopes of the conversionists apart), society did not expect the total absorption of the Jews. They were looked upon by many as an irretrievably surviving ancient people whose role, character and external relations were bound up with a particular faith. Absorption would require the erosion of that faith, especially its national elements. See Israel Finestein, 'Anglo-Jewish Opinion during the Struggle for Emancipation', 'Post Emancipation Jewry: The Anglo-Jewish Experience', 'The Uneasy Victorian: Montefiore as Communal Leader' and 'Some Modern Themes in the Emancipation Debate in Early Victorian England', in *Jewish Society in Victorian England* (London, 1993); L.P. Gartner, *The Jewish Immigrant in England, 1870–1914* (London, 1960; 2nd edn 1973); V.D. Lipman, *Social History of the Jews in England, 1850–1950* (London, 1954); V.D. Lipman (ed.), 'The Age of Emancipation', *Three Centuries of Anglo-Jewish History* (Cambridge, 1961), pp. 69–106; and H. Pollins, *Economic History of the Jews in England* (London, 1982).
5. For Goldsmid's electoral address, see D.W. Marks and A. Lowy, *Memoir of Sir F.H. Goldsmid*, appendix 5 to part I.
6. See in particular: Lucy Cohen, *Arthur Cohen, a Memoir* (London, 1919); Lucy Cohen, *Lady de Rothschild and her Daughters* (London, 1935); Lucy Cohen, *Some Recollections of Claude Goldsmid Montefiore* (London, 1940); Lady Battersea (Constance Flower, née de Rothschild), *Reminiscences* (London, 1922); and Hannah F. Cohen, *Changing Faces* (London, 1937).
7. For the emergence and growth of the United Synagogue, see S.S. Levin (ed.), *A Century of Jewish Life* (London, 1970), and A.N. Newman, *The United Synagogue 1870–1970* (London, 1976). Geoffrey Alderman, *The Federation of Synagogues* (London, 1987); Stephen Sharot, 'Religious Change in Native Orthodoxy in London, 1870–1914', *Jewish Journal of Sociology*, 15, no. 2 (1973), 167; and Steven Singer, 'Jewish Religious Observance in Early Victorian London', *Jewish Journal of Sociology*, 28, no. 2 (1986), 117.
8. For Adler's personal and public explanation of this policy and of his late change of attitude in terms of the changing needs and character of the community, see his important published lecture (1905) 'The Sons of the Prophets', in *Jews' College Jubilee Volume* (London, 1966), part 2, p. 1.
9. The idea of the Jewish mission was stressed in the mid-Victorian era as a justification for Jewish separateness. In the following generation it was stressed as an explanation of a moral justification for Jewish dispersion in face of political Zionism. In widely noted sermons at the Bayswater Synagogue in 1869 (published in London in that year), Adler expounded the doctrine of Jewish Messianism and explored its biblical and rabbinic sources. He rejected Christian assertions that the ruined condition of Jewish Jerusalem was by its nature permanent and later advocated support for Jewish settlements in the

Holy Land. He was less to the fore with these ideas when confronted with political Zionism, which he vehemently opposed. The influx of Eastern European Jews into Britain from 1881 (totalling almost 150,000 entrants by 1914 into a community which in the 1870s barely totalled 60,000) presented Adler and his lay associates with ready-made centres of resistance to the style of the Anglicised, centralised and anti-Zionist Judaism of which he was deemed the main exponent.

10. O. Chadwick, *The Secularization of the European Mind in the Nineteenth Century* (Cambridge, 1975), p. 17.

11. A telling demonstration is afforded by the efforts of some members of the Sephardi Synagogue in 1852 to discover from the congregation's religious heads (David Meldola and Abraham Haliva) whether it was 'inimical' to their religion for them 'to associate for the purpose of adopting constitutional measures to promote the idea of our nation regaining possession of Palestine'. This interest was in the wake of Judah Alkalai's efforts to arouse support for his proto-Zionist endeavours. With the concurrence, if not at the request of, the Mahamad, Meldola and Haliva avoided giving a reply. In response to publicly expressed dismay at this seeming abdication of authority, Meldola wrote to the Jewish Chronicle on 23 July that the 'future deliverance' will be by divine intervention as distinct from human agency. The spokesman of the enquiring members, Solomon Sequerra, wrote to that journal in the next issue that they made their enquiry as 'Englishmen' and that their object was 'to see the Jewish nation assume rank and standard amongst the nations of the earth, that millions of our suffering brethren may be released from the despotism and unheard-of oppressions and national degradation'. Meldola's reply and Sequerra's rejoinder was typical of that age, and are not necessarily mutually exclusive in their implications. The aforementioned 'object' was pursued by the emancipationists and their early successors but without any express cultivation of the Jewish national idea.

4

Religious Disabilities at Oxford and Cambridge and the Movements for Abolition 1771–1871

The Universities of Oxford and Cambridge were Anglican preserves. This circumstance was part of the settlement of Church and State following the Reformation. With the authority of Elizabeth I, the Earl of Leicester as Chancellor of Oxford University procured the inclusion in the statutes of that university the express requirement that admission was to be conditional upon the entrant's prior acceptance of prescribed Articles of Faith of the Church of England, and recognition of the monarch as supreme head of the Church. The principal object of these stipulations was to exclude Roman Catholics. In order to tighten further the ties between Oxford and the Church, both in fact and in appearance, James I further secured in 1616 the express exclusion from degrees of those who failed to subscribe to the Articles. This rule was directed principally at the Puritans, now a strong force in theological and intellectual debate.

Twenty years later, under the influence of William Laud, the Archbishop of Canterbury, and with the authority of Charles I, comparable restrictions were extended to Cambridge, save that subscription to the Articles was not required there as a condition of admission. This difference reflected the stronger spirit of independence at Cambridge than at the older University, the personal links between Cambridge savants and continental theologians and philosophers, and the greater influence at Cambridge of individual

102

Colleges in some of which the Puritan element had expanded. With the overthrow of the Cromwellian Commonwealth and the restoration of the Stuarts and the Church in 1660, the Act of Uniformity (1662), *inter alia*, required that all Heads of College, Fellows, and university teachers at both Universities, should as a condition of office subscribe to the Articles and accept the Anglican liturgy. These over-riding legal obligations were additional to the operation by the Universities and Colleges of their own statutes. The Act of Uniformity was deemed a necessary ultimate safeguard against the local impact of dissent in any quarter.

In his *Life* of Dr Johnson, Boswell reports a conversation with him about the recent Petition to Parliament, drawn up in 1771, calling for legislation to relax the restrictions for admission to Oxford. It was signed by 250 Oxford graduates, most of whom were Anglican clerics, and including 'gentlemen of the professions of law and medicine'. The Petition was presented to the House of Commons in 1772. It was lengthily debated and heavily defeated. Lord North (Prime Minister and newly appointed Chancellor of the University) and Edmund Burke were the leading opponents of the proposal. A similar renewed measure in 1773 was likewise defeated.[1]

'Sir', said Johnson to Boswell, the Petitioners 'talk of making boys at the University subscribe to what they do not understand (namely Articles of the Church)' whereas the Petitioners 'ought to consider that our Universities were founded to bring up members of the Church of England, and we must not supply our enemies with arms from our arsenal. The meaning of subscribing is not that they fully understand all the Articles, but that they will adhere to the Church of England.'[2]

Johnson's opinion, perhaps reported somewhat crudely by his biographer, reflected on this issue the views of the English political and ecclesiastical establishment of the day. Whatever may have been the intentions of their medieval Roman Catholic founders and their pre-Reformation status in the Roman Catholic world, the ancient universities were now national institutions in the sense in which the Church of England, as established by law, was a national institution.

Far into the next century, many continued to believe that the exclusive connection of the Universities with the national Church was necessary to ensure the peace and moral well-being of the Church and society. The removal of William Frend, theologian, scientist, Hebraist, and a recent convert to Unitarianism, from the office as Tutor at Jesus College, Cambridge, in 1788, heightened tensions over the religious tests. In 1787 he had been prominent in the abortive campaign to persuade the Senate at Cambridge to open degrees without prior subscription to the Articles. Each discrimination, such as suffered by Frend, strengthened the agitation of the Petitioners and their successors in what clearly promised to be a protracted contentious public debate. One such further dramatic event was the refusal to allow James Edward Smith to lecture on botany in Cambridge on the grounds of his Unitarianism. It was a period of growing interest in botanical studies, as part of the expanding exploration in the natural sciences. Smith, founder of the Linnaean Society in 1788, was the country's major botanical scholar.

The Petitioners regarded admission unfettered by religious disabilities, as not only a likely strengthening of the Universities and the nation by the enlisting of hitherto excluded talent, but also a plain tenet of justice. Some of them were also increasingly restive over the fact that the Articles were a political-style compromise hammered out long before in the midst of bitter religious, intellectual and political conflicts, and now caused confusion. They were seen as an exclusionary irritant harmful to conscience. The Petitioners were aware of the rising tide of a new 'enthusiasm' within the Church (later developing into the secessionist Methodist movement), often on the part of its brightest spirits who were especially troubled by the complacency of the Church, the power of the Bishops, and the limits set to free expression. The Petitioners and their supporters wanted to encourage a retentive accommodation within the Church.[3] There was also an increasing vocality and natural resentment on the part of the older groups of Protestant Dissenters at their own exclusion. The growing economic and social prominence of the old and the new dissenting bodies sharpened the incongruous image of exclusion and of the disabilities generally.

The protesters had long found in the Church an influential spokesman in Archdeacon Francis Blackburne. His book, *The Confessional* (1766), which went into a series of editions, castigated the whole system of subscription. He deemed the insistence upon it to be a self-defeating artifice since many who subscribed were known to do so with tongue in cheek.[4] He went indeed beyond what many of the protesters called for. He wanted, he declared, to see the Church 'brought back to the terms of the original record ... with respect to those points in which it has deviated from it, namely by discharging all superfluous traditions and systematical doctrines with which the Christian religion hath been incumbered by the craft and vanity of men presuming to be wise about what is written'. Blackburne opened up for debate matters which were thought to have been long settled. His opinions resulted in his being denied a Fellowship at Cambridge.

The spirit of opposition to change, combined with the power of vested interests and the overwhelming Anglican and clerical character of the Universities, were such that the study of subjects not associated with the training of clergy often became atrophied. Pluralities and sinecures became common. Among the younger men of calibre in the new age, and with the support of some seniors, a clamant movement of opinion developed. It gained added force after the expulsion of Frend from Cambridge in 1793. It was a movement for improvement and reform, including the relaxation of the religious tests.

Intermittent progressive moves, such as the creation of the Mathematics Tripos at Cambridge in 1748 and the marked advance in classical studies, had set examples which could not but be standing challenges to the Heads of the Colleges. Their arbitrary rule aroused increasing antipathy. The respective governing bodies of the Universities – Convocation at Oxford and the Senate at Cambridge – were largely under their personal control. In particular, the powers of the Heads included the authority to veto any discussion of 'undesirable' topics at those councils. They decided what was undesirable.

The academic repute of the Scottish Universities, free of religious tests, encouraged the English reformers. The opening of Trinity College, Dublin, to Protestant Dissenters and Roman Catholics in 1793 was an added stimulus. The inception of the University of London, test-free and non-denominational, in 1826, with the support of prominent Jews (notably Isaac Lyon Goldsmid), leading Nonconformists (as the Protestant Dissenters were increasingly coming to be called), and Jeremy Bentham, the philosopher-father of the scheme, was much noted both by the reformers at the ancient

13. University College London, c.1828

Universities and by their opponents.[5] In his *Nationalisation of the Old English Universities* (1901), Lewis Campbell, liberal theologian and formerly Professor of Greek at St Andrews University and Fellow of Trinity College, Cambridge, wrote that the 1820s at Cambridge, especially Trinity College, were 'marked by intense intellectual activity, the new spirit of free enquiry showing itself in historical criticism, in theological speculation, and in the bold assertion of Liberal and even Radical opinions'.

The civic and political emancipation of Roman Catholics and Nonconformists in 1828/9 and the changed House of Commons following the Reform Act of 1832, were propitious circumstances for the reformers.[6] In December 1833 and February 1834 the Heads of College at Cambridge disallowed any consideration by the Senate of proposals directed to having the tests question submitted to a special committee. Their decision provoked a lengthy battle of pamphlets between protagonists on both sides, on this issue and related topics. Three Fellows of Trinity College came to the fore in the campaign of opposition to the Heads. They were Connop Thirlwall, later Bishop of St David's; Adam Sedgwick, later Professor of Geology and a founder of the Cambridge Philosophical Society; and Thomas Musgrave, Senior Proctor and later Archbishop of York.

106

Thirlwall had for some time been under the influence of the German schools of Bible criticism, especially after his visits to Germany.[7] His personal associations with members of the critical schools in Tübingen and elsewhere, together with his general intellectual interests (and his concern for the welfare of his College and University, as he perceived it) had inclined him to move to a theological position somewhat 'to the left' of Sedgwick[8] and Musgrave. This did not interfere with their collaboration against the tests.

Notable in the controversial literature was the 45-page brochure by Thirlwall. Its appearance quickly led to an invitation from Christopher Wordsworth, the Tory Master of Trinity, to Thirlwall to resign his Assistant Tutorship. He complied. This substantial publication had been his instant response to an even longer booklet by Thomas Turton, Regius Professor of Divinity, setting out the dangers to the religious life and discipline of the Universities if degrees were opened to 'persons without regard to their religious opinions'.

Thirlwall made three main points in his broadside, each of which raised major issues in principle and public policy.

First, he denied that the Colleges were or ought to be theological seminaries, or had or should seek to exercise any right to teach dogma by compulsion. This view was related to his idea of a university as a place of learning to which many would wish to resort without intention of involvement in any ecclesiastical vocation.

Secondly, he argued that obligatory attendance at Chapel, which Turton had defended, was harmful in that it rendered the services artificial, militated against devotion, and alienated those upon whom it was imposed. Thirlwall's opinion on this subject probably attracted the most hostility at that time.

Thirdly, Thirlwall contended that the presence of non-Anglicans at the Universities, and their admission to degrees, presented no danger to the Church. Their presence and graduation would secure greater academic distinction for the Universities, improve relations between the social classes and between the differing sections of intellectual society, and put the Church on its mettle.

The Turton–Thirlwall affair was a landmark in the history of the movement for the abolition of the tests.[9] Wordsworth's reaction proved a short-term gain for the retentionists. It did not impede

Thirlwall's career. His scholarship, independence, and comparatively advanced opinions commended themselves to liberal-minded Whig politicians such as Melbourne – as they did to Macaulay in India who applauded Thirlwall's publication. When Prime Minister, Melbourne caused him to be elevated to the episcopal bench (1840). In the House of Lords, Thirlwall was a persistent advocate of the civic and political emancipation of the Jews (with, on his part, publicly expressed conversionist hopes).

Sedgwick and Musgrave were firmly of the view that only through an appeal to Parliament would relief be likely. In 1834 they presented to the Prime Minister, Lord Grey, a petition organised by them. It sought the abolition of tests for entry and for degrees. It was signed by 63 resident members of the Senate (including two Heads of College and nine Professors), totalling about one-third of all resident members. It elicited a 'counter-memorial' signed by 110 resident members, including 11 Heads of College. The debates on these approaches were marked by the clarity of the implications drawn therefrom.

The proposals of 1834 were limited. They did not seek any parliamentary enactment which would compel the Universities and Colleges to allow entry and degrees without tests. The Petitioners were content to seek freedom for them to decide the issues for themselves. They feared any parliamentary interference with collegiate independence. In particular, they were concerned that at Oxford, where entry was subject to the tests, any proposal to render the tests unlawful by Act of Parliament, might well arouse greater opposition to the whole scheme of the Petition. Soon after the Petition was presented, a Nonconformist M.P., George Wood, sought and was given leave to introduce a Bill which went beyond the Petition and proposed to exercise statutory compulsion on the Universities and Colleges. Sedgwick managed to procure an amendment deleting the proposed compulsion. In any event the Bill (carried in the Commons) was defeated in the House of Lords.

The passage of the measure in the Commons did more than demonstrate the increased weight therein of Nonconformist opinion.[10] It also revealed the impact on political opinion of the university debates and the polemical literature. On 25 March 1834, *The Times* gave strong support to the reformers of that year. The editor, Thomas Barnes, sharply criticised the Tory Party, especially its leaders, Wellington and Peel, for their 'too narrow' interpretation of the 'spirit of the Church of England', observing that 'to an enlightened mind' the question 'does not admit of argument'. Peel knew that if such a measure became law, the implication would be drawn that the composition of the Fellowships, and thus the teaching posts and the governing bodies of the Universities and Colleges, could not indefinitely be left outside the scrutiny of Parliament.

It is a mark of the ideological and political importance of the university issue that in 1835, Peel, now the leader of the party, included his opinion thereon in his party proclamation, the famous Tamworth Manifesto. He denied that non-Anglicans had any intrinsic right to admission or to the taking of degrees at the ancient universities. The Colleges, he declared, were founded for purposes in which they could have no part as of right. To grant their requests would be hostile to the principles on which the Colleges were established. The subversion of those principles would have by extension and example far-reaching consequences for Church and State.

Some Anglicans, while opposing the Bill, thought that the Universities and Colleges would be likely of their own volition to seek to modify their own rules.[11] Gladstone, who began his political career as a Tory, opposed the Bill of 1834, while expressing his belief in that likelihood. That confidence was not shared by the promoters of the Bill. In fact many of its supporters may well have shared the belief that the present measure would be the prelude to wider and to them welcome changes imposed by Act of Parliament.

To the older school, represented in Parliament by a resolute body of Tory opinion (which Peel may not have unreservedly shared), a whole range of legislative reform in that epoch was dangerous and unwelcome. Measures such as the reforms of 1828/9 to which Wellington and Peel (then in Government) gave their unwilling approval, or the vesting of ultimate appellate authority over the ecclesiastical courts in a lay tribunal (the Privy Council) in 1832, seemed to them to be directed to weakening the ecclesiastical and religious element in national life. The institution of civil marriage in 1836 and civil divorce in 1857, like the opening of municipal office to Jews in 1845 and of the House of Commons in 1858, were likewise to be seen by them as stages in that trend. To the more practical and less ideological politicians such as Peel, there was in the new intellectual climate and in the changing political, social, and economic structure, a political inevitability about such measures – even if it seemed desirable to defer their realisation as best as one could.

The issues which were raised at the Universities were in some respects the most delicate and difficult of all. They touched upon what were perceived to be not only prescriptive rights of ancient foundations (inherited from the medieval world under the new post-Reformation dispensation), but also vital ancient privileges of the Church.

In particular the proposals foreshadowed the question of the opening of teaching posts at the Universities without any tests, whether of an Anglican kind or indeed of any Christian or of any religious kind. This last concern lay too far ahead to be prominent in the Parliamentary debates in the 1830s, but there was expressed (by John Keble, the Anglican cleric and poet, and others) an abiding anxiety over the widening impact of the rationalist and secularist philosophies of the eighteenth century.[12]

The reformers kept the issue before Parliament and the reading public by sustained publicity. In the 1840s James Heywood emerged as a most significant figure in the continuing campaign. Heywood was a member of a Lancashire Unitarian banking family. Among his social enterprises, he was a pioneer in the provision of free lending library facilities in London, believing in the virtue and practical value of extending to larger sections of the people the opportunities of education and self-help.

Heywood had been a contemporary of J.J. Sylvester[13] at Trinity College, Cambridge. Like Sylvester, he did not take his degree because of religious scruples. He declined as a Unitarian to subscribe to the required Anglican formula. In the 1840s, he caused to be published at his own expense English translations of the Latin statutes of Oxford Colleges, at a time when that was held by many in authority at the Universities to be undesirable and even subversive. Perhaps there was some comfort in the obscurity of the Latin.

From 1847 to 1857 Heywood represented North Lancashire in Parliament as a Radical, generally in support of the liberal wing of the Whigs. Before his election he had long been an important link between the Radical and Nonconformist members and their supporters outside. These connections gained him, then and later, much political influence. In April 1850, in a long and learned speech in the Commons, he proposed that the Whig Government of Lord John Russell should institute a wide-ranging enquiry into the administration and revenues of the Universities, including the operation of the religious tests. His motion was the immediate occasion for Russell's announcement of the Government's intention to appoint Royal Commissions to enquire into those matters, save that their terms of reference were expressly to exclude the tests. Gladstone was among those who opposed the setting up of the Commissions. He described such a proposal as 'an unprecedented exercise by the Crown of a novel and undefined prerogative, albeit exercised on ministerial advice'. His opposition reflected the widely-held view among seniors at the University of Oxford, which he represented in Parliament, as well as that of a body of opinion at Cambridge.

The Commissions included men well-known for their support of abolition.[14] There was an increasing number of people who thought that the degrees might best be protected by ending the obligatory test for admission at Oxford. Among them were some who preferred that decision to be taken, if at all, by the Universities and Colleges themselves. Both the retentionists and the abolitionists had their own reasons for caution; the former for fear that comprehensive opposition might prove conducive to wider Parliamentary intervention (perhaps affecting before long the crucial matter of the Fellowships, and possibly even the ultimate inhibitions enshrined in the Act of Uniformity); and the latter for fear that pressure for large reform might deter acceptance of the more limited and currently demanded measures.

Meanwhile the Commissions proceeded with their investigations, hearing evidence from parliamentarians, ecclesiastics, and University personalities. Heywood was one of the most industrious witnesses. He published documents bearing on the tests as well as on structures and procedures, seeking to demonstrate the anomalies, and reveal the Heads' arbitrary government and the injustices. Among the petitions was one organised by him and signed by himself and other Cambridge non-Anglicans, including Sylvester and Arthur Cohen.[15] The non-cooperation with the Commissions by some leading University figures strengthened the feeling for reform. The Commissions' Reports were the bases of the seminal Acts of 1854 (relating to Oxford) and 1856 (relating to Cambridge), save for the additional statutory clauses relating to the tests which emerged in the parliamentary debates.

The Oxford University Reform Bill of 1854 was presented in the House of Commons by Gladstone. He was then the Chancellor of the Exchequer in the coalition government of Lord Aberdeen during the Crimean War. He had mastered the Commission's Report, and was persuaded by it.[16] On being put in charge of the Bill, there was 'excited in him', wrote a much younger contemporary, 'a fury of interest with the problem',[17] which was manifested in an extraordinary profusion of correspondence by him. In the face of the merits of the argument and the changing tide of opinion, and notwithstanding prestigious opposition in Oxford, he made the Bill his own policy with impressive vigour. He was strongly supported by *The Times* under John Delane, who succeeded Barnes as editor in 1841. Gladstone was in any case much influenced by the need, as he saw it, to try to avoid further pressure for reform, by way of agreeing to the measures of modernisation propounded by the Commission.

The Bill was drafted principally by Gladstone and Benjamin Jowett, Fellow and Tutor at Balliol and later Master of that College. Jowett was the leading figure at Oxford in favour of reform. The Bill prescribed a more democratic and accountable system of government for the University. It also required the appointment of statutory commissioners with power to rationalise College endowments, abolish academic sinecures and revise antiquated trusts. College wealth was increasingly to be put to the use of study, research and teaching. The Government measure had the support of a majority in the House. The Bill was silent on the tests, and the Government hoped that it would remain so. Gladstone continued to assert his preference that this should be the prerogative of the University authorities.

Heywood and his friends had no confidence that the majority of those who ruled the University and Colleges, even under the new system, would act speedily or at all. He moved an amendment to the Bill to abolish religious tests for entry. The abolitionists were well organised. Many sat for constituencies, especially in the north,

112

where Nonconformist opinion was strong in electoral votes and in *esprit de corps*. His amendment was eventually carried by 252 votes to 161. The Government was surprised by the size of the majority. Fortified thereby, Heywood moved a second amendment aimed at opening the B.A. degree in like manner. This was defeated. Some of his supporters were concerned lest this amendment might endanger the whole Bill, including his first amendment, in the House of Lords.

The Government had opposed both amendments. Gladstone, ever sensitive to majorities, together with his principal colleagues, was sufficiently impressed by the extent of support for the first amendment as to consider the Government now obliged to explore whether this did not also reflect the true opinion of the House in regard to the second amendment. There was also a desire to seek to call a halt to this long-standing divisive issue in politics. The awareness of that need was heightened by an anxiety to retain the ready confidence of the House in the war-time coalition. Larger numbers were coming to think that it was injurious to the nation and empire (as well as unjust) to exclude a substantial and growing segment of the people, often among the most industrious, from the opportunities and honours available through the Universities. The exclusion appeared especially out of place at a time when the philosophy of self-improvement increasingly mattered in religion and politics.

The Government sought legal advice on whether, should the second amendment be reintroduced and carried, there would remain adequate legal safeguards against the admission of non-Anglicans into the Fellowships and thus into the governing bodies and teaching posts. Assurance was given that the Act of Uniformity, as well as certain University provisions, were a legal barrier to such an advance. Content with this advice, Gladstone, on behalf of the Cabinet, announced support for the second amendment on its agreed reintroduction on the Third Reading of the Bill. It was overwhelmingly carried. The Bill, as amended, was likewise passed by a majority in the House of Lords. By agreement the B.A. in Divinity was not included in the amendment.

The Cambridge University Reform Bill was introduced in 1856 by Edward Bouverie, a leading member of Palmerston's Whig administration. It largely followed the recommendations of the

Commission on Cambridge as far as the greater democratisation of the system was concerned. As at Oxford, a body of commissioners was to be set up with statutory powers to revise antiquated rules and outmoded trusts. The Bill, which was adopted by majorities in both Houses, also opened the B.A. and M.A. degrees (save for Divinity degrees) to non-Anglicans. The measure further provided that the M.A. degree was not to qualify its holders, as it otherwise would, for membership of the Senate without their prior declaration of membership of the Church of England.

Ideological and political differences on university issues had somehow been converted, at each stage (and were at later stages also to be so converted) into immediate questions of practical politics. Preconceptions gave way to a pragmatism, formulated in the questions: What is now possible? What is now retainable? What present concession does the future now require?[18] In a collection of Gladstone's correspondence on 'Church and State' in 1910, D.C. Lathbury significantly observed: 'The question that had to be answered was one in which the conception of an ideal University had little place. It was what should be done with the existing Universities of Oxford and Cambridge' (p. 212).

Writing to a correspondent in June 1854, at the time of Heywood's amendments, Gladstone revealingly commented that the second amendment 'is one of those incomplete arrangements which seem to suit the practical habits of this country, and which, by taking the edge off a matter of complaint, are often found virtually to dispose of it for a length of time'. He added: 'As regards the integrity of the teaching and governing power in Oxford, ... I hardly knew what concession should not be made, rather than to impair the hold of the Church over that power' (p. 218). With regard to the later opening of the Fellowships (1871), Gladstone never wholeheartedly accepted that new system, even though in practice he did much to bring it about.

Both the opponents and advocates of abolition were aware of the underlying transformations which were taking shape in society, regardless of their respective ideologies. John Stuart Mill had caught the mood of the new intellectuals when he wrote in 1833: 'If we were asked for what ends, above all others, endowed Universities exist, or ought to exist, we should answer – to keep alive philosophy.' Others would have substituted the word 'religion' for the bare, indeterminate and to some the dangerous word 'philosophy'. Twenty years later, John Keble wrote regarding Oxford: 'It is not so much Dissent (from the Anglican standpoint) that I fear, nor even Radicalism, but it is the complete secularisation of men's minds there ...'.

In November 1869, at a critical point in the events which were to lead to the Act of 1871, Adam Sedgwick spoke as follows: 'I have not outlived my love of liberty. I believe the removal of tests (on Fellowships) would tend to perpetuate our great institutions. Fears have been expressed of the predominance of Dissenters. That is a white-livered opinion. If Dissenters should command a predominance in the intellect of the nation, let them take the place to which they are entitled. ... I am a Churchman because I believe the Church of England right; but I deprecate the University hiding itself in any little nook of prejudice out of the general spirit of the community'.[19] This was by then the authentic voice of the reformers, uttered by their oldest member.

From their different vantage points, Keble and Sedgwick wanted the same thing. As D.A. Winstanley, wrote, the protagonists by the mid-century, for the most part, wanted 'peace at the Universities'. Some feared that the changes, already achieved and those possibly pending, would cause disarray and discord. Others believed they would bring a degree of harmony and a greater sense of cohesion between the Universities and the nation at large. If the Universities were indeed to be at one with the nation, then some reformers would have added that if scepticism, disbelief and secularism were to permeate wide sections of 'the intellect of the nation', their exponents should not be prevented from finding their place at the Universities. If this was perceived as an implication of Sedgwick's remarks, he may nevertheless not have considered that it was in practice a likely development. Others thought that it was likely and desirable.

Supporters of abolishing the University tests were generally also in favour of granting relief from other religious disabilities in society, including those affecting professing Jews. Among the striking exceptions was Lord Lyndhurst, Lord Chancellor in Peel's Government of 1841–46. This former patron of the young Disraeli and whose second wife was the daughter of Lewis Goldsmith (Jewish notary and volatile journalist), actively supported the Acts of 1845 and 1858, but opposed the admission of non-Anglicans to Fellowships. He was sometimes taunted with being unwilling to 'de-Christianise' the governing bodies of the Universities while ready to 'de-Christianise' Parliament.[20]

Perhaps a more significant figure was Thomas Arnold, the head-master of Rugby who in 1841 was appointed Regius Professor in Modern History at his own University of Oxford. He encouraged in his pupils a belief in the virtue and utility of free enquiry. He saw Church and nation as one, with the former moulding and sustaining the character of the latter. He wanted the Church to be broad enough to include all Christians, save for the Roman Catholics who, for him, entertained a different allegiance from that of the English nation. Nor did he evince enthusiasm for the inclusion of Unitarians and Quakers, who seemed to him to be outside a recognisably Christian ambit. As for Jews, he did not regard them as Englishmen. He opposed their civic and political emancipation, and was troubled by the notion of freeing them from the religious tests at the Universities, whose Christian character he wanted to uphold, as that of Parliament. He readily accepted the idea of abolishing the religious tests at the Universities for the Protestant Dissenters, which tests he regarded as hostile to the prospect of a comprehensive Church and as an undesirable relic of earlier centuries.

Campbell Tait, former Tutor at Balliol and a long-standing supporter of university reform, was appointed Archbishop of Canterbury (1869) early in Gladstone's first administration. He and Sedgwick had been members of the Commission on Oxford. They regretted that the tests question had been excluded from the Commission's purview, but they ensured that the Report made clear the extent of concern at Oxford over the disabilities, as indeed did the Cambridge Report. The joint secretaries of the Cambridge Commission were Goldwin Smith and Arthur Stanley, both known for their advocacy of the reforms. Goldwin Smith, historian and prominent Liberal, had a deep aversion to Jews, resulting only in part from his distaste for Disraeli as man and politician. He was well-known for his acerbic expressions of his dislike of the 'exclusivity' of the Jews, especially when combined with their demands for equality and their incorrigible 'foreignness'. At the same time he hated what he called 'clericalism', which he said had long degenerated into the narrow interests of the clerics. Smith's zeal for reform, his scholarship, and his talent for lucid presentation, led to his appointment as Stanley's colleague in the secretariat of the Commission, which was judged a triumph for the reformers.

Disraeli, who supported Jewish emancipation, was not greatly interested in the University tests question. He tended to follow the line of his party's leadership, of which he was a senior member. In 1854, like many of his colleagues, he made clear that he deplored any onslaught on 'prescription', upon which it was his long-held view – like that of Burke – that the institutions of England rested. He disliked policies which interfered with the self-government and independence of the Universities. His leader, Lord Derby, who had supported the proposals for abolition as a member of Melbourne's administration in 1834, continued to favour abolition in principle, but hoped that the University authorities would be left to decide such questions for themselves without Parliamentary interference. He opposed Jewish emancipation as long as he could. The Jewish Relief Act of 1858, passed during his administration, was not directed by any principle on his part but by the wish to settle the perennial divisive issue of Jewish admission to the House of Commons once and for all and thus avoid the long and distracting turmoil provoked by the issue.

In some respects the 1860s was the first modern decade. Darwin's *The Origin of Species* and Mill's *On Liberty* appeared in 1859. Geological studies had already cast the planet in a new light and affected the opinions of many as to its antiquity. New notions, in particular the theory of natural selection, presented to many minds personal challenges to traditional ways of belief and thinking. The sharp antithesis, as it was perceived to be, between contending bodies of opinion, led some to conclude that there was no choice other than an either/or opinion as between the Christian faith and its rejection. On the younger Fellows at the Universities this approach had a considerable impact. A dramatic and infectious example of the effect of the new era was the surrender of his tutorship at Trinity College, Cambridge, by Leslie Stephen in 1862,[21] followed by the giving up of his Anglican priesthood and his Fellowship, and his public abandonment of the Christian faith. All this followed his declaration that he was no longer able to accept the biblical narrative or the Articles of the Church.

The theological controversies of the 1840s were now followed in the 1860s by conflicts over the acceptability of any dogma or creed. Lecky's monumental study of the history of rationalism (1865) quickly became a textbook for sceptics, atheists, and all critics of organised religion. In the section entitled 'The Secularisation of Politics', Lecky referred to what he called the 'Church and State theory'. He observed that 'in its most definite form (its upholders) demanded that every nation should support and endow one form of religion and only one ... and that the rulers and representatives should belong exclusively to the established faith. ... The invasion and partial destruction of the sectarian character of the universities represents the last stage of the movement which the earliest advocates of toleration had begun.'

Leslie Stephen, who became the first editor of the *Dictionary of National Biography*, and his friend, Henry Fawcett, Fellow of Trinity Hall, Cambridge, were highly popular university personalities. They entered the lists of powerful advocates for the complete abolition of tests; they injected into the debate a sharper acrimony. Fawcett, a disciple of Mill and from his early manhood entirely blind, was Professor of Political Economy at Cambridge, a Radical M.P. and by temperament an enemy of compromise. He thought the universities of England should be the culminating points of a great national system of education.[22] He pressed for an expanded system of school building with public aid, and for the abolition of the tests, with equal zeal. In 1861 Fawcett organised a widely noted Petition signed by 70 Cambridge Fellows calling for abolition. His pressure for the opening of the Fellowships at Trinity College, Dublin, contributed much to that achievement in Dublin.

Of those who in the 1860s decided on grounds of conscience to resign their Fellowships, Henry Sidgwick's decision in the summer of 1869 attracted the most attention. This was partly because of his academic standing and partly because of his family connections. His wife was a sister of Lord Salisbury, who in that same year became Chancellor of Oxford and was the senior political opponent of abolition. Mrs Sidgwick's cousin, Arthur Balfour, was himself thought to be a philosophic sceptic but was certainly loyal to Salisbury, his uncle and mentor in the Tory party. Sidgwick's sister was married to Edward Benson, a senior master at Rugby, and adjudged to be a prospective Archbishop of Canterbury (becoming such in 1882). Sidgwick was acknowledged to be among the leading

14. Henry Sidgwick (1838–1900), *c.*1894, Fellow, Trinity College, Cambridge

Cambridge intellects of his time. Philosopher and classicist, he had been increasingly affected by the intellectual and scientific trends of the day, and in particular was much influenced by Mill.

Son of an Anglican cleric and devoted to his family circle, Sidgwick had in recent years grown increasingly uneasy over the retention of his prized Trinity Fellowship, as a precondition for which he had followed the rule of subscribing to the Articles of the Church. When Benson informed Sidgwick that he found his decision to resign 'sad and puzzling', he replied that for some years he had laboured under strain on account of that subscription. He had written to a friend in 1866 that 'this remaining in the Church of England is humbug. ... The terrible thing is that ... to be humbug in one thing is to make a terrible breach in the citadel of morality'. To another, after his resignation, he wrote that 'for long I have had no doubt except what arose from the fact that most of the persons whose opinions I most regard think differently'.[23] His mixture of agnosticism and theism drove him in conscience from Christianity.

119

During the 1860s it became more widely recognised that it was impracticable to exclude non-Anglicans from the higher honours. In addition to the changing nature of society and political and intellectual opinion, there were specific reasons. First, having been allowed to take University degrees, the artificiality of their exclusion grew more patent with every year as increasing numbers of them received their degrees. Secondly, the movement for abolition attracted the support of growing numbers of people of the highest academic distinction, as well as of political weight inside and outside the Universities. Retentionism was taking on the character of a lost cause.[24\]

Further, there emerged in that decade a sequence of non-Anglican graduates of outstanding academic prowess, whose claims to Fellowships could not justly or sensibly be resisted. In 1860 James Stirling, a Presbyterian at Trinity College, Cambridge, was Senior Wrangler, that is to say he headed the year's Mathematics list, a position of historic prestige and special distinction. He was excluded from further advancement in that field at his University. He turned to the study of law, and became a Lord Justice of Appeal. The three Aldis brothers, all of them Baptists, became respectively Senior Wrangler (1861), Fifth (1863), and Second (1866). In all, between 1860 and 1871, 16 non-Anglican graduates were excluded from Fellowships at Cambridge because of their religious conscience, including Numa Hartog (1869), nine of whom, including Hartog, were of Trinity College. It was Stirling's case in particular which stimulated the reformers at Trinity, headed by Sidgwick, to continue their public pressure with added vigour.

This was the background against which the protagonists in Parliament brought forward their succession of Bills in the 1860s, accompanied by University petitions and followed by counter-petitions. Among the vocal abolitionists in the Commons were Edward Bouverie, the Palmerstonian Whig; John Dodson, an Oxford classicist, who urged Parliament in 1863 to give the University authorities power to undo religious tests; George Goschen, a pupil of Thomas Arnold, Oxford classicist and later a leading advocate of the University Extension movement, whose notable speech in 1865 as a recently elected Liberal M.P. for the City of London, was much taken up by his proposals for abolishing the tests; and Sir John Duke Coleridge, Solicitor General in

Gladstone's Government and later Lord Chief Justice, whose effort to end the tests was made in his private capacity. Gladstone warned Coleridge that his Bill 'will be taken ... to be an absolute secularisation of the colleges, a reversal of what was deliberately considered and sanctioned in the legislation of 1854 and 1856'. He added: 'I am inclined to think that this work is work for others, not for me.'

Coleridge's Bill came forward at a time of rapid political change. In 1867, a majority in the House of Commons had for the first time voted in favour of opening the Fellowships. It was one of the many issues behind the election in 1868 of a substantial Liberal majority in the House. That result reflected the coalescence under Gladstone of the old Peelites, of whom he had been a prominent member, the progressive Whigs, the Radicals, and the large body of Noncon-formists. John Bright, Radical and Quaker, became President of the Board of Trace, the first Nonconformist member of Cabinet. Bright would often draw public attention to the numerical strength of the Nonconformists as revealed in the religious census of 1851. He regarded Gladstone's political reliance on them inside Parliament and beyond, as the strongest lever for change. The disestablishment of the Anglican Church of Ireland in 1869 indicated to many the existence of a new approach by Government to the relationship between State and Church. Gladstone, now representing a Lanca-shire constituency, described himself as 'unmuzzled' when compared with his long years as Member for the University of Oxford.

By 1869 there was a long history of negotiations between politicians and diverse groups from the Universities. Out of Coleridge's proposals of 1869 there developed the prospect of a widely supported measure relating to the two ancient Universities and the recently founded University of Durham. Sedgwick's above-cited remarks in November 1869 were made at a meeting of some Heads of College and prominent Fellows in the Master's Lodge of St John's College. The meeting resolved to urge upon the Govern-ment that the envisaged Bill should become a Government measure in the next session of Parliament. The meeting was followed by a parallel gathering under Jowett's influence at Oxford. Both groups resolved that a joint deputation should attend upon the Prime Minister, who had encouraged the leaders to think that he was with them on these matters.[25]

A demonstration of the lengths to which some of the old school were prepared to go was provided in 1868 by Henry Liddon, Canon of St Paul's and Professor of Exegesis at Oxford. He publicly proposed that each College at Oxford should give one-half of its property towards the establishment of Colleges for non-Anglicans, while the existing Colleges would remain Anglican preserves. Alternatively, he suggested that one-half of the existing Colleges might be assigned to Nonconformists, while the remainder would remain an Anglican monopoly. These proposals were indeed desperate counsel. Liddon's plans were earnestly debated, but came to nought.

Many saw plainly that most Fellows were now in favour of abolition. There was no escape from the reality that they were the future leaders of the Universities. It was perhaps also noteworthy that in 1869 the Cambridge Union for the first time voted in favour of opening the Fellowships. The voting was 70 to 62, a small majority in a forum of no constitutional importance, but a pointer.[26] Liddon's proposals represented on his part a sad acknowledgement of the extent of reformist opinion in Parliament and the Universities.

Salisbury and his circle in the House of Lords as well as prominent Tory Members of the Commons such as Gathorne-Hardy and Spencer Walpole, and even conservative clerics such as Liddon and Edward Pusey (Regius Professor of Hebrew at Oxford) might have found it possible, if driven, to accept non-Anglican Christians or even men of non-Christian religious faiths. It was less easy for them to contemplate non-believers (in which category they included not only atheists but also agnostics, sceptics, scientific positivists and Unitarians, usually referred to as Socinions) in teaching posts or in offices responsible for the appointment of University teachers. They regarded their philosophies as dangerous to the moral basis of society. They realised the difficulty, once the Fellowships would be opened to Nonconformists, in resisting their being opened to all; and once they were open to all, they feared the decay of 'religion'. In particular they wanted safeguards against anti-religious indoctrination.

In 1869 the House of Lords rejected Coleridge's Bill. It was reintroduced in 1870, backed by the growing weight of academic opinion. In the House of Lords Salisbury procured the setting up of a select committee of the House on the Bill, thus ensuring that the Bill would in any event not be enacted in the current session. When the Bill was again introduced in 1871, the select committee resumed its consideration of it. Salisbury had been appointed its chairman.

The purpose of the committee was defined as being to enquire 'into the best mode of giving effect' to the resolution of the House in July 1870, namely 'that in any measure to enable non-Anglicans to hold offices for which they were not now eligible' in Oxford, Cambridge, Durham or in the Colleges thereof, 'it is essential to provide by law proper safeguards for the maintenance of religious instruction and worship and for the religious character of the education to be given there'. The committee which represented different opinions on the issue heard a large array of witnesses, lay and clerical, from the respective diverse schools of thought.

Two broad sections of opinion found expression among those who addressed the committee. One, whose principal spokesman was Jowett, objected to tests in principle on the plain grounds of unfairness to the talented and loss to the Universities. The second, of whom Liddon was probably the most notable, sought above all the protection of the teaching posts. Salisbury enquired whether the feeling of injustice might not be met by allowing Fellowships to be 'the rewards of learning or excellence' without conveying eligibility 'to the government of a college' or to the teaching posts. One witness, Charles Neate, former Professor of Political Economy at Oxford and now Liberal Member of Parliament for the City of Oxford, replied that 'so long as you have tests of any sort at Oxford you will have a spirit of more or less open hostility to the Church and you will only strengthen that hostility – by any attempt to maintain tests …'.

Jowett went further. He thought that the only safeguard was 'the general religious feeling of the community, which is not likely to be violated in the University. … What society is, the University will be'. When asked by Lord Stanley of Alderley whether the 'apparent hardship' of a Jew being excluded from a competition for Christian endowments, is not lessened by the fact that it is open to any Jew, Parsee or other, to establish scholarships or to open colleges for their coreligionists on Oxford or Cambridge', Jowett agreed that it may be so.

Lord Colchester raised a more general question with E.H.

Perowne, historian, theologian, and Fellow and Tutor at Corpus Christi, Cambridge. Would it make a 'great difference' whether the Professor of Modern History was an Anglican, Roman Catholic or Positivist since it was 'scarcely possible for a man to lecture on modern history very extensively without any kind of religious bias'. Perowne agreed that it would. Their shared view was that without the tests there was no method to prevent the teaching of the unwelcome positivist notion as to religious belief being but 'the infancy of thought'.

Liddon expressly acknowledged to the committee that 'under our natural circumstances a modification of the existing tests is undoubtedly desirable'. This was chiefly 'on account of what I suppose to be now the political necessity of admitting Noncon- formists and other classes of Her Majesty's subjects ...'. He said he now took it for granted that all degrees were to be free and likewise all professorships and lay Fellowships. Yet he would retain tests for Divinity Professors and also, if it were possible, for Professors of Moral and Metaphysical Science, and History, 'because everybody knows how closely those subjects are connected with most funda- mental problems in theology'.

Liddon considered that 'the present strong feeling in Parliament' was 'probably' the result of 'considerations of social justice' – the desire of 'the great body of dissenters to be admitted on social equality terms to the Common Rooms at Oxford'. He said he would be glad 'as far as possible, to conciliate' that feeling.

The many lengthy presentations and exchanges over ten days of sitting between 22 July 1870 and 21 March 1871, constitute a graphic portrayal of the age and a multiple commentary thereon, largely as seen by churchmen and in university common rooms. It did not appear that anyone's opinions were changed by the proceedings, either among the questioners or the questioned. It was clear to all that while the numbers affected by the tests were at present small, the proposed changes were likely to be substantial in their future effects. There was also an underlying sentiment which at times was made explicit, that 'religion' was not endangered by Nonconformists – many of whom, it was said, came from 'humbler homes' or 'lower orders' than most at the Universities and that in those sections of society 'religion' tended to be taken more seriously. It was also noted that Mill, Lecky and other 'contentious' authors were currently part of university reading, which also included some of the 'contentious' German philosophers. The Committee was also reminded that a conscientious Presbyterian, James Bryce (historian, and later British Ambassador to the United States) had already been appointed a Fellow at Oriel and was Regius Professor of Civil Law at Oxford, without detriment.[27]

One of the later witnesses to address the Committee was Numa Hartog.[28] He was the only Jew to do so, and the only one to do so of the non-Anglicans who had because of their faith been denied a Fellowship. Those circumstances may have impressed the committee in a personal sense. His main themes were the hardship to those who would otherwise qualify and the injury to the Universities by the deprivation. 'Any test' he averred, 'tends to produce dishonesty. ... It lets in every man who is unconscientious'. Hartog's replies to the questions put to him rested upon those propositions. He was not drawn into the wider issues concerning the character of the Universities in relation to Church and State on which other witnesses had spoken.

This conscious or instinctive restraint typified the attitude of the Jewish community to its 'external' relations. Those who pressed for 'improvement' in the Jewish civic or political status did not do so with the wider intention of changing the social or political system, nor with the purpose of going beyond remedying what they saw as anomalies bearing upon themselves within the established system. They had no wish to transform society. The significance of Hartog's evidence was that he, a Jew, testified at all, in relation to an area of public life in which the Jewish community had for long showed no special interest.

Hartog's Senior Wranglership deeply affected the Jewish communal approach to the university tests. A much more robust attitude became the fashion; some considered that Hartog had not urged the cause with sufficient vigour. *The Times* later described Hartog's testimony as 'important evidence', and added: '... it is due perhaps to the sympathy which his exclusion excited that the Lords proposed a measure which would have admitted him a Fellow of Trinity'. Having regard to the weight of opinion on the part of a series of prominent witnesses who argued for the abolition of tests, one may reasonably doubt any assertion of a major influence on the outcome springing from his evidence. The Committee's principal concern related to admitting non-believers. Hartog's personality, his staunch religious faith, and the evident care with which he responded to a form of cross-examination by members of the Committee, especially the chairman, may have played a confirmatory role in their minds. On the particular question of the Fellowship tests, regarding which in his evidence Hartog made no concessions to his questioners, former opponents of abolition had already come to share Liddon's acceptance that the restriction, as exemplified by Hartog's case and other cases, could not as a matter of practical politics be sustained.

On 24 April 1871 the Committee resolved to recommend to the House of Lords that no test be required for Fellowships, or in respect of any degree (other than in Divinity) or for the holding of any college or University office (other than Professorships in Divinity). These recommendations were accepted by the Lords and by the House of Commons, which was by now long known to favour these measures.

The Committee had also recommended and the Lords had agreed that the tests be retained for Heads of College. At Gladstone's suggestion, this proposal was rejected by the House of Commons – by a majority of 106. The House further rejected without a division the Committee's proposal that university statutes should not be revoked without the authority of Parliament. The Committee had also proposed *inter alia* that any teaching contrary to scripture should be prohibited. The vagueness of that prohibition and the impediment which it might introduce to the course of free enquiry had aroused some opposition in the House of Lords against such provision. It was adopted by that House under Salisbury's influence. It was rejected by the House of Commons without division.

The Bill, in the form in which it left the Commons, returned to the upper House on 13 June 1871. The House shared Salisbury's opinion that no useful purpose would be served by dividing the House on the amendments made in the Commons, save as to the matters of teaching. Their Lordships were pressed by Salisbury to insist on the maintenance of the said prohibition, as had been recommended by the Committee and approved by the Lords. He said that the measure was aimed at unbelievers and represented a necessary compromise in return for the opening of the Fellowships.

He regretted that more support was not forthcoming from the Nonconformists. By 129 to 89 votes the House of Lords decided not to insist upon the clause.

Whatever further changes lay ahead the Universities Tests Act of 1871 was the crucial parting of the ways between old and new worlds at the Universities. It was seen as such, and as reflecting a new age in society.

From time to time before the foundation of the University of London, writers against the religious tests referred to the Jews as among those wrongfully deprived of the opportunity of an English university education. As early as 1789 the Unitarian, John Dyer, in his *Inquiry into the Nature of Subscription to the Thirty Nine Articles*, made this point. The record of Jews who became students at the new University in London certainly indicated the ample availability of young men of adequate interest, talent and ambition in the Jewish community of barely 30,000, to justify the kind of critical comment made by Dyer. Before Sylvester's arrival at Cambridge in 1831, there is no evidence of any professing Jew at either of the ancient Universities.[29]

The reality was that those institutions were seen by Jews as citadels of entrenched privilege remote from Jewish aspiration, save largely for some members of the upper layer of the Jewish plutocracy. But the aspiration was there. On 27 March 1846, the *Voice of Jacob* reported David Salomon's expression of belief that 'the day was not far distant when (Parliament) would initiate the example of foreign states (he was thinking in particular of recent decisions in Prussia) and admit all creeds to the Universities'. The leadership of the Jewish community remained engaged in campaigns for the opening of Parliament to Jews. Further, even at Cambridge where admission did not depend on religious tests, there was the handicap of the duty to attend college chapel. William Christie who had graduated at Trinity in 1838 and was a Member of Parliament from 1842 to 1847, told the House of Commons that he knew of a Jew who while at Magdalene College was given leave not to attend chapel, but that when that Jew transferred to Trinity that indulgence was not allowed.

When Alfred de Rothschild was at Trinity in 1859, it was through the intervention of his father and his tutor, the noted liberal theologian J.B. Lightfoot (later Bishop of Durham), that the Master granted him leave of absence from chapel.[30] In Hartog's day there was usually no difficulty in obtaining leave of absence from chapel and from religious instruction on grounds of religious conscience. The indulgence became general at both Universities. In 1868 Balliol formally abolished compulsory chapel, a decision reflecting the influence of Jowett, which example was followed by other colleges. At Oxford, C.P. Scott, a Unitarian and later editor of the *Manchester Guardian*, records that he reached a novel agreement with the Dean of his college whereby he would attend chapel mid-week provided he was free not to attend on Sundays and on other special days.

On 11 August 1854, following the Oxford University Reform Act, Abraham Benisch wrote in the *Hebrew Observer* with some euphoric flourish that now the University was open to professing Jews, 'we see no reason why they should not have a private hall at Oxford of their own'. It would be permissible by law and would prove cheaper than living in college. In such a hall there would no doubt be a greater facility for meeting Jewish dietary requirements in such a hall. The suggestion was not taken up. Prominent Jewish emancipationists were not likely at that stage of their campaign to embark upon what might appear a gratuitous act of self-segregation. But the Act of 1854 did stimulate some enthusiasm among Jews. It represented for those in the Jewish reading public and who were interested in public trends, an omen of wider 'liberalisation'. Sir David Salomons made public references to the Act as raising hopes for wider measures at the Universities and elsewhere. It was significant that among non-Jewish guests fêted at the recurring Jewish charity dinners, Heywood was a notable figure. In April 1856 at the dinner in support of the West Metropolitan Jewish School, Heywood presided. David Woolf Marks, of the Reform Synagogue with which the School was associated, urged the need for yet wider reform at both Universities. With Heywood's concurrence, he expressed regret that Sylvester and Arthur Cohen had not been able to take their degrees because of the restrictions, which at the date of the dinner were still operative at Cambridge. Cohen in his response deplored the restrictions. His eloquence and his family connections attracted wide attention to his address.

It is noteworthy that in the above-mentioned editorial in the *Hebrew Observer*, Benisch, describing the Act as 'great and unexpected', observed with some licence that the Act did no violence to the wishes 'of the original testators'. Parliament, he added, had interpreted their wishes 'according to the increasing light and knowledge of the age in which we live – by giving to their benevolence a wider range of usefulness than they in their day – were capable of conceiving ...'. He urged that the M.A. degrees be opened.

If Benisch spoke for a comparatively limited segment of the Jewish community, the Jewish press could not fail to acclaim Jewish students, wherever they might be, who showed merit. On 27 July 1843 the *Voice of Jacob* typically rejoiced in the academic prizes awarded to B.H. Ellis, son of a treasurer of the Great Synagogue, at Haileybury College, the staff college of the East India Company. Ellis had studied at the University of London. At Haileybury he had refused to attend church. 'An intelligent Jew', commented the editor, 'has but to preserve his self-respect in order to command that of all honourable men'. Ellis's career was one of those cited in the Parliamentary debates on the disabilities. On 10 April 1845 Christie referred to Ellis's recent appointment as a Magistrate in India, as an object lesson to those who opposed the lifting of the restrictions at the Universities and in municipal government, the latter sphere being in immediate issue at the time. As Sir Barrow Helbert Ellis, he eventually served as a member of the Viceroy's Council and later became Chairman of Jews' College. Jewish editorial expressions became more frequent (and more effusive), with successive Jewish distinctions gained over the years. Notable reference was made to the election of Alfred H. Louis (admitted to Trinity College, 1847) as President of the Cambridge Union, in 1850, a prestigious post occupied by Arthur Cohen in 1853.

The opening of the House of Commons in 1858 did more than render the anomaly of the restrictions more grievous to those affected. It also gave greater freedom to those who had been strenuously involved in the now successful 'political' campaign. Interest was encouraged by the succession of university reform Bills in the 1860s, and in particular by the career of Numa Hartog. It was the resonance of that career which precipitated a veritable Jewish campaign, stirred in particular by the *Jewish Chronicle*, for the opening of the Fellowships. Editorial references were frequent during that decade, but the editorial of 10 July 1868 may be said to begin a sustained Jewish effort on the issue. Michael Henry, appointed editor in that year, a former pupil at the City of London School and a one-time operator of a patent agency, pushed the matter hard, and with a measure of self-righteousness.

'The connection between Christianity and education', wrote Henry, 'is simply artificial. ... It has no warranty in Christian writings'. The editorial contrasted this with the case of Judaism, wherein 'learning is a religious duty to the Jew'. The Church of England cannot 'fairly' claim 'a monopoly of academical privileges'. This editorial must have seemed to some to dispatch the Church's case with excessive journalistic zeal; but it demonstrated a new mood of confidence in some quarters. 'True religion', Henry concluded, 'bids us throw those portals widely open.' It was a slogan to which interested Jews might adhere, but it was not primarily or indeed at all a Jewish issue. It was a national issue, in which Jews had an interest, as did also the much larger Christian bodies not in conformity with the established Church. In assessing communal opinion in 1870, David Woolf Marks was nearer the mark when he declared: 'It is not to be supposed that University tests can be maintained after political disabilities have been removed'.[31] That was the real ground for confidence.

During 1870 there were exceedingly few Jewish communities in Britain, and few synagogues in London, which did not send Petitions to Parliament urging the opening of the Fellowships. They were encouraged by the Board of Deputies to do so. The petitions were sent via Sir David Salomons, or the local Bishop, or the Board, or direct to the Government, and added to the combined welter of pleas from all sections of the Nonconformists. The enthusiasm for the change was shared by all the political groups which made up the Liberal Party. Hartog disclaimed the extent of the share attributed to him by fellow Jews in the bringing about of the present phase. He had 'simply followed where others had led the way', he said; realistically adding that 'prejudices were being thrown down in other walks of life' and not only 'in the Universities'.[32]

Hartog instinctively shared the prevailing belief among the Jewish communal leadership in the importance of emphasising the value of education in the inculcation of good citizenship, especially technical education, among 'the working classes'. Addressing Jewish working men in 1870, he said that he 'hoped the working classes would follow (the advice given at that meeting) and strive

15. Numa Edward Hartog
(1846–71), 1871

16. Marion Hartog
(1821–1907), writer of
historical sketches and poems

to educate themselves and cultivate their faculties and thus become better citizens and better Jews'.

Hartog was born in Mansell Street in Whitechapel. His mother was Marion Moss, daughter of a Portsmouth shopkeeper, a writer of popular Jewish historical tales and a journalist. In 1845 she married the Parisian Jew, Alphonse Hartog, who taught languages in London. They founded a Jewish school attached to their home, which moved successively from premises in the City of London to Camden Town and Maida Vale. Numa was the eldest of a large and talented family. His youngest sibling was Sir Philip Hartog, scientist and university administrator. The family was reared in an Orthodox household, where literature and education were serious subjects of discussion.

Numa's education was financially assisted by Mayer de Rothschild's wife who had been a pupil at the Hartog school. From University College School he passed to University College, gaining scholarships and graduating with high honours in mathematics, classics and modern languages. He entered Trinity College, Cambridge in 1865 and was assisted thereat by the winning of further scholarships. He gained a First in each of his years at

Cambridge, his heading of the Mathematics list in 1869 causing no surprise. It was noted that Hartog demurred over the Christian form of words to be used by the Vice-Chancellor in bestowing the B.A. degree upon him in 1869. His request was that when he came to kneel in the customary fashion, those traditional words be omitted. The Senate granted his request. The precedent was increasingly followed.

Hartog was a member of the Cambridge Union. His speeches there against religious disabilities attracted much attention in the University. After he left Cambridge in 1869 he continued to give public addresses in support of that cause. In 1870 he was one of the founder members of the Society for Hebrew Literature, and served as Joint Secretary with Israel Davis.[33] He was appointed to the Council of Jews' College, and was often seen on Jewish public occasions. If he was treated as a celebrity, that was in spite of himself. Beset by ill-health, a man of nervous temperament (but not without courage), and uncertain as to his future occupation, he was not always easy in public company. The Act in whose pre-history he had played a part, received the royal assent on 16 June 1871. Hartog died a few days later at the age of 25, smitten by small-pox.

If the instance of Hartog and his evidence were reported in the national press and cited in the Parliamentary debates, there were also other distinguished young scholars affected by the tests. In 1871 much attention was drawn to the case of John Hopkinson (one of those referred to by Hartog to the select committee as Senior Wrangler of that year), a Manchester Nonconformist whose inhibition in respect of the tests was, at that moment, especially topical. Hopkinson, who later became Professor of Electrical Engineering and head of the Siemens Laboratory at Trinity College, London, was granted a Fellowship at Trinity College, Cambridge, shortly after the passage of the new Act.

The anonymous biographical sketch of Hartog in the Dictionary of National Biography, states that his evidence to the committee 'made a considerable impression'. This was not the universal view. On 26 May 1871, the *Jewish Chronicle* published a long article signed 'I', expressing some implied but clear regret that Sylvester had not given evidence, adding that Hartog 'having suffered little or nothing did not speak with all the ... thoroughness that was deserved'. It is a reasonable assumption that Hartog's outlook on public affairs, combined with his natural reticence (consistent though it clearly was with forthright and clearly articulated replies), disinclined him from expressions of outrage (which Michael Henry may – or may not – have preferred), and from taking up with Salisbury and others (as later commentators may – or may not – have preferred) issues which were important to Salisbury but not directly related to Hartog's own particular complaints. The better opinion is that Hartog probably made a more helpful contribution by 'speaking to his brief.'[34] There was a universally expressed belief that by his early death public life and the Jewish community had suffered an immense loss.

NOTES

1. William Cobbett's *Parliamentary History of England*, Vol. 17 (pub. 1813 under T.C. Hansard's 'superintence') records the debates (6 February 1772 and 23 February 1773), and recounts the preceding events, including the history of the original Petition, whose presenter to Parliament was Sir William Meredith, M.P. for Liverpool, a liberal Whig politician and an Oxford graduate in law.
2. Among the boys who were to gain admission without subscribing to the Articles because they were adjudged too young to understand them, were Jeremy Bentham and James Bryce.
3. The exclusion of the six students from St Edmund's Hall, Oxford in 1768 who were pronounced guilty of preaching and praying as 'calvinistic methodists', had added to the sense of grievance and injustice. The charge and the judgment thereon by the Heads of College who considered their cases, were long remembered and denounced as inconsistent with the purposes of a university which, it was urged, related to wider purposes than the enforcement of a creed. W.R. Ward, *Georgian Oxford: University Politics in the Eighteenth Century*, 1958, pp. 239–55, and *passim*.
4. Blackburne proposed and drafted the Petition of 1771. A Christian philosopher of yet longer and wider influence was the celebrated William Paley, who in his *Principles of Morals and Political Philosophy* (1785), and in his lectures at Cambridge where he had been Fellow and Tutor at Christ's, addressed what he argued were the many inconsistencies within the Articles of the Church. In his account of Paley in the *Dictionary of National Biography*, Leslie Stephen notes that the book went into 15 editions by the time of his death in 1805. Among later editions, was one edited in 1859 by Richard Whateley, Archbishop of Dublin, a liberal churchman and an influential advocate of Jewish emancipation. Stephen referred to Paley's 'curious compromise between orthodoxy and rationalism'.
5. The college opened as the University of London. With the University expansion, it was incorporated in 1836 as University College, part of the

University. H. Hale Bellot, *University College London 1826–1926*, 1929. The calibre and achievements of many of its students and graduates reminded Oxford and Cambridge of their own loss. Lord Acton, the most prominent Roman Catholic lay figure, began his inaugural lecture as Regius Professor of Modern History at Cambridge in 1895, by informing his audience that in the late 1840s three Colleges in Cambridge had refused him admission. He was at the time a student in Edinburgh and 'fervently' wished 'to come to this University': *Lectures in Modern History*, 1921, p. 1. See also Acton's letter to Gladstone about this in January 1896: David Matthew, *Acton: The Formative Years*, 1946, p. 72. The Quaker, W.E. Forster, the father of the Education Act of 1870, reminded a deputation of supporters canvassing in Liverpool for the opening of the Fellowships in 1869, that he had been excluded from the Universities and that he had 'felt an interest in the question all his life': *The Times*, 11 November 1869. John Bright, fellow-Quaker and the first Nonconformist to enter the Cabinet (appointed President of the Board of Trade in 1868) did not conceal his like personal experience and reaction. Sir George Jessel likewise gave public expression to his regret over his exclusion as a Jew – without any diminution in his attachment and active devotion to London University and University College, where he had proved to be a gifted student.

6. In the early part of the nineteenth century there emerged what Professor (Lord) Annan, adopting a famous phrase, called 'the intellectual aristocracy': *Studies in Social History*, ed. J.H. Plumb, 1955. In addition to Quakers, Unitarians, and philosophical radicals, they included members of the Evangelical wing of the Church of England and Christian Nonconformists. Whatever their differences, they were marked by intellectual talent and sharp social conscience. They were members of a rising self-conscious middle class, influenced by libertarian ideals and the political philosophy of social amelioration and utilitarianism. They added considerable intellectual stimulus towards that century's political, social, and administrative reforms, including university reform, and were individually prominent in public advocacy and public action in their respective chosen fields. Many of them (not all) could not but share Mill's belief (whatever they may have made of some elements in his sceptic philosophy) that enforced subscription was not helpful to private or public morality.

7. Henry Milman's *History of the Jews* (1830) was publicly and solemnly denounced by Professors Faussett and Blunt, respectively Professors of Divinity in Oxford and Cambridge, because of the author's historical approach to scripture. His friend, Arthur Stanley (later Dean of Westminster), described Milman's work as 'the first palpable indication that the Bible can be studied like another book, that the characters and events of sacred history could be treated at once critically and reverently'. Bryce wrote of Stanley that 'it was generally believed that his own opinions were what nine-tenths of the Church of England would call unorthodox': *Studies in Contemporary Biography*, 1903, p. 80. Divisions such as over Milman's work tended to coincide (though not invariably) with divisions over the tests.

8. T.W. Clark and T.M. Hughes, *Life and Letters of Adam Sedgwick*, 1890.

9. In his short history of Trinity College in 1943, G.M. Trevelyan, then Master of Trinity, raised the question of how far the strong reactions against Thirlwall were due to his views (which Trevelyan shared) and to his boldness *vis-à-vis* Turton and Wordsworth. He seemed to think that Thirlwall may have over-played his hand and that his boldness in the face of authority may have been excessively provocative. The episode certainly projected the issue to a wider audience outside the Universities. In 1940 D.A. Winstanley, then Vice-Master of Trinity, noted that the Cambridge Commission commended the revisions of the University's statutes proposed by the syndicate which had already been appointed by the Senate 'in anticipation' of the Commission. In relation to the mid-century in particular, he described Sedgwick as 'aggressive, dogmatic and too ready to think of himself as battling against the forces of evil and darkness', and added that the Heads were not 'the tyrants that Sedgwick and his friends represented them to be': *Early Victorian Cambridge*, 1940, pp. 43–4, 57, and 83–96. See generally D.A. Winstanley, *Unreformed Cambridge* (18th Century), 1935, and *Later Victorian Cambridge*, 1947; and G. Midgley, *University Life in 18th Century Cambridge*, 1996.

10. For more than a century an effective role in influencing opinion was played by the Committee of Protestant Dissenting Deputies. It was London-based, and represented the 'old' dissenting bodies, namely the Presbyterians (many of the English Presbyterians turned to Unitarianism in the late eighteenth and early nineteenth centuries), the Independents (inheriting the Puritan tradition) and the Baptists. Many of their leaders were prominent in the City of London and some entered Parliament. Their main purpose was to press for the termination of religious disabilities in public life. Some of them supported the separate 'liberationist' movement for the disestablishment of the Church – a movement which also brought pressure to bear against the disabilities. The Committee of Protestant Dissenting Deputies was founded in 1732, and achieved its maximum impact between the cessation of the French Wars in 1815 and the rise of the Liberal Party in the 1860s. It was the model in name and early structure of what became the Board of Deputies of British Jews. The Committee consistently supported the movement for Jewish emancipa-tion. Ashley Pellatt, M.P. for Southwark, a London glass manufacturer and a City of London Common Councillor, was Vice-Chairman or Chairman of the Committee from 1853 to 1863, and, as was characteristic, frequently attended Jewish public events. He was typical of the leadership of the Committee, which continued its work beyond the 'freeing' of the Universities from the tests. See generally B.L. Manning, *The Protestant Dissenting Deputies*, 1952. The *Nonconformist Weekly* (founded 1841) was a significant mouthpiece for the Committee. The Wesleyans or Methodists (divided into several groups in the nineteenth century) often shared the same anxiety over the spread of 'bible criticism', as experienced by many Anglican Evangelicals and some of them had their own concern over opening the Universities to 'non-believers'.

11. For many at the Universities, the issue of self-improvement where necessary, as distinct from obligation under Parliamentary intervention, became in itself

one of principle. Wellington, for many years Chancellor of Oxford, regarded suggestions for direct statutory action as part of what he considered the predatory and inquisitorial habit of the reformed House of Commons. In effect he urged the Vice-Chancellor and others to seek to remedy palpable and injurious anomalies and raise standards of teaching and study within their own powers, if Parliamentary intervention was to be resisted realistically.

12. Mark Pattison, the sceptic in holy orders, who became Head of Lincoln in 1861 and was second only to Jowett in the matter of university reform, later wrote: 'In 1846 we were still the old Oxford .... In 1850 all this had suddenly changed'; such was the sharp impact of the agitation for reform and such also was the dramatic realisation of how far the University had already moved in opinion and internal reform. Pattison told the Oxford Commission that 'the ideal of a national university is that it should be co-extensive with the nation'. The reforms of the 1850s were a long stride to that end, and greatly strengthened the spirit of modernisation at both Universities, with all the open-endedness as to the results which that might bring. The moods of complacency and change are likewise pictured in the *Autobiography* of Professor Max Muller (1901), who had arrived in Oxford from his native Germany in 1848. 'Long before the Commissioners came' he observed, 'a new life seemed to be springing up (in Oxford) and what was formerly the exception became more and more the rule among the young Fellows and Tutors. ... I often tried to persuade my friends at Oxford to make the Fellowships really useful ... but the feeling of the majority was always against what was called derisively Original Research, and the fellowship funds continued to be frittered away ... so that often there remained payment only but no results' (pp. 259–61). Muller catches both the mood of improvement and the need for the kind of impetus administered by the Reports and the legislation of 1854–56.

13. James Joseph Sylvester (1814–97) was Second Wrangler in 1837 and received his B.A. and M.A. degrees at Cambridge in 1872. Among the appointments held by this world-famous mathematician was his Professorship in Natural Philosophy at University College, London and the Savilian Chair in Geometry at Oxford.

14. A factor which weighed with members of both Commissions is seen in the following observation in the Report of the Commission on Oxford: 'It is certainly desirable that the manufacturing and mercantile (interest) which has arisen by the side of the landed aristocracy, and which is exercising a great influence in the public counsels, should seek to have its sons brought up where so many eminent statesmen of the past and present times have been trained, and that the Universities should not cease to send forth a succession of persons qualified to serve in the State as well as the Church': James Heywood, *The Recommendations of the Oxford University Commissioners* (with selections from their Report and a history of the University Tests), 1853, p. 177. The somewhat patronising tone of the language did not obscure the implied reference in the passage to Heywood and his associates in industry and commerce.

15. Arthur Cohen (1829–1914) was Fifth Wrangler in 1853 and took his degree in 1857. He was President of the Board of Deputies (1880–95), and Standing Counsel for the University of Cambridge and the India Office. He was a Liberal M.P. and a leader of the commercial bar: Israel Finestein, 'Arthur Cohen, QC, 1829–1914' in *Jewish Society in Victorian England* (London, 1993), pp. 305–26.

16. Gladstone was 'shaken by its arguments' and even more by the supporting evidence: J.B. Conacher, *The Aberdeen Coalition 1852–55*, 1968, p. 333. In general for Gladstone's thinking on university issues, including the tests, see his *Diaries* (12 vols. ed. H.C.G. Matthew).

17. Francis Birrell, *Gladstone*, 1933, p. 51.

18. Yet the difference in principle remained wide and unbridged. 'So rife,' wrote George Corrie, Master of Jesus College, Cambridge, 'have indifferentism and strange principles become among us here, as elsewhere, that I often feel as if I were one of the last remnants of a bygone race.': *Memorials of the Life of G.E. Corrie*, ed. M. Holroyd, 1890, p. 248 (1847). Of Corrie, Winstanley wrote that 'the last ditch was his spiritual home'. A far different notion, widely held, was expressed by *The Times* on 17 March 1869 in the context of the public debate of that year, but which reflects a view often heard over the whole period. 'When Oxford and Cambridge', wrote the editor, 'are made national institutions, with religious limits coterminous with those of the nation itself, not a single real safeguard to the morality and religion of any undergraduate will have been taken away'. There was a widening expression of concern over what was called 'sophistry in the interpretation of solemn obligations' arising from 'careless assent in the matter of tests': Randall T. Davidson and W. Benham, *Life of A.C. Tait*, 1891, Vol. 1, pp. 162–7. Forster went further. He said that 'in some measure (he attributed) the degeneracy which we must acknowledge has been observed of late in the English character for straightforwardness in all business matters ... to (how) good ... and able men have got into the habit of faltering with words in these matters'. He was 'struck by how (they) got over scruples ... in signing tests and making declarations ...': *The Times*, 11 November 1869.

19. Note 8, *supra*, Vol. 2, p. 451.

20. From 1847 Gladstone supported proposals for the admission of Jews into Parliament but long continued to oppose the statutory opening of Fellowships to non-Anglicans. In the 1860s Gladstone, in the spirit of compromise, suggested that instead of the old requirement of Fellowships being limited to Anglican clerics, one half of the Fellows in each College might be so obligated: W.R. Ward, *Victorian Oxford*, 1968, pp. 253–4, and P.T. Marsh, *The Victorian Church in Decline: Archbishop Tait and the Church of England 1969*, pp. 83–4.

21. F.W. Maitland, *Life and Letters of Leslie Stephen*, 1906. He resigned the tutorship at the Master's request when he declared he could no longer take part in Chapel services.

22. Leslie Stephen, *Life of Henry Fawcett*, 1885, p. 231.

23. For Sidgwick it was a question of morality, a theme examined by him in his

published paper, *Ethics of Conformity and Subscription* (1870). The Trinity Fellowship was restored to Sidgwick in 1885; he had already resumed his lecturing in Political Economy.

24. Typical of the extensive exercise in public relations on behalf of abolition was the large assembly in the Manchester Free Trade Hall on 6 April 1866, addressed by Frederick Temple, later Archbishop of Canterbury. He called for admission to all honours regardless of creed, a course which would 'advance learning', extend opportunities for a 'liberal education' and 'promote the unity of the nation'. The issue had become a major national question among the reading public. Characteristic of the changed approach was Maitland's observation at the Cambridge Union in 1869 that 'there are two things which we have learned by costly experience that the law cannot control – religious belief and the rate of interest': H.A.L. Fisher, *F.W. Maitland 1850–1906*, 1910, p. 13.

25. The two groups were not agreed on every particular but, two Bills having been rejected by Parliament since Gladstone came to power, they pressed upon him that the measure to be introduced in the next session should now be a Government measure. He agreed with the request but could not promise a date for any Bill because of other business, inviting them to secure the widest harmony in the meantime. The Queen's speech in February 1870 envisaged 'a legislative settlement of this question as may contribute to extend the usefulness of those great institutions and to heighten the respect with which they are justly regarded'. On 16 December 1869 *The Times* had reported the exchanges between the deputations and Gladstone.

26. In 1865, when the Union last debated the question, the proposal was overwhelmingly rejected.

27. Charles Appleton, Fellow of St John's, Oxford and an 'unreserved abolitionist', reminded the Commission that 'a well-known Jewish *savant* is at present employed in the Department of Oriental Literature (who) is on the best of terms with the Professors of Divinity and Hebrew'. He said the latter and 'many other clergymen' are 'very glad to apply to him for help in their biblical studies'. He added: 'I do not see any harm would arise from setting up a Jewish faculty of theology, provided a considerable number of Jews went to Oxford. In fact it would be an exceedingly useful institution.' The Duke of Somerset (who in 1872 published his *Christian Theology and Modern Scepticism*) asked Appleton how he would secure 'the orthodoxy' of the teachers in such a faculty. Appleton replied that he had considered that and 'it would not be at all objectionable as far as he could see to have a test ...'. Two Jewish *savants* were at Oxford. One was Adolf Neubauer (1831–1907), the Orientalist and bibliographer. He was a senior librarian at the Bodleian Library, cataloguing its Hebrew manuscripts, and was later Reader in Rabbinic Hebrew at Oxford. The other was Solomon Schiller-Szinessy (1820–90) who in 1866 was appointed teacher (later reader) in Talmud and Rabbinic Literature at Cambridge. Appleton's reference was to the latter. See Professor Raphael Loewe's paper on Schiller-Szinessy in *Trans.*, J.H.S.E., 21, 1967, pp. 148–89. The above exchange is in House of Lords Reports, 1871, 179,

ix, 85, pp. 58–9. In his book the Duke, of liberal disposition and on many issues a supporter of Gladstone, commented that 'truth is the daughter of time and not of authority' (p. 173).

28. Mrs Beth-Zion Lask Abrahams (now deceased) kindly drew my attention to the following references to Hartog in the autobiography of Sir Charles Rivers Wilson (1915), who was Private Secretary to Robert Lowe, Gladstone's Chancellor of the Exchequer (1868–74). Mrs Juliana de Rothschild, Mayer's wife, asked Lowe to help Hartog in the task of making a living. Lowe requested Wilson to see what might be done, and Wilson interviewed Hartog. Wilson writes: 'I found him to be a timid, retiring little man, very modest and apparently unconscious of his mental superiority'. Hartog informed him that he had tried to find work as private tutor but in vain, as he was thought to be too good for it. 'He assured me that he was in such extremities that he would take anything that would bring him enough to live on'. Hartog accepted Wilson's offer of a 'clerkship' in the Revenue Office at thirty shillings a week. Lowe seems to have thought that the work fell below Hartog's quality and to have authorised the offer reluctantly. Some weeks later on an official visit to that Office, Lowe and Wilson saw Hartog in his shirt-sleeves sorting out old documents. Lowe shared Wilson's view that this was a waste of talent and asked Sir Henry (later Lord) Thring, the Parliamentary draftsman, to employ the Senior Wrangler in his office where high ability was required, whither Hartog was transferred and where 'he worked most satisfactorily'. (Wilson, *supra*, pp. 3–4). Mrs de Rothschild was a grand-daughter of Levi Barent Cohen, the eighteenth-century London magnate, synagogue leader and philanthropist. By the time of his fatal illness, Hartog had begun to read for the Bar. Whether he contemplated practice in the Courts, one does not know.

29. See H.P. Stokes, *Studies in Anglo-Jewish History*, 1913, pp. 212–40; Cecil Roth, 'The Jews in the English Universities' *Trans.*, J.H.S.E., Misc., 1942, pp. 102–15; and Raphael Loewe, 'Cambridge Jewry: The First Hundred Years', in William Frankel and Harvey Miller, *Town and Tallith*, 1989, pp. 13–37. See also the Book of Memorial in the last-mentioned volume, p. 159 etc.

30. D.A. Winstanley, *Early Victorian Cambridge*, *supra*, p. 83. Alfred de Rothschild's father was (Baron) Lionel de Rothschild.

31. *Jewish Chronicle*, 15.4.1870. Marks was Professor of Hebrew at University College London as well as Senior Minister at the West London Synagogue of British Jews.

32. Ibid. The enthusiasm was such that in Manchester and elsewhere local Jewish religious dissensions were not allowed to stand in the way of joint meetings and combined efforts to assist the cause.

33. Israel Davis, later proprietor and editor of the *Jewish Chronicle*, was a former pupil at the City of London School and had gained a First Class degree in classics at Christ's College, Cambridge, whereafter he practised for some years at the Bar.

34. Hartog's evidence to the Select Committee was given on 3.3.1871, pp. 131–8 [Nos. 1226–95], House of Lords Reports.

5

British Opinion in the Mid-nineteenth Century on the Idea of Jewish National Restoration

The fashion of men and women of social distinction in London to travel to the East brought London society directly into contact with local conditions in Palestine. The country was visited by the Prince of Wales and entourage in 1862. The region was of concern to British imperial and commercial interests. It also held a natural attraction for Christian conversionists. The emphasis on the authority of Scripture within the increasingly influential Evangelical sector of the Church of England, and the importance attached to the Old Testament in the outlook of the Nonconformists (especially among the Presbyterians), reinforced the study of the literal meaning and, as they saw it, the potential contemporary significance of biblical prophecy. Interest in the history, geography and topography of Palestine was evident at many levels of society.

One of the most influential writers in this field was the Oxford theologian, George Stanley Faber. His *Dissertation on the Prophecies*, published in London in 1807, which surveyed post-biblical history and its relation, as perceived by him, to 'the Restoration of the Jews', ran into many editions. Macaulay recorded a striking recollection in a letter to his sister in November 1859. He wrote: 'When I was a boy [he was born in 1800] no human being doubted that Buonaparte was the principal subject of the prophecies of the Old Testament. ... I heard my father [Zachary Macaulay, London merchant and prominent Evangelical] say that the prophets were then wilder than ever he remembered them [on Napoleon's entry into Egypt]. They fully expected the [prophesied] battle in the valley of Jehosaphat and the restoration of the Jews within a year.'[1]

In his highly popular *Short History of the English People*, the Victorian historian J.R. Green, observed: 'No greater moral change ever passed over a nation than passed over England during the years which parted the middle of the reign of Elizabeth [around 1580] from the meeting of the Long Parliament [in 1641]. England became the people of a book, and that book was the Bible. It was as yet the one English book which was familiar to every Englishman.'[2] The cultivation of Hebraic studies at the Universities reflected the special place of biblical study in intellectual enquiry.[3] It also revealed the importance attached in some quarters to what was deemed the virtue of pursuing close knowledge of the role of the Jewish people in history.[4]

When William Howley, Archbishop of Canterbury, declared his opposition to the civic and political emancipation of the Jews in 1833, he spoke of the Jews with compassion over their historical woes, with admiration for their steadfastness, and with conviction both as to their ultimate conversion and their ultimate restoration to Palestine. On the other hand, Richard Whateley, the Archbishop of Dublin, was a consistent advocate in the House of Lords on behalf of Jewish emancipation. He shared his colleague's belief in the conversion of the Jews and their national restoration in Palestine. They differed over the propriety of accepting unconverted Jews as full citizens and over the efficacy of emancipation as a step towards the anticipated conversion. But both schools of thought had no doubt that the Jews retained a role within a continuing providential design in which that restoration was an element.

In the 1840s public discussion in the national press and literary periodicals seemed to transform the debates on the future of Palestine from the distant, imponderable reaches of time to the here-and-now. The sights and sounds of the land experienced by soldier, explorer, adventurer, businessman, pilgrim, diplomat and traveller, who were now all assisted in their travels by the new forms of transport, added colour to the continuing public curiosity aroused by the possible consequences of the contemporary palpable weakening of the Ottoman Empire. The ambitions of the Great Powers, the expectations of the millenarians, the aspirations of missionaries, and the thoughts of the plainly curious, mingled in the developing interest. If this interest was mainly confined to a section of the reading and travelling public, it was a section whose influence on public debate and national policy was not insignificant and was to grow.

Lord Shaftesbury, Tory social reformer and a leading Evangelical, was a conversionist who long opposed Jewish admission to Parliament. He was a firm believer in the propriety and necessity of British encouragement of Jewish residence in Palestine. He was much influenced by the evangelical preacher, conversionist and restorationist, Edward Bickersteth, who was a trained lawyer and Secretary of the London Society for promoting Christianity among the Jews from 1816 to 1830. For Shaftesbury, the creation of the British consulate in Jerusalem in 1838[5] and the joint Anglo-Prussian bishopric in Jerusalem in 1841, were acts of religious dedication as well as of political strategy. To Palmerston, the Foreign Secretary, the political strategy was uppermost. So too was the case in respect of his instruction to the consulate in 1841 to extend British protection to the Jews of Palestine.[6]

The ambition of Mehmet Ali, Viceroy of Egypt, for independence from the Sultan, further weakened the Ottoman Empire. In the 1830s he extended his control to include Syria, inclusive of Palestine. Britain was prepared to treat with him as the *de facto* master of the region. In 1839 Sir Moses Montefiore negotiated with him for concessions to Jews in Palestine for the purchase of land for agricultural settlements. But British interests lay with sustaining the Porte, while the French supported Mehmet Ali. Palmerston's diplomatic initiatives secured the assistance of the major European powers in persuading the Viceroy to vacate the disputed territories. Montefiore's plans were not carried out. In 1841 Palmerston authorised Montefiore to inform the Jews in the East that British consuls would send to the British Ambassador in Constantinople any serious complaints regarding their treatment, for submission to the ministers of the Porte. In January 1839, Shaftesbury wrote a widely noted article in the *Quarterly Review* calling for Jewish settlement in Palestine under the protection of the major powers. It was in the form of a review of *Letters on Egypt, Edom and the Holy Land*, by Lord Lindsay, traveller and restorationist, one of a mounting genre of books by those categories of publicist.

The earliest travel guide to Palestine that I have seen (by courtesy of Mr Harry Schwab of London) is dated 1824. In that year an announcement appeared in London of the intended publication of a series of 'Popular Descriptions' of 'the various countries of the globe'. The series was to be entitled 'The Modern Traveller' and was to be concerned with the 'geographical, historical and topographical' features of the respective lands. The volume on the Holy Land was the first volume in the series. It is a 372-page, pocket-size book entitled *Palestine or the Holy Land*. 'Every acre of the Holy Land,' declared the editor, James Duncan, in the preface, 'is connected with associations interesting to the antiquary, biblical critic and Christian reader.' Accordingly, it was 'thought necessary to go far more minutely into topographical details than will be either requisite or desirable in the case of other countries. ... There is ample scope for the investigation of future travellers.'

Among the contemporary explorers relied on by the editor for information and illustrations were the brothers-in-law Captains James Mangles and Charles Leonard Irby. Their letters concerning their travels in the region in 1817–18 were privately printed in 1823 and then published in 1844 in John Murray's famous 'Home and Colonial Library', where they attracted wide attention. Prominent among travellers whose works were used in the travel guide of 1824 was James Silk Buckingham. James Duncan was undoubtedly aware of what would attract purchasers. Thus, the book provides detailed accounts of past explorations and recent surveys. The historical, especially biblical, background of numerous sites and buildings is set forth, and extensive information of current interest to the traveller is included.

Such publications illustrate the increase in foreign travel, after the long years of war, on the part of the wealthier classes in Britain, particularly the rising middle classes in the new age of expanding industry and commerce. The fact that the first volume in the series related to Palestine was more than a matter of piety, although that element was undoubtedly present. The sheer weight of detail in the book reflects the sharp interest that was rightly thought to exist in intellectual circles concerning the history of the land, its future, its 'desolation', its possible 'rebirth' and the prospective political and commercial roles of the West in the Eastern Mediterranean.

Among the prominent public figures who travelled in Palestine and wrote accounts of what they saw and experienced were John Carne, the Cornish-born *litterateur* whose descriptions of his tour of 1821 were first published in serial forms in the *New Monthly Magazine* before appearing as a book (in three editions); William John Bankes, Tory Member of Parliament and friend of Lord Byron; John Madox, who in 1834 published an extensive (two-volume) record of his *Excursions* to the Holy Land and neighbouring territories; and Lady Egerton, who in 1841 printed for private circulation a diary of her tour of the Holy Land during the previous year. The diary included copies of illustrations drawn by her husband, Francis, later the first Earl of Ellesmere.

With its widening authority and mounting prestige, Britain's role was perceived as clearly marked out by providence. On 17 August 1840, *The Times* observed that 'the proposal to plant the Jewish people in the land of their fathers,' with international support, was a subject for 'political consideration.' The confinement of Mehmet Ali to his Viceroyalty of Egypt a year later meant that if such ideas were to take root, the Sultan, now restored to his hegemony in the relevant provinces, would need to be persuaded to help.

Palmerston saw an advantage in an arrangement whereby the Sultan would approve of Jewish settlement and land purchase, with Britain as a protecting power of the same. His instructions to the British ambassador in 1840–41, to acquaint the Ottomans with the benefits of encouraging Jewish settlement – the introduction of Jewish wealth and enterprise, the gaining of Jewish friendship, the strengthening of international alliances – reflect a mixture of senti-ments. His efforts coincided with the aspirations of the Christian advocates of Jewish restoration (his proposals would have facilitated a resumption of Montefiore's plans), but his predominant concern was to seek a British presence in the area or an opportunity for influence. Palmerston exaggerated the importance of Jewish influence, and underestimated the contrast between the Jewish nature of Montefiore's schemes for self-reliant Jewish agricultural settlements and the conversionist hopes over what they thought might follow if the British Government backed Jewish settlement in the Turkish dominion.

The Damascus Affair of 1840, which prompted Montefiore's mission in the East, had reinforced the sense of Jewish need. There was also a sharper sense of the feasibility of fruitful intervention to enhance Jewish and British interests. Considerations of humanity, long-term Jewish needs, British imperial policy, and restorationist expectancy mingled. While the reassertion of the Porte's control over the disputed regions, with British support, dampened the mounting enthusiasm, the intermixture of those considerations remained a theme of public discussion in England. There was the presumption of a distinct Jewish nation whose future was closely associated with a national restoration in Jerusalem. The image of a Jewish nation did not fit in with the policy or outlook of the Jewish emancipationists.[7]

If some Christians used restorationist hopes as a basis for opposing Jewish emancipation, others used them to support the cause. The proponent of the abortive bills in Parliament in the early 1830s for the removal of Jewish disabilities was Sir Robert Grant, barrister, landowner, Whig politician, and conversionist. In urging the wisdom of his measure on the House of Commons in 1833, he compared his era to that of the Exodus and drew some remarkable analogies.

Grant quoted extensively from the work of Dr Claudius Buchanan, traveller, educationist and millenarian, who had journeyed widely in the East in the early years of the nineteenth century. In his *Christian Researches in Asia* (London 1811), he had written: 'It is predicted ... that Israel shall return to the Lord.' He called on 'our Christian nation' to proceed without delay 'to take away the reproach of the Jewish people and announce an Act in the most public and solemn manner as an example to the rest of the world.' In this way, he explained, Britain would demonstrate that the Jews no longer merited their afflictions. 'The time,' he commented, 'is now come when Parliament may restore to the Jew the franchise of a fellow-creature without contravening the divine decrees.'

The Jews, Grant declared in the House of Commons, 'are proceeding ... to the ultimate restoration of their former greatness. They carry with them ... though under dark and unbroken seals, the mighty charter of Heaven's favour, the ultimate reversion of more than their original glory.' Although the Jewish emancipationists did not disclaim the restorationist belief – indeed, they avowed it – Grant's presentation was neither in their style nor in accordance with the substance of their own public relations. For them it was at most a far-off contingency, and without any bearing on the here and now. Not so for the English Christian restorationists, even if they were in alliance with the Jewish leadership in the campaign for the removal of Jewish disabilities.

In his speech Grant argued that just as in the biblical narrative divine anger was aroused against those who impeded the progress of the Israelites to Palestine, so now those who failed to ease their lot might be acting in sin. He directly related the welfare of Britain to the question whether, at the time which he considered to be witness to a comparable modern Jewish journey, Britain would extend friendship to the ancient people by granting them the civil rights they claimed. Few speeches in Parliament revealed so clearly the atmosphere in which the Jewish question was debated, or the deep-rooted conviction on the part of leading British politicians that Jewish national restoration was at hand and that they could not remain indifferent to it.

When Grant's bill reached the House of Lords, the former Chancellor of the Exchequer, Lord Bexley, used similar words, but gave them a different emphasis. He said that a large body of Christians agreed with the Jewish belief 'that their nation will at some time be restored to the land divinely granted to their forefathers,' even though they might differ as to the manner and time of the restoration. While there was a Christian belief that 'the Jewish polity shall not be restored in Jerusalem ... before the expiration of a period called the Times of the Gentiles,' nowhere could he find it predicted 'that individual Jews should not be promoted in foreign countries to situations of honour and distinction'. In fact, he declared, such a course would facilitate their conversion.

If Grant's sense of immediacy was lacking in Bexley's address, their views did not differ in principle. For both, the prospect of Jewish restoration was within a calculable period of time. The events around 1840 and in the mid-1850s caused people of their stamp to consider most seriously whether the time was indeed not at hand. It is noteworthy that when Sebastopol finally fell to the allied forces in 1855, and the end of the Crimean War came into sight, Stanley noted that the siege ended on the same date as the siege of Jerusalem ended in the year 70.[8]

It was by no means the case that influential opinion always had clear-cut thoughts about what ought, or was likely, to lie ahead. On 26 August 1840 *The Times* captured the mixture of feelings well:

> Even to those who like ourselves mix much more of what is worldly than divine in their speculation respecting the future fate of Syria, it does not seem among the most improbable of suppositions that the restoration and nationalisation of the Jewish people, however improbable at present, may ultimately become the means of reconciling conflicting pretensions and of establishing a new focus of civilisation in that interesting region. It is, however, we acknowledge, among the most improbable of suppositions that the Great Powers of Europe will be moved by any such representations as those to which we have referred [i.e., Scriptures] unless the Jews themselves come forward and show in some definite form what is desirable to be accomplished for their benefit, how it is to be attained, and in what manner its attainment may conduce to the security of the neighbouring states and the maintenance of the general peace.

The careful language of this acknowledgement and plea sprang from the fact that there was no political direction or any organised response to the various schemes and hopes that came under discussion. The Palmerstonian ambition to acquire political footholds in the area depended for success on the changing fortunes of British relations with the Porte, and the changing ties between the Porte and the Great Powers. Yet travel, exploration, archaeology, and Semitic language study were all accompanied or fostered by a continuing examination of the role of Jerusalem in the long-term evolution of history. The long-term and short-term interests of Britain were sometimes linked with the possibility of Jewish national restoration, irrespective of conversion.

What was being considered was either the involvement of Britain in an impending or contemplated eschatological epoch, or the enlightened use by Britain of those who believed in it, or the mutually advantageous use by Britain of the idea and the actuality of Jewish settlement. Some gentile publicists came close to the advocacy of political Zionism by referring to a self-governing Jewish polity in Palestine, based on the concept of Jewish nationhood, under certain circumstances. If the Jewish leadership sought to divest the Jewish national idea of any political connotation, there were times when gentiles criticised the Jews for appearing not to be ready or willing to grasp or foster opportunities.

It is typical of the age that some individuals detected a parallel between the innovations in transportation and the growing interest in the fate of the Holy Land. Thomas Waghorn had long experimented with the idea of overland routes across the Suez region to India for mail, commercial goods, and personal travel, and in 1835 he initiated a successful regular service. He urged the British Government to link that region by rail to Cairo and, via the Cairo–Alexandria line, to a major port. The spirit of the times is caught in the self-congratulatory words of *The Railway Chronicle*, which *The Voice of Jacob* gladly adopted in its issue of 1 February 1845. 'Surely,' *The Railway Chronicle* wrote, 'there was never a time which fulfilled the prediction that many shall go to and fro and knowledge be increased, and nation shall no more go to war with nation, and when all the kingdoms shall come up to Jerusalem once a year with their offerings, so perfectly as this our era of railroads, when all these predictions cease to be hyperbolical and become possibilities.'[9]

Opponents of the Jewish case for civil emancipation warned fellow Christians again and again about what they regarded as the true nature of the Jewish national hope. Notable among them was the leading Tory lawyer Sir Frederick Thesiger, later (as Lord Chelmsford) Lord Chancellor. In 1848 he vigorously opposed the bill introduced by the Government of Lord John Russell, which would have opened Parliament to Jews. 'The Jewish race,' he stated, 'look forward to the time when they should be called together [under divine providence] … and when their religion should be the religion of the whole world.' He does not appear to have set much store in conversionist hopes or to have attached much weight to the prospect of British interests being served by British involvement with Jewish restoration.

The creation of the bishopric in Jerusalem in 1841 was met with reservations in the High Church party. Its association with Prussian Lutheranism seemed to them to represent a dilution of Anglicanism. The lack of definition in the theology of the Christians who might fall within the new diocese struck them as being in line with the broadening of the doctrinal bounds of the Church that had been a precipitating factor in the creation of the Oxford Movement. Apostolic Christianity appeared to them to be in danger of attenuation in the interests of a corrosive liberalism. For John Henry

Newman, the leading light in the Oxford Movement, the creation of the bishopric was the final act. It led him to cease to work as an Anglican priest and constituted a major propelling force that, in due course, led to his conversion to Roman Catholicism. In an article in the *Bible Critic*, the organ of the Oxford Movement, in July 1841, Newman, while still an Anglican, gave expression to his dismay at what seemed to him to be the British and Anglican policy in the East. His interesting reference to the Jews was an uncharacteristically loose expression. But it says something about the air in which projects concerning the Jews in the East were discussed, and the vague, uneasy impact they left upon some minds. His expression has irony and a touch of parody about it, but, coming from that source, it is no less interesting historically for all that.

Newman quoted that passage when he set out the history of his religious opinions in his *Apologia Pro Vita Sua* (1865). 'When our thoughts turn to the East,' it ran, 'instead of recollecting that there are Christian Churches there, we leave it to the Russians to take care of the Greeks, and the French to take care of the Romans, and we content ourselves with erecting a Protestant Church at Jerusalem, or with helping the Jews to rebuild their Temple there, or with becoming the august protectors of Nestorians, Monophysites, and all the heretics we can hear of, or with forming a league with the Mussulman against Greeks and Romans together.

Newman was impatient with what he regarded as the disagreeable mixture of ecclesiastical and political considerations in British policy, and its association with religious movements that were either hostile to Christianity or conducive to what for him was a vapid kind of Christianity with which, at home, the Oxford Movement was in verbal conflict. In a private letter of 12 October 1841, he wrote: 'We have not a single Anglican in Jerusalem; so we are sending a Bishop to *make* a communion, not to govern our own people. Next, the excuse is that there are converted Anglican Jews there who require a Bishop; I am told there are not half-a-dozen ... for them he is a Bishop of the circumcision ... Thirdly, for the sake of Prussia, he is to take under him all the foreign Protestants who will come; and the political advantages will be so great, from the influence of England, that there is no doubt they will come ...'[10]

In the Roman Catholic Church there was an even sharper sense than elsewhere of the succession of the Church to Israel, and

theories concerning the Jewish restoration were difficult to recon-
cile with the idea of the succession. English High Churchmen were
equally sensitive to the difficulty. The persistent Evangelical interest
in Jewish restoration tended to confirm the High Church view of
the dangers, as they saw them, represented by the evangelical
influence in the Anglican Church. Just as Jewish emancipation was
a test case between the old and the emerging order of society in
England, so too, in some minds, interest in Jewish national
restoration further highlighted the different shades within English
Christianity.

Not every Christian supporter of Jewish emancipation was
prepared to accept the validity of any belief in 'the Return'. Some
advocates rejected any analogy with the Christian doctrine of the
Second Coming. They regarded the restorationist feature of Jewish
tradition as divisive and sought to explain it out of existence. Charles
Egan's *The Status of the Jew in England* (London, 1848) is a survey
by a legal historian of the historical evolution of the status of the
Jew in English law and the various schools of opinion on the subject
in his day. He challenged the view that any restorationist hope or
expectation was justified by the prophecies. Egan believed that the
Jews would be restored to divine favour upon their conversion;
after that, their residence, wherever it might be, would cease to
press adversely upon them. It was in that sense that 'their time
would come'.

In addition to relying on seventeenth- and eighteenth-century
divines, Egan cited a contemporary, Joseph Lightfoot, the notable
theologian who later became an Anglican bishop. Lightfoot's view,
shared by many Anglicans, was that the rebuilding of Jerusalem was
not contemplated in the Gospels, and that Christianity was not to
be regarded as upholding the 'peculiarity' of that city or as defining
'the calling of the Jews' in any sense that touched upon geography.
Their eventual 'calling' was to be where they lived, and would be
comprised in their ultimate conversion.

Ironically, even those Jewish leaders who sought to divest
Judaism of the idea of Jewish nationhood resisted the contentions
of Christian spokesmen who preached the permanence of Jerusalem's 'desolate state'. Those Christians preserved the image or
inspiration of Jerusalem in the spiritual sense; sometimes they
tended to lay particular emphasis on the continuation of the then

150

physical condition. It was against that emphasis that the future Chief Rabbi, Hermann Adler, reacted in particular. Long before he became deputy for his father in 1880, Adler – independently of his detachment from restorationist activism – publicly repudiated the efforts to decry Jewish messianism. The high point of his response was the publication in 1869 of the series of addresses he gave at the Bayswater Synagogue in London, devoted to passages in the Bible on which Christians relied. In his third address, Adler declared that it was 'our duty to labour for the speedy realisation of [the] great future' set out in the 53rd chapter of Isaiah.

The Jewish publicists were confronted with a delicate issue. It was easier for them to disown the conversionist elements in the movement for Jewish emancipation – whether or not those elements were linked to restoration schemes – than to deny any interest in Jewish restoration. They felt it was incumbent on them to retain those strands of Jewish tradition in which this belief was rooted. Christians who advocated Jewish restorationism, whatever their motive, were encouraged by the Jewish responses to those who preached that 'Jerusalem is trodden down' and beyond re-settlement.

The title of an article in *The Spectator* magazine in July 1843, 'A Romance That May Become a Reality,' is revealing. The writer was impressed by the body of Jewish support, not only in England, for the idea of a Jewish agricultural settlement in Palestine. As was often the case, the weakness of the Ottoman Empire was stressed as the important contributing factor. 'In the present temper of the Jews, a large body of immigrants might apparently be attracted to Palestine.' If the Ottoman Government were 'to enter into a definite contract with them and induce England or a committee of European Powers to become guarantors for its observance,' benefits would accrue to the Ottomans in revenue, improved law and order, and international ties.

Such public debate helped to fuel the addresses of opponents of Jewish emancipation. It is not surprising that in their counter-arguments, the Jewish spokesmen often returned to the topic in a defensive spirit. Typical of this literature was Henry Faudel's 39-page pamphlet *Few Words on the Jewish Disabilities*, circulated in 1848 and ostensibly addressed to Sir Robert Inglis, a doyen among the opponents. 'The wealthy Jews,' wrote Faudel, 'do not send their money to Palestine, the land to which they are so gratuitously assumed to belong and to claim to be their country ... they become landowners in England in the hope of remaining in it.' Inherent in Jewish belief was the proposition that Jewish restoration would come by way of miracle. For example, in *The Arguments Advanced against the Enfranchisement of the Jews Considered in a Series of Letters* (London, 1833), Francis Goldsmid observed in the second letter that 'it is an admitted principle' of the Jewish religion that 'whenever their re-establishment in the promised land may occur, it will be brought about by means wholly miraculous.' When he republished his arguments 15 years later (largely but not wholly in identical terms), Goldsmid omitted that passage. The more articulate the Christian exponents of Jewish restorationism, the more reticent were the leading Jewish emancipationists on the subject of Jewish messianism.

There were few more articulate presentations concerning the 'Jewish Nation' than E.L. Mitford's *An Appeal on Behalf of the Jewish Nation in Connection with British Policy in the Levant*. Mitford, a British colonial civil servant who had travelled widely in the Levant and Central Asia, wrote his 51-page work in 1845, while serving in Ceylon; it was published in London the same year. As a British imperialist, he hoped to see his country 'have the privilege of being the instrument' of divine providence in connection with the Jews, a people long 'unprotected and wronged'. He proposed the 're-establishment of the Jewish nation in Palestine in two stages,' first as a 'protected State' under British auspices, and second as an 'independent State' when the time proved ripe for the tutelage to end. Among the circumstances essential to justifying independence would be that the 'national spirit' had 'sufficiently recovered from its depression to allow of their governing themselves.'

Mitford rested his case on two grounds: the scheme would benefit the Jewish people, and would also increase British power in the Levant and secure Britain's communications with 'her Eastern possessions'. He envisaged no difficulty in negotiating the cession of the necessary territory with the Turks, but added that, in the last resort, Britain should take the territory by force, since, he contended, all parties stood to benefit.

Of the Jews, Mitford wrote: '... the condition of this extraordinary race of people has long been to me a consideration of deep sympathy and absorbing interest'. He noted their universal belief in their restoration, and he expected them to welcome the proposed opportunity. Their industry would restore the 'original fertility' of the land. British assistance, he stated, should be conditional upon their not attempting to restore their 'obsolete ceremonial', by which he presumably referred to Temple worship and priestly cult. In any event, he did not expect that any such attempts would be made.

The various proposals for Jewish settlement in Palestine, or in relation to the Jewish Return, did not always specify the nature or extent of the Jewish self-government that was expected. Where the designs of providence were uppermost in the contemplation of the proposer, there was little motivation for particularisation, save that in the meantime there should be no physical protection of the Jews by the Ottoman authorities, or by Britain as a guardian power. Where immediate political considerations were uppermost, the references to British influence would be direct. Mitford made it clear that, in the first instance and for an indefinite period, there was to be British control.

The Rev. Samuel Alexander Bradshaw's *Tract for the Times, Being a Plea for the Jews* (London, 1844) rests upon the belief that the restoration was a prelude to Jewish conversion. Bradshaw regarded interim attempts to convert the Jews as uneconomic and wasteful. It was better by far to provide the means for substantial migration to Palestine from Eastern Europe than to spend resources to achieve the occasional conversion, he argued. The divine covenant with Abraham subsists, he went on, and it is incumbent on the nations of Christendom, as a moral duty, to advance the restoration in view of the suffering experienced by the children of Abraham at their hands. Bradshaw called on the British Government to elicit from Parliament a grant of £4 million for this purpose, and urged that the churches raise an additional million. 'The temporal and national prosperity' of the Jews is bound up with the ultimate designs of divine providence, he declared.

The sense of due Christian reparation to the Jews weighed heavily with a significant number of Christian supporters of Jewish emancipation. Sir Robert Peel gave powerful expression to it in the House of Commons in 1848, as one of the grounds for his advocacy of the opening of Parliament to Jews.

Some Christian supporters of Jewish emancipation noted with

much interest that English Jews rarely visited Palestine. James Silk Buckingham, journalist and traveller, stated in the House of Commons on 22 July 1833 that he had 'never heard of a single English Jew having visited Palestine even as a matter of curiosity or recreation'. He appears to have forgotten Montefiore and to have treated Disraeli as falling outside the category of Jew. Suffice it to say that there was point in Buckingham's remark. He employed what he contended to be the current lack of interest by Jews in Palestine as part of his argument in support of Grant's bill of 1833 for the removal of Jewish disabilities.

The Rev. Henry Highton, a master at Rugby School, was a friend of Morris Raphall, the minister of the Birmingham Hebrew Congregation and a noted representative in England of the *Haskalah* and of Jewish messianic thought. In 1842, Highton addressed a public letter to Montefiore, and through him to the Jewish community. In printing this letter, *The Voice of Jacob* on 15 September 1842 rightly called Highton's address a 'rebuke ... for [the community's] indifference to our national interests'. Highton asked whether it was not 'a shameful thing that a Gentile should be reminding you of these things'. He pointed out that there were 'many signs ... in the political events of the world ... in the movements of the Jewish mind ... in the feelings towards your nation awakened far and wide among the Gentiles'. In explaining why he sent his letter to *The Voice of Jacob*, Highton wrote that he felt 'exceedingly anxious to see the Jews throughout the world unite together as a nation' and that he thought 'a Jewish press may be a great means to that end.'

When Jacob Franklin founded *The Voice of Jacob* in 1841, he certainly entertained high hopes that his newspaper would serve to increase the sense of common purpose among the geographically scattered, socially disparate, and to some extent religiously diverse elements within the Jewish community in the United Kingdom. He also saw it as a means of strengthening ties among the Jewish communities of the British Empire, as well as of enhancing the mutual awareness of the needs and efforts of English-speaking Jews wherever they lived.

The Damascus Affair, and the coordinated action it aroused on behalf of the Jewish cause, revealed the extent of international Jewish solidarity in the face of threat. The eminence of Montefiore in that response and the support given to his mission by the British Government seemed to give the Anglo-Jewish community a special task, which was reinforced by the wealth and power of the ruling families. The Anglo-Jewish press sought to rise to the responsibilities thrust by events upon that community, which prided itself upon its English character and whose pride was accentuated by the fact of British power.

In *The Voice of Jacob* of 7 October 1842, Franklin reported the 'common rumour' that the Board of Deputies had considered a plan at its last meeting by a 'gentleman officer recently returned from the East.' There was some impatience to know more about the plan and the response it had elicited. The officer was Charles Henry Churchill, traveller, aristocrat, and a friend of Montefiore. He proposed nothing less than that 'the Jews of England conjointly with their brethren on the Continent of Europe' ask the British Government to send out a 'fit and proper person to reside in Syria' for the sole purpose of watching over the interests of Jewish residents there. The territory thus designated included Palestine.

Churchill's object went beyond the important purpose of protecting the Jews. He probably regarded himself as the natural candidate for the post. He had made his home in the region; he had been appointed British representative in Damascus; and Montefiore had confided in him while on his mission to the East in 1840. In Damascus and in London, Churchill publicly advocated the creation of a Jewish state in Palestine, with British support and through negotiations with the Porte. That state would be allied with Britain. He pressed for Jews to be seen in the vanguard of the movement. Mehmet Ali's withdrawal left open the question of whether and how far the Sultan might be ready to facilitate such schemes. This was the background to Churchill's approaches of 1841–42.

The Anglo-Jewish leadership declined to take the initiative. Political prospects seemed uncertain; the British Government's attitude after the return of the Sultan's authority over the region was problematic. Moreover, the campaign for Jewish emancipation was reaching a critical stage. Here was one of the 'other Jewish interests,' which the opponents of emancipation brought up again and again. However, Christian advocacy of Jewish restoration persisted. Churchill himself, in his *Mount Lebanon* (London, 1853), wrote that if 'Mount Lebanon' were to cease to be Turkish, 'it must either become English or else form part of a new independent State which ... shall [have the capacity] to unite the hitherto divergent races of mankind in the humanising relations of fraternity and peace ...'

One of Montefiore's companions on his visit to Palestine in 1849 was Col. George Gawler, a former British Governor of South Australia. This practical-minded civil servant was convinced that Britain was a providential agent in the evolution of the 'Jewish Return'. He gave his patronage to the Association for Promoting Jewish Settlements in Palestine, organised by Abraham Benisch in 1852.[11] Among its leading Christian sponsors were John Mills, the Welsh Calvinist Methodist pastor, whose survey, *The British Jews* (London, 1853), emphasised the national element in Judaism, and William Henry Black, a prominent antiquarian and Seventh Day Baptist and the principal founder of the Anglo-Biblical Institute and the Palestine Archaeological Association.

In 1845 there appeared Gawler's slim but impressive work, with the carefully phrased title *Tranquilisation of Syria and the East; Observations and Practical Suggestions in Furtherance of the Establishment of Jewish Colonies in Palestine – the Most Sober and Sensible Remedy for the Miseries of Asiatic Turkey.* Gawler saw opportunities in the state of uncertainty over the future of the eastern Mediterranean, in the need to cure lawlessness in the region, and in what he deemed to be the readiness of Jews and of Christendom to try to settle the long-standing problems arising from the national homelessness of the Jews. The desolate condition of much of the region seemed to him in itself to be a reproach to Christian intelligence.

Gawler's call was for the land to be replenished by 'the energetic people whose warmest affections are rooted in the soil'. He explained:

> Men of worth and education throughout the world now look upon this extraordinary people with respect and interest ... The Jews, rising again to life and vigour, are eagerly entering upon those researches in the different branches of human knowledge for which they were once distinguished, and as individuals are taking rank and station according to the common gradations of society ... Every nation ... which has participated in the persecution of the Jewish

people, owes to that people a heavy debt of retribution; and every civilized nation, including every individual in it, be his particular creed what it may, which has received from the Jews, as a source, its principles of religion, owes to those Jews ... a heavy debt of grateful acknowledgement ... If then an opportunity is now before us rendering to Jews an acceptable service, in addition ... to the important duty of rescuing the East from ... degradation, why should not the first instalment of those debts be paid.

He ascribed a special duty to Britain, 'which divine providence has remarkably constituted as an instrument of welfare to the world', and which also had a particular indebtedness to the Jews. Gawler continued to publicise his views, not least in the *Jewish Chronicle*, to which he was a frequent contributor on this subject.

Without sharing Disraeli's attachment to the idea of Jewish superiority – an idea the Jewish emancipationists did not seize on and which was not central to Christian thought – Gawler had in common with Disraeli a strong conviction that the British way of life owed much to Jewish influence. There was the Judaic source of Christianity and, in particular, the pervasive influence of the language and thought of the Bible. Such were the considerations behind the public thought of Gawler, in addition to his assumptions regarding providential favour and the resultant responsibility resting upon the British nation.

Disraeli had visited the East in 1830–31. The impact of his journeys through Palestine and his visit to Jerusalem on the romantic and mystical sides of his mind, and on his emotions as a Jewish Christian, was considerable and enduring.[12] Among the group of novels in which he dwells on the relations between the two faiths and on the past and future role of the Jews in the family of mankind, *Tancred or the New Crusade* (1847) contains his most explicit references. For example, on the festival of Succoth, the central character declares: 'The vineyards of Israel have ceased to exist, but the eternal law enjoins the children of Israel still to celebrate the vintage. A race that persists in celebrating the vintage, although they have no fruits to gather, will regain their vineyards.' Reacting to the experience of his Christian pilgrimage to Palestine, *Tancred* makes the connection, as he sees it, between Britain, in whose upper-class society he is a notable figure, and the regeneration of the ancient nation. 'Vast as the obligations of the whole human family are to the Hebrew race, there is no portion of the modern populations so much indebted to them as the British people,' he comments, adding, 'There never was a race who sang so often the odes of David as the people of Great Britain.'

Even allowing fully for Disraeli's courage in his advocacy of Jewish civil emancipation, it is difficult to believe, with regard to his extensive and detailed presentation of the image of the national 'Jewish Return' and the British many-sided interest in it, that he did not sense that his sentiments would strike widespread echoes in the minds of his substantial reading public. Behind the grandiloquence of his language, there was a residue of opinion that met with a degree of sympathy and understanding. Gawler would have subscribed to the above-cited views of *Tancred*.

In some provincial cities, Christian exponents of Jewish restorationism acquired considerable influence by applying their passion and energy in pursuit of Christian ideals to the advocacy of that cause. As preachers, schoolmasters, and publicists, they enjoyed acclaim among their flock and their readers, whose religiosity they shared and to whose belief in the fulfilment of prophecy they sought to add practical contemporary dimensions.

One such cleric was Henry Hawkes, an Anglican preacher of Portsmouth. In 1846 he published a booklet entitled *The Colonisation of the Holy Land by the Jews; Introduction to the Return of the Children of the Dispersion*, in which he based his exposition largely on passages in the second and third chapters of Zachariah. His perception of the potential bearing of contemporary events is exemplified in another booklet, *The Colonisation of the Holy Land Considered in Reference to India and the Prospects of a General War*, published in the same year. He appears, as did a number of the Christian advocates of Jewish restorationism, to have regarded the Czar as a fetter upon the realisation of prophetic designs. This view was hardly out of accord with the practical policies of the Foreign Office. Pitt, Palmerston, and Disraeli were highly sensitive to possible Russian designs on European Turkey, the Indian frontiers, and British-Eastern communications.

In the middle of 1847, Hawkes delivered a local sermon entitled 'The Position of the Jews'; it was published and circulated in London shortly thereafter. After describing the 'preservation' of the Jews as part of a divine plan, the author is 'awestruck' at the connection between their survival and its 'great purpose,' the detail of which remains inscrutable. His reverence for that mystery is matched by his 'grief' that the revelation of the divine hand in human affairs, as evidenced by that survival, should be 'so little heeded.'

Hawkes was a regular guest at Jewish charitable events. In December 1850 he was the principal speaker at the annual dinner of the Portsmouth and Portsea Hebrew Benevolent Institution, which the civic leaders of Portsmouth and Southampton and a number of naval and army officers also attended. What gave the occasion added interest was the presence of a group of naval officers from units of the Turkish fleet, in port on a friendly visit to Britain. The opportunity was not missed. Hawkes commended the practical purposes of Montefiore's missions to the Holy Land in terms of relief and the encouragement of self-help, and spoke of his own hopes in careful terms. The chairman of the evening, Emanuel Emanuel, referred diplomatically to the 'tolerance and goodness' shown to the Jews by the Turks. The local press reported the event in great detail. The proceedings were typical of the growing intimacy between local Jewish communities and the society in which they lived, of the broadening recognition by civic leaders of the role of the Jewish citizenry in local social, economic, and literary life, acknowledgement of the fact of international Jewish kinship and the national (even if, for some, the metahistorical) element within Judaism.

One of the most influential preachers and theological writers in the early nineteenth century was the Hebraist, Thomas Scott. Appointed rector at Aston Sandford, Buckinghamshire, in 1801, Scott was a leading member of the Anglican conversionist body (founded in 1808), the London Society for Promoting Christianity Amongst the Jews. His sermon, *The Jews, a Blessing to the Nations and Christians Bound to Seek Their Conversion*, which he delivered at the Church of St Lawrence Jewry in the City of London on 12 June 1810, attracted wide attention when it was published. It was a classic presentation of the philosophy of those Christians who believed that the ultimate conversion and national restoration of the Jews were based on biblical prophecy.

While exponents of this dual belief differed among themselves over which event was to come first, for Scott this appeared an idle debate. He preached for active conversionism while believing that the restoration would come about by direct divine providence. 'The bulk of the … nation will, after a time, be collected into their own land and its environs,' he declared, adding that he felt for them 'as I should towards a father who had … disgraced himself but who after all was still a father.'

Writing in 1814, in a letter made public in his son John's biography of him soon after his death in 1821, Thomas Scott referred to 'the precedency, honour and love' that should be accorded to the Jews on their restoration. Scott was at pains to prove his thesis solely from the Old Testament. His most extensive work on the topic was a reply in 1814 to 'Rabbi' Joseph Crooll's *Restoration of Israel* (London, 1813),[13] an elaborate Jewish messianic work amounting to a fierce repudiation of all conversionist doctrines and efforts.

John Scott was an Anglican clergyman in Hull and headmaster of the old local grammar school. Messianic in inspiration, missionary in purpose, and historical in method, his *Destiny of Israel* (Hull, 1813) became virtually compulsory reading for Christians interested in the position of the Jews in history and their possible role in the future. In it Scott sought verification of the Biblical prophecies in historic events. Both the conversion of the Jews and their restoration were directed by divine providence, he argued. Active conversionist work was not necessarily related to distant events, he explained, since the restoration might well be at hand.

This sense of approaching dramatic change was not only retained but also strengthened as the century advanced. A typical expression of such thinking appeared in the *Jewish Herald*, the organ of the British Society for the Propagation of the Gospel Amongst the Jews, set up by the Nonconformists in 1842. 'We hail [the Jews'] literal restoration,' it proclaimed in April 1852, 'as an event fast approaching. Let us strenuously labour to discharge the paramount and urgent duty of seeking their spiritual restoration.' From their vantage point in the Evangelical wing of the Anglican Church, the Scotts, father and son, would have concurred with that prescription. 'Is it not encouraging', asked the article in the *Jewish Herald*, 'to learn that (the Jews) are losing confidence in their own traditions, and consequently are the more open to instruction from the (Christian) oracles?' John Scott's biography of his father ran into seven editions within four years of Thomas Scott's death.

The considerable strength of evangelicalism in Hull, a thriving and expanding Yorkshire port, was due to a number of factors. There was the wide local attachment to Nonconformity. Methodism, especially, appealed to the individualistic merchants and industrialists in and around the region. The enthusiasm, seriousness and emphasis upon public works, stimulated by the revivalist spirit of that movement, were conducive to the growth of like sentiments in the Established Church, wherein, in any event, the commercial classes were by instinct and policy inclined in those directions. The great personal influence of Joseph Milner (died in 1797), John Scott's predecessor as head of the local grammar school, a preacher, ecclesiastical historian, and persuasive personality, extended beyond local opinion. Thomas Scott's addresses in the town, which he frequently visited during his son's tenure there, reinforced the influence of Milner and of John Scott, who became the organising secretary of the local branch of the London Society for Promoting Christianity Amongst the Jews.

Hull, being the main point of arrival for immigrants after London, held a special attraction to the conversionists. Local features relating to commercial and industrial expansion, the spread of evangelical influence, and the growth of conversionist effort both within the Established Church and on the part of the Nonconformists, were typical of many of the newly growing cities. Restorationist advocacy was common in the widening bodies of opinion propelled into prominence and influence by the industrial and commercial revolutions. It accompanied the growing popularity of radical Bible-based forms of piety. The interest aroused by issues concerning the Jews went beyond their local numbers. The few tens of thousands of Jews in England were only a segment – on the English doorstep, so to speak – of a larger whole which, whatever its internal differentiating features, was seen as having a common fate.

William Ayerst, was a scholarly and influential figure in the Anglican movement for converting the Jews and in the advocacy of restorationism. He edited the organ of the London Society, *Jewish Intelligence* (founded in 1825), and maintained contact with missionaries in Germany and Eastern Europe, where he had travelled widely on behalf of that cause. In 1847, he published a series of historical and contemporary studies entitled *The Jews of the Nineteenth Century.* Ayerst was impressed by the Jews' persistent adherence to their own tradition, literature, and hopes, despite poverty and suffering. His work, he believed, was likely to assist them in their temporal plight and hasten conversion.

The Crimean War gave new life to restorationist thinking. Ostensibly the conflict between the Ottomans and Russia had been over the control of the Holy Places, but wider considerations set in. Anglo-French support for the Sultan encouraged Shaftesbury and others to consider that the Sultan might now be amenable to concessions that would advance Jewish restorationist goals. His suggestion that the British Government should consider the possibility that the Sultan might allow Jews to hold land, was passed on to the British embassy in Constantinople. He also asked Montefiore to assess how the Jews might respond to such a move.

But the Porte's lack of positive response and Britain's reluctance to press the matter militated against any optimism. Poor harvests and the Crimean War's disruption of commerce brought acute local distress. As periodic reports of poverty, oppressive taxation, and brigandage reached London, the Anglo-Jewish community organised public appeals. On one such occasion, in 1854, an appeal headed by Montefiore and the Chief Rabbi, Nathan Marcus Adler raised £20,000. To this sum Montefiore added his own monies and funds from Judah Touro's substantial legacy to alleviate distress and initiate self-help projects in Palestine. Montefiore also bought a plot of land to the west of Jerusalem, near the Jaffa Gate, for the building of a hospital. Louis Loewe proudly recorded that Montefiore was the 'first Englishman' to be given permission by the Ottomans to acquire land.[14]

The close relationship in the mid-1850s between Britain and the Porte strengthened the efforts of the Anglo-Jewish leadership to induce the British Government to urge the Ottoman Government to improve the status of the Jews under the Turks. This was allied to Britain's policy of seeking to persuade the Ottomans to make concessions to their Christian subjects in the form of greater freedom of movement and more effective protection. Similar concessions, and the right to hold land, were among the claims made by and on behalf of the Jews.

In April 1854, Lord Clarendon, the Foreign Secretary, informed Lionel and Anthony de Rothschild that there was ground to believe that the Porte's projected concessions to the Christians were also under consideration as far as the Jews were concerned. Later that month the Board of Deputies appointed a committee (on which the Rothschilds, after Sir Moses Montefiore, figured most prominently) to consider with the Consistoire Général, acting on behalf of the Jewish community of France, the most appropriate procedures for securing the intervention of the British and French Governments with the Porte on behalf of the Jews. When Montefiore, as President of the Board, wrote to Clarendon on 10 May 1854 to urge the British Government's further attention to this matter, the Foreign Secretary assured him that the request would receive favourable consideration.

In a leading article in the *Hebrew Observer* on 12 May 1854, Abraham Benisch was quick to detect in the coordinated actions of the leaders of the Jewish communities of France and Britain a move towards the accomplishment of 'a common national object in the East.' Such collaboration, the writer hoped, would eventually encompass Jewish leaders and communities in other lands, including the United States.

The long public discussion kept alive trends of thought whose influence survived their eschatological character. The fact was that the old hopes remained, in whatever blend of the metaphysical and the practical, or even solely in the practical.

Zionism is the antithesis of conversionism. Jewish restorationism had, and has, its own ethos. The old Jewish creative passivity gave way, under the force of unrelenting history, to practical Jewish measures to foster that cause. There was a welter of gentile restorationist literature in Britain. The idea that there was or should be a link between British policy and Jewish national restoration was a seminal idea whose longevity – despite its diverse formulations – did not weaken its appeal.[15]

NOTES

1. Macaulay's *Letters*, (ed.) Thomas Pinney, Vol. 6, 1974, p. 253.
2. 'The revival of religion ... pervaded all society, challenged men and women of every level of society or of education, and become fused with the objectives of most political parties and the hopes of every class.' George Kitson Clark, *The Making of Victorian England*, 1962. In these processes the influence of

the Bible was immense. National success in commerce and empire was thought to betoken a chosenness. The biblical tone of English religion endowed 'Protestant thought and practice, and especially the English and Scottish varieties of it, with 'a Judaic air', and this 'was due entirely to a following of the Old Testament ...': F.C. Burkitt, 'The Debt of Christianity to Judaism', in (eds) E.R. Bevan and Charles Singer, *The Legacy of Israel*, 1928, p. 69.

3. Hebraists such as John Selden and Edward Pococke in the seventeenth century and Benjamin Kennicott in the eighteenth, were successors and precursors of notable lines of Christian Hebrew scholars in Britain. See G.H. Box, 'Hebrew Studies in the Reformation Period and After' in *Legacy of Israel*, supra; R. Lowe, 'Jewish Scholarship in England', in (ed.) V.D. Lipman *Three Centuries of Anglo-Jewish History*, 1961. In Scotland the importance of Calvinism (through Presbyterianism and Congregationalism) in national life was stronger than elsewhere in Britain. New College, Edinburgh, was the divinity school of the Free Church community, the well-organised 'separatist' segment of Scottish Christianity. There was a marked emphasis in the Free Church upon the significance of the Hebrew Bible. The methods and substance of biblical study and presentation which were developed at New College, influenced the study of Hebrew and the pursuit of theological enquiry at Oxford and Cambridge. From 1843, John Duncan served as Professor of Hebrew and Oriental Languages at New College for twenty years, succeeded by Andrew Bruce Davidson, the noted Hebraist and theologian who held the post until his death in 1902. His annotated editions of books of the Prophets reveal his attachment to the Hebrew Bible as literature having contemporary significance in matters of public policy and private practice. Davidson's most famous pupil was Sir George Adam Smith, traveller to Palestine and author of the celebrated *Historical Geography of the Holy Land* (1894) who became Professor of Old Testament Language, Literature and Theology at the Free Church College in Glasgow and later Principal of Aberdeen University.

4. Among works of this kind Henry Milman, *The History of the Jews* (1830) and Arthur Stanley, *History of the Jewish Church* (three volumes between 1863 and 1876), were of enduring influence on Victorian opinion. 'Such a history as that of the Jews', commented the *Gentlemen's Magazine* on Milman's work, is one 'which all persons should read not as a mere matter of entertainment or interest but as a study of the highest moment and an indispensable companion to the Bible'.

5. Meir Vereté, 'Why was a British Consulate Established at Jerusalem', *English Historical Review*, Vol. 85, 1970; Beth-Zion Lask Abrahams, 'James Finn, Her Britannic Majesty's Consul in Jerusalem 1846–63', *Trans.*, J.H.S.E., 27, 1982; V.D. Lipman, *America and the Holy Land through British Eyes 1820–1917: A Documentary History*, 1989, *passim*.

6. Sir Moses Montefiore, *Diaries*, ed. Louis Loewe (1890) 1983, Vol. 1, p. 303. When Montefiore in due course pressed upon Palmerston's successor Lord Aberdeen, 'the desire of the Jews of the East to be brought under British protection', Aberdeen doubted its practicality on the ground that the European powers were jealous of British interference, but he added that he

would consider the best means of affording them protection for the sake of humanity and justice. Montefiore referred to Palmerston's directive when he called on Sir Stratford Canning prior to the latter's departure for the embassy in Constantinople in 1840. Canning said he would be happy to do all that his duty permitted: ibid., pp. 303–4. In 1848 the British Consul in Beirut informed Montefiore that the Jews would receive every protection: ibid., Vol. 2. p. 14.

7. Some indication of the enthusiasm prevalent in restorationist (including some Jewish) circles is found in the editorial in the *Voice of Jacob* for 29 September 1843, probably written by the Zionistic Abraham Benisch: 'Israel' was no longer being held 'to signify some chimerical, fictitious abstraction but that Israel who lives ... Jerusalem [was no longer being construed as] some fantastical, visionary prefiguration but the real Jerusalem, the restored capital of Palestine.'

8. R.E. Prothero and G.G. Bradley, *Life of A.P. Stanley* (London, 1893), p. 489.

9. The first reference in Montefiore's published *Diaries* to the desirability of constructing a railway between Jaffa and Jerusalem was in 1838. For his discussions in 1845 about plans for such a project, see *Diaries*, Vol. 1, pp. 56–60, and in 1862, p. 133.

10. Jewish spokesmen were anxious over the implications of the bishopric from the Jewish point of view. The Anglo-Jewish press repeatedly expressed concern at conversionist efforts generally and among the Jews in the Holy Land. The first bishop was Michael Solomon Alexander, a convert of Prussian origin and formerly Minister at the Plymouth Synagogue.

11. See the study of that eminent journalist, editor, and pre-Herzlian Zionist by J.M. Shaftesley in *Trans.*, J.H.S.E., 21 (1968).

12. Regarding his visit, see Robert Blake, *Disraeli's Grand Tour*, 1982. Much later, Disraeli's success at the Congress of Berlin in 1878 in achieving in effect the cession of Cyprus from the Ottoman Empire to the Crown after the Russo-Turkish War, was seen by some, not only by conversionists, as a significant pointer, geographically as well as figuratively, to Palestine. Following the collapse of the Anglo-French dual control in Egypt, a British force in the summer of 1882 seized power in the country, which had been under the nominal rule of the Khedive and the formal sovereignty of the Sultan. In March 1882, the Church Congress met in Derby, opened by the Archbishop of York. The Dean of Ripon expressed hopes that 'England would now use her grand opportunity in Egypt of breaking up' the Turkish dominion and 'bringing about a Jewish Restoration in the East of the Mediterranean'. 'Whoever holds Abraham's territory' declared the Rev. Edward Horne, 'would hereafter have the command of the commerce of the world ... Turkey could not hold it and we should never allow the Russians to hold it'. A special session of that Congress was devoted to 'The Jews'. The first and principal paper was delivered by J.C.S. Kroenig, Vicar of Hull (himself a talmudist, yiddishist and convert, and leader of the local missionaries). His address, later published under the title, *The Present Religious Condition of the Jews*, surveyed the Jewish religious schisms and considered how existing conditions might lend themselves to conversionist efforts.

13. Crooll, of Hungarian birth, was an eccentric scholar of literary verbosity, with a dread of what he perceived as the de-judaising consequences of emancipation. His fears were reinforced by the expressions of some Christian advocates thereof, including conversionists. 'By passing this measure' said the Bishop of St David's in the House of Lords on 25 May 1848 in terms characteristic of a certain species of support for Jewish admission to Parliament, 'you will be hastening the approach of the time when the veil shall be taken away from the eyes of the people for whose relief it is designed'. Crooll, was described by the Bishop of Oxford as a 'learned person'. The occasion was the debate in the House of Lords in May 1848 on the current emancipation Bill, the Bishop citing 'Rabbi Krule' as indicating that Jews opposed the measure. Crooll had written *The Last Generation* (1829) to warn against the dangers of emancipation. Jews would say 'London is our Jerusalem – we have no need for another Jerusalem.' In *The Fifth Empire* (1829) he envisaged the final turn of the world's cycle, when the hegemony of the earth would be 'the inheritance of the people of Israel'. He castigated the conversionists for the 'sin' of attempting to draw them away from their providential 'separateness'. The derisive sketch of Crooll in the *Jewish Encyclopaedia* (Vol. 4) is based on the hostile description of him by Dr F.R. Hall, Rector of Fulbourn and former Fellow of St John's College, Cambridge (following the debate of May 1848, long after Crooll's death) which was quoted by the *Jewish Chronicle* at length on 30 June 1848. Crooll was a preacher in Manchester in 1803, and was later employed as a private teacher in Hebrew in Cambridge for some years. In his *Studies in Anglo-Jewish History*, (1913), H.P. Stokes describes him as 'of considerable if not profound learning and of curious not to say eccentric habits' (p. 231). See Cecil Roth, *Rise of Provincial Jewry*, 1950, p. 87; Israel Finestein, 'Some Conversionists in Hull in the 19th Century', *Gates of Zion* (journal of the Synagogue Council of the English Zionist Federation, London), Vol. XI, No. 4, July, 1957; Bill Williams, *The Making of Manchester Jewry 1740–1875*, 1976, pp. 19–20; H.W. Meirovich, 'Ashkenazic Reactions to the Conversionists 1800–1850', *Trans.*, J.H.S.E., 26, 1979, pp. 6–25: N.C.N. Salbstein, *The Emancipation of the Jews in England*, 1981; and *Encyclopaedia Judaica*, Vol. 5. A history of the London Society by its Secretary, W.T. Gidney, was published in 1908. Among Jews who published notable remonstrances against the conversionists were Solomon Bennett, engraver and communal controversialist; Moses Samuel, the scholarly silversmith of Liverpool; Charles Salaman, liturgical composer; and Stanislaus Hoga, a convert who returned to Judaism. Opposition among the Jews of Hull to the conversionists found strong expression in *High Street* (1862), a collection of papers by the local historian, John Symons, jeweller and civic leader (later Alderman).

14. *Diaries*, Vol. 2, Ch. VI.

15. Foregoing themes are examined in Barbara Tuchman, *Bible and Sword: England and Palestine from Bronze Age to Balfour*, 1956: Franz Kobler, *The Vision was There: A History of the British Movement for the Restoration of the Jews to Palestine*, 1956; N. Bentwich and J.M. Shaftesley, 'Forerunners of

Zionism in the Victorian Era', in (ed.) J.M. Shaftesley, *Remember the Days*, 1966; M. Scult, 'English Missions to the Jews: Conversion in the Age of Emancipation', *Jewish Social Studies*, (New York), Vol. 35, No. 1, 1973, pp. 3–17; Lionel E. Kochan, 'Jewish Restoration to Zion Christian Attitudes in Britain in the late 19th and early 20th centuries – Comparative Approach', in (ed.) Moshe Davis, *With Eyes Toward Zion*, Vol. 2, Praeger, 1983; V.D. Lipman's paper in the Palestine Exploration Fund and its origins (founded in 1865) in *Palestine Exploration Quarterly*, Vol. 120, 1988; pp. 45–54; V.D. Lipman, 'Britain and the Holy Land 1830–1914', in (eds) Moshe Davis and Yehoshua Ben-Arieh, *With Eyes Toward Zion*, Vol. 3, Praeger, 1991; and see Yehoshua Ben-Arieh, 'Jerusalem Travel Literature as Historical Source and Cultural Phenomenon', Sarah Kochav, 'The Mission to the Jews and English Evangelical Eschatology', and Martin Luckhoff, 'Political and Religious Controversies Surrounding the Foundation of the Jerusalem Bishopric' in Yehoshua Ben-Arieh and Moshe Davis, *With Eyes Toward Zion*, Vol. 5, 1997.

6

Morris Jacob Raphall (1798–1868): The English Career of Popular Preacher and Lonely Publicist

Raphall was the Minister-Preacher of the Birmingham Hebrew Congregation from 1841 until he left for high ministerial office in New York in October 1849. In Victorian England the five pre-eminent figures in this vocation, apart from the Chief Rabbis, were Raphall, David Meyer Isaacs (Liverpool and Manchester), Asher Levy Green (Sheffield and the Central Synagogue, London), David Woolf Marks (West London Synagogue of British Jews) and Simeon Singer (New West End Synagogue). Of these Raphall was in many ways the most remarkable. He lacked the influential lay patronage enjoyed by Green, Marks and Singer. He was not attached, as those three were, to any fashionable metropolitan congregation. He stands out in his own generation by the range of his learning. No Anglo-Jewish preacher of that century, including the Adlers, exceeded Raphall in the extent of his preaching and lecturing. Nor, save for Hermann Adler in his day, were any as much to the fore as Raphall in the public repudiation of calumnies against Jews and Judaism. His public robustness in the latter connection did not always attract the approval of the Jewish community's lay leadership of his time.

He was born in Stockholm in 1798 and was a pupil for five years at the Copenhagen Hebrew Grammar School, where he was recognised as a child prodigy. He arrived in England with his father in 1812. Following the final overthrow of Napoleon, his businessman father (described in some reports as having been a banker in Sweden), sent the young Raphall to the continent for his higher education. He studied philosophy at the Universities of Giessen and Erlangen, travelled widely in western Europe, and imbibed much of the spirit of the *Haskalah*. He retained the attachment to the traditional Jewish religious observances which he inherited, as well as the outlook of the school of thought which later attracted the epithet of Orthodox.

Raphall had a flair for languages, a feeling for poetry and an aptitude for philosophical speculation. By the time he finally settled in England in 1824, he had mastered several European languages and was at home with classical and modern philosophers. The Directories in 1822 list J. Raphall, probably his father, as a general merchant, off Broad Street in the City of London, and in 1824 M.J. Raphall appears in that capacity. He married in 1825 and supplemented his income by private teaching and public lecturing. He was an occasional speaker in London synagogues, and he sought out therein and elsewhere like Jewish minds. He served Solomon Hirschell as secretary and translator from the late 1830s until he left for Birmingham. His association with Hirschell did not impose upon him any constraint in his intellectual pursuits, which did not always meet the priorities or style of his old-world master.

The relationship between the young secularly-lettered *savant* and the old and ailing Chief Rabbi must have proved somewhat ambivalent for Raphall. He must have noted with regret the hostility to the early movements for synagogal change.[1] Nothing in the initial requests for change would have in the slightest disturbed Raphall.

Continuing his wide reading and private study, he became imbued with the desire to fuse into a rational whole, so far as he could, the doctrines of Judaism, the implications of Jewish history, and the system of the modern advanced philosophies. He deplored what he regarded as the loss of the freedom of style and originality of thought which marked the principal medieval Jewish classics. 'The mystics of Poland,' he later wrote, 'had spread the opinion that it was sinful to read any books other than Hebrew or Rabbinical. ... The Jews used a corrupt jargon of their own. ... Pulpit oratory [a phrase which he curiously used in reference to a time before the advent of what his century would have understood by the term "pulpit". I.F.] degenerated into imitations of the useless public disputations that had disfigured the Christian universities of the Middle Ages.' He discerned in Moses Mendelssohn the renaissance of the old freer thought and style.

Raphall described the century which followed the death of Menasseh ben Israel (1604–57) as 'the most barren in Jewish annals'. He equated the outlook and method of Maimonides with those of Mendelssohn, despite the differences of circumstance, and insisted that what was lawful to the Jew in the age of the former could not be sinful in the modern age. He was to describe Wessely[2] as 'the most eminent of Hebrew poets since the close of the scriptural cannon'. Raphall wanted to widen the bounds of Jewish study beyond the Talmud and the *halachic* codes, so as to incorporate Bible, Hebrew poetry (old and new) and post-biblical Jewish history.

It was natural that Raphall should become an immediate and welcome entrant into the circle of Hebraists and Mendelssohnians in England, among whose principal patrons was the philanthropist and Hebrew man of letters, Michael Josephs (1761–1849). In 1830 it was from this group that there arose the short-lived Society for the Cultivation of the Hebrew Language and Literature, of which a notable member and a kindred spirit to Raphall was David Aaron de Sola (1796–1860).[3] Raphall lectured to the Society on Hebrew poetry. The Society ceased to exist after its first year, de Sola attributing its demise to 'excessive speechifying'. What he probably meant was that its members paid inadequate attention to organisation and to the gathering of support, moral and material.

Raphall quickly understood the deeper reason and consistently declared that the leadership of the Jewish community was largely uninterested in any cultivation of the ideas reflected in the Society. His was as a voice crying in the wilderness. He did not cease his efforts to remedy the situation, which he considered to be all the more regrettable by reason of the wide and growing freedoms enjoyed by the Jews in Britain. His failure, as he thought it to be, to change that situation was a major factor in his decision to seek a new life across the Atlantic.

In his famous paper on 'The Queen's Jewry',[4] Lucien Wolf commented that from this Society 'all the intellectual impulses of the Reform movement came'. While Wolf's wide sweep may require some qualification, it is clear that the events which precipitated the Reform secession, including Orthodox responses to the initial demands, took place against the background of a sense of contemporary intellectual advance and the spirit of adventure, both associated with the Society. These sentiments acted as a philosophic and ideological stimulus, which rendered any breach with authority less daunting than might otherwise have been the case. But the people principally associated with the Society were generally more interested in the progress of Hebrew study than in such contentious issues as liturgical change, the adoption of a synagogal choir, the authority of the oral law or the creation of a synagogue in the West End. Change was certainly in the air.

It is significant that, as de Sola's son and biographer later observed, it was de Sola's lectures to the Society that led the Mahamad of the Spanish and Portuguese Congregation at Bevis Marks to invite him to deliver English sermons in their Synagogue.[5] He gave his first English sermon there in March 1831, a highly influential example. The Society reinforced the spirit favourable to change and this encouraged critics of the existing system. The Society's early failure may also have persuaded some that something more than a literary society was required if the hold of the old century upon the life of the new was to be released.[6]

A subtler but yet more direct sign of changes in outlook, particularly in attitudes towards authority, arose some years later. There developed a movement within, but not confined to, the Mahamad in favour of the production under the auspices of the Mahamad of an English translation of the Mishna. It was desired that this Hebrew halachic source-book, the basis of the Talmud and with it the Oral Law, should be easily available for all who might wish to read it in the vernacular. The Mahamad at first declined to commission such translation, but soon did so, albeit without enthusiasm and under much pressure from those with influence in their Congregation and who were regarded as the party for synagogal change. Their attitude was: 'You tell us to abide by the Oral Law; then open up to us its sources.' Raphall, the Ashkenazi onlooker, had no doubt as to the propriety and desirability of such a course. He saw in the request a 'Mendelssohnian' tone and an educational opportunity.

The Mahamad in 1838 commissioned de Sola and Raphall to translate the work, which they proceeded to do with impressive speed. Most of it was completed in 1839. The Mahamad did not

171

17. Morris Jacob Raphall (1798–1868), c.1860

publish the work. In 1842 Benjamin Elkin, a prosperous shipper in West Indian trade, caused the translation of the then ready 18 tractates to be published at his expense and without authority. It was said that he had bought the text as it stood with the private intention of getting it through the press in any event. The Mahamad seems to have intended that the translated text should be available for inspection, rather than for general instruction. Elkin named the translators in his Preface but did not disclose that they had no involvement in the decision to publish. He implied the contrary. Matters of protocol soon expanded into a long public debate which went beyond the role of Raphall and de Sola and the unauthorised nature of the publication. It became concerned with doctrine and rabbinic authority. Elkin's 'reformist' zeal was evident from the Preface and was further given expression in the ensuing private and public exchanges, which were not confined to the Jewish press. No one comes out of this affair well. Of sharp practice, I think there was none. Of naiveté, much, all round. And thus emerged the first English translation at Jewish hands of the major portion of the Mishna. Advertisements for the second edition in January 1845 recorded that the translators were in no way connected with the Preface or with the publication.[7]

172

18. David Aaron de Sola (1796–1860)

Another literary partnership between Raphall and de Sola was in the English annotated translation of the book of Genesis. Each undertook the translation of a large segment of the work, and the limited remainder was translated by Israel Lindenthal, the learned secretary and occasional preacher at the New Synagogue in the City of London. The work was published in 1844. The trio intended to produce a translation of the whole Pentateuch, their Prospectus stating that their model was to be Mendelssohn's German version thereof. That they did not get beyond the first volume was only partly due to Raphall's other commitments. It was mainly the result of the lack of public response. The public may readily be excused the absence of warmth. The notes were described by one critic at the time, with some charity, as 'exceedingly philosophical'. They were far too prolix for comfort. They incorporated much from classic commentators, including Rashi, and extracts from Mendelssohn, but added thereto were extensive sections of notes on genealogy, geography and grammar. In 1936, the Chief Rabbi, Dr J.H. Hertz, justly described the translation as 'fantastic', a term which at that date had not yet acquired the complimentary sense with which it has since been invested.[8]

The ethos of the Society of 1830 found its best expression in the *Hebrew Review and Magazine of Rabbinical Literature*. It was Raphall's creation. He edited it throughout its 78 weekly issues (1834–35). It was later said that he abandoned publication through ill-health. If that played any part at all in his decision, it was not the major factor. The publication failed because of lack of support. Raphall give up in face of the unrelenting climate of indifference. It did not surprise him, but he was hurt by this kind of communal rebuff. It sprang, as he saw it, from an entrenched disinterest on the part of significant numbers of those who held power in communal life. Their public support would have been a fruitful example.

In the final number of the journal, Raphall confidently looked forward to its resumption. He was loath to accept that the Jewish community would retain indefinitely its unconcern for the promotion of serious Jewish study. He was most conscious of the fact that the *Review* was the major pioneer of Anglo-Jewish periodic literature. Its literary standard was high. Some of its English translations of medieval and modern Jewish classics still read well.

Many of its articles – by Raphall, de Sola, Tobias Theodores and others – are either scholarly essays or pungent assessments of the Jewish scene and communal issues. Some of the papers, such as on the Sabbath in the modern world, have a strikingly modern ring. In 1840 Raphall republished his articles on the Sabbath and Festivals as a separate volume. The editor's messianic beliefs and his adherence to rabbinic Judaism were manifest in the journal, as was his broad approach to other points of view.

In a two-column four-page Introduction in the first issue on 3 October 1834, Raphall set out his characteristic views, reflecting his typical combination of Jewish national pride and his belief in the necessity of apprising the Christians of the true nature of the Jewish mind and attainment.

'The Jewish nation,' he wrote, 'dispersed over the face of the earth, is more generally known and less correctly appreciated than perhaps any other. ... [The knowledge of them] consists in characterising them as a people exclusively devoted to the pursuit of gain. And the prejudices that have been raised against them ... have prevented mankind from doing them justice, and from ascribing this blot on their character to its true cause, [namely] the oppression and degradation which during a succession of centuries it has been their lot to experience.[9] Their history proves that this trait was not originally in their character and that they are supremely gifted with intellectual power; and that even whilst groaning under the most tyrannical oppression they have never been without men pre-eminently able to instruct and improve the human mind. ... But time ... [and] the slow ... steady and beneficial progress of reason, have wrought a change in men's ideas on this subject [namely, hatred of the Jews] as on most others, ... which [renders an] opposite course of duty [on] the Israelites of the present day [namely no longer one of reserve in respect of making their literature known to the world] ... In Britain no efforts worth naming have been made by Jews to diffuse the knowledge of the writings of their learned and wise men save for the late David Levy, Tobias Goodman, Professor Hyman Hurwitz.[10] Yet in Britain more than in any other land it behoves the Israelite to unfold to the world the literary treasures of his nation, and in return for the instruction which the Rabbis will afford, to call upon mankind to render them that justice to which their merits and sentiments entitle them.'

175

Those extracts illustrate not only Raphall's style of address but also his high optimism (widely shared at the time) about the impact of the acquisition of knowledge – and in particular through the written word – upon the dissolution of prejudice and the attenuation of gentile reserve in respect of Jewish separateness and over the special character of Jewish interests. The Introduction in high-minded tones is vivid testimony to the deep-rooted nature of the apologetic approach by Jewish publicists, however proud their attachment may have been to their own national or religio-national inheritance. In particular it expressed the pervasive belief among Jewish spokesmen in the quality of British society, the wisdom of the constitution and the merits of the religious 'toleration' within the British system. To Raphall these were characteristics of the English-speaking world, derived from English example and nourished by knowledge of the Bible; notwithstanding William Cobbett, Thomas Arnold, Sir Robert Inglis and others in public life who were antipathetic to Jews, Judaism and the advances of the role of Jews in society and the life of the State. In his prolific projection of these opinions in speech and print, Raphall did not seek or imply any diminution in his adherence, in belief and practice, to rabbinic Judaism and the authority of the oral law. He was more a *maskil* of the eighteenth century than of the nineteenth.

While it was common form on the part of Jewish spokesmen to eulogise Britain in their public addresses, Raphall was the main exponent of the theme by way of the huge number of his addresses up and down the land. Typical of his formulation was his long speech (lengthily reported in the Jewish press) at the 35th anniversary dinner of the Liverpool Hebrew Philanthropic Society attended, as was usual in Liverpool and elsewhere on comparable occasions, by prominent politicians and businessmen. Raphall's toast was to 'The land we live in'. He typically referred to the assembly, including himself, as 'us Britons'. He emphasised the duty of Jews to have 'good feelings' to all men. In his course of lectures in London and elsewhere on 'The Fall of Napoleon', he laid stress on the self-defeating character of tyranny and contrasted the British system with that of continental despotisms. In his course of lectures on the effect of geography and climate on national character, he related British qualities to those natural forces.

On 1 October 1842 Raphall delivered an hour-long speech at

the New Synagogue in the City of London during the Sabbath afternoon service. The synagogue was described in the Jewish press as 'crowded to overflowing'. His name and interests were well known. This was his first extensively reported address. The *Voice of Jacob* wrote: 'He is generally considered the most eloquent preacher that has recently appeared on the scene.' He stressed the need for 'religious discourses' to be adapted to the times. He spoke of the unique authority of the Bible, and the duty of Jews to discharge their 'high office' among the peoples of the world, with the aid of 'faith founded on knowledge'. How far, despite the acclaim, his Mendelssohnian associations account for his not finding ministerial office in London is a matter for speculation. He did not desist from the public pursuit of the themes of this address.

The *Review* often made the particular 'apologistic' point that it was desirable that the Christians should see that Jews have a respectable post-biblical history as well as an enlightened literary tradition. Raphall treated that objective as a special part of the journal's rationale. The flavour and direction of the journal were such that he thought prominent Jewish figures who were engaged in the campaigns for Jewish civic and political emancipation would have welcomed its publication as demonstrating their own attachment to 'enlightened' forms of Jewish thought and worship. Was it the case that, with all their sophistication, the governing families of the Jewish community, including the fervent emancipationists, were as yet by nature and habit strangers at the gate of any elevated form of presentation of Jewish learning? That is how Raphall tended to view them. Or was it that intrinsically the advancement of Hebrew literature, especially when written by foreign Jews, or their translations of the writings of medieval Jewish legalists or philosophers, could, in their eyes, have neither practical use for any communal purpose nor carry any personal appeal of interest to them?

The latter states of mind were attributed to them by later observers. The closure of the *Review*, a common fate of other Jewish literary periodicals of the age, might be said to demonstrate with special clarity the force of the editorial comment in the *Jewish Chronicle* ten years later: 'The men of the last generation had accustomed themselves to look on Hebrew scholarship as superfluous.' Not without provocation did one observer write at the time: 'We almost despair ... of obtaining any improvement as long as the monied interest of leaders of our congregations rule over both laymen and ecclesiastics ...'. James Picciotto in his *Sketches of Anglo-Jewish History* in the '70s, wrote that the *Review* 'was written for the few'. He added: 'It did not seek popularity, and with all its merits it certainly did not achieve it. That is a fair comment on Raphall's self-imposed standards concerning the substance and character of the *Review*.

In 1860 Marcus Heyman Bresslau sought in his own way to revive the *Review* in more popular form and style under the title *The Hebrew Review and Magazine of Jewish Literature* (a small but, he thought, relevant and significant change of title). He was acutely conscious of the perils of the attempt. In the opening number – his journal lasted barely one year – he made the following sharp but realistic comment upon the emancipationist leaders, who had often expressed the wish for a more 'acceptable' image of the Jews: 'This state of isolation and dead calm (in England) on the ocean of our vast national literature, has afforded (by contrast with the Jewish productions of Jewish communities abroad) and still affords much plausibility to the accusation that we are a people absorbed in commercial disputes and exclusively devoted to the accumulation of wealth.'

In an interesting comment in his foreword to his book on the Sabbath and Festivals in 1840, Raphall refers to the *Review* as having been 'expensive' at six pence per week. He hoped that the book, priced at two shillings and sixpence, would reach more readers. The paper tax had not been lifted, and sixpence had not been treated as cheap. The price cannot be wholly ignored in assessing the causes of its demise, but Raphall did not think that this could explain or justify the neglect of it by those who might have been expected to perceive its wider importance and who either failed to do so or shirked what he regarded, even on their own grounds, as a public duty.

There were also cases such as that of Zevi Hirsch Edelmann, the distinguished 'foreign' explorer of Hebrew manuscripts at Oxford. Early in 1849, while Edelmann was engaged in that task with slender and declining financial resources, it was left to Raphall, with the help of David Barnett of Birmingham and M.H. Simonson (the scholarly *shochet* in Manchester) to raise private subventions to provide Edelmann with a modest wherewithal. His *Ginzei Oxford* was translated into English by Bresslau in 1851 under the title *Treasures of Oxford*. Bresslau was, at that time, editor of the *Jewish Chronicle*. Edelmann, of Russian birth, left England for Berlin in 1852. 'The taste for light reading and satire,' wrote one observer, 'which amuses but not instructs, monopolises all minds.' In due course, effort was made by Nathan Marcus Adler to encourage the preparation and publication of Hebraica in the original and in translation. Indeed, A.L. Green was driven to enquire whether too much effort was not now being put into that type of production and not enough into more popular works and bible study. Raphall was anxious to stimulate both types of work, and in diverse ways contributed to both at a time when neither greatly flourished inside the Jewish community.

In 1840 Raphall became prominently involved in the public relations side of the Damascus Affair. Events in Damascus and the allegations against Jews and responses thereto, including Montefiore's visit to the East and its outcome, attracted considerable international attention. Many reports appeared in the British newspapers, notably in *The Times*. Hirschell's repudiation of the blood libel against Judaism and Jews appeared in several languages and was published in European capitals. The translations of the original Hebrew, and some have said the Hebrew itself, were by Raphall, all of which he executed in Hirschell's name. In October *The Times* published a letter signed T.J.C. from Oxford, in which the blood libel was expressly revived. This correspondent was the Rev. Theodore Cartwright, former Fellow of University College, Oxford. He presented his thesis on this and related topics with an air of objectivity and even concern for the Jews.

On reading Cartwright's letter and his rejoinder to replies, Jewish readers, already shaken by the apparent credence given to the allegations in high places in Europe, were astonished that in a new era of presumed enlightenment and 'progress' there should appear in so 'liberal' a newspaper as *The Times* the expression of such views by an Oxford personality. Under the current editorship of Thomas Barnes, that newspaper had adopted a favourable stance on legislative changes and proposals in support of greater freedom of conscience and the widening of civic rights for Jews and others. Even if the newspaper was minded in like spirit to open its columns to all points of view, however eccentric, there remained the question as to how far the enlightenment had truly penetrated academic milieux if such opinions of medieval vintage found acceptance therein.

Cartwright did more than challenge the denials that Jews are required to use and, where they could, did use Christian blood for ritual practices on the Passover. He attacked Jews on a broad front. He contended that they were by nature anti-social, hated the gentiles, prayed for their ruin and regularly supported the rabbis' subversion of the divine word, quoting in support of his charges a variety of liturgical and other passages. He charged Sir Moses Montefiore with carefully avoiding Damascus and evading any enquiry into the circumstances of Father Tomaso's murder for fear that the Jewish guilt might be revealed. Montefiore, Hananel de Castro (who acted as President of the Board of Deputies in the latter's absence) and Barnard Van Oven had separately replied to the respective charges, followed by Cartwright's public rejection of their presentations by his further letter.

At this stage Raphall chose to enter the correspondence under his own name. His lengthy essay, for such it was, amounted to an extensive marshalling of the Jewish case. It was unlikely to persuade Cartwright out of his convictions, nor others who shared them, just as in earlier times the deep-set beliefs of like nature were impervious to contrary argument or explanation. What mattered perhaps more was that while the particular allegations might be repudiated, there would remain a pervasive sentiment as to the peculiarity of the Jews, their quintessential alienness, their irretrievable separateness and their somewhat mysterious concerns and aspirations. How to disabuse Christians of the specific charges without in some manner sustaining the racial or national particularity of the Jews, was an anxious question for the emancipationist leaders. Lengthy public argument, including the 'explaining away' of biblical or rabbinic passages by drawing distinctions between Jewish attitudes to heathens in ancient times and later Jewish attitudes to gentile monotheists, was not always regarded by them as necessarily helpful.

Raphall thought it right to publish without delay his 'essay' together with Cartwright's letters in a booklet which was circulated generally. It was often quoted in the continuing debate over the fitness or otherwise of the Jews for civic and political emancipation. Henceforth he was the foremost Jewish polemicist in Britain in this field. Politics and the general debate were in the hands of others. On the religious, historical and socio-religious argument, he was during that decade a principal figure. Those in ultimate charge of the emancipationist campaigns regarded his contributions with a mixture of undoubted gratitude and somewhat troubled reserve. They preferred to rely on the contemporary 'self-evident' nature of the fairness of their cause and the benefits which they argued had accrued to State and society from the role of Jews therein.

In 1841, the Birmingham Hebrew Congregation appointed Raphall Preacher and headmaster; for a time he also served as secretary of the Congregation. He consciously set out to use the pulpit to teach, rather than exhort. He had long mastered English, with but a barely perceptible foreign accent. An American commentator, by no means uncritical, later spoke of him as 'silver-toned'. He proved to be a public speaker of considerable eloquence. The versatility of his interests was reflected in the wide range of his pulpit themes in his weekly addresses – post-biblical Jewish history, Hebrew poetry, prophecy, Palestine in retrospect and prospect, and Jewish–Christian relations. His solemn demeanour in the pulpit did not jar. He soon came to be treated in Birmingham with genuine and marked deference. Despite this, his remuneration fell short of the level which he thought his efforts justified; indeed, despite occasional improvements thereto, it fell short of what he deemed adequate to provide for his wife and their four children in reasonable comfort.

Raphall advertised for boarders in their Birmingham home. He gave private lessons. He lectured widely in the city and beyond. Before he left London for Birmingham, Raphall had become accustomed to professional Jewish public speaking. He was surprised in 1848 to learn that the Birmingham Hebrew Congregation had decided that it was obliged to reduce his salary – because of the growing pressure on its funds for the relief of the Jewish poor in the city. This information led him to embark on a lecture tour in the United States. There was made known to him the readiness of the prestigious Bnai Jeshurun Synagogue in New York to appoint him as Preacher at what was described as the highest salary of any Minister in America at the time. It is clear that his departure for the lecture tour was made with knowledge of what awaited him.

Raphall was known nation-wide before he was appointed in Birmingham. By the time he left that city for New York, he had become by far the best known Jewish Preacher and lecturer in England, not excluding the newly appointed Chief Rabbi. His reputation was more than that of Minister. He had become the major spokesman for Anglo-Jewry and for Judaism to the wider society. Throughout his eight years in Birmingham he did not allow his multifarious public involvements to detract from the perfor-mance of his congregation duties – though it is evident that towards the end of his tenure there was some concern over the balance of his time between the latter responsibilities and his larger agenda.

There is abundant evidence that in the arts of Preacher and lecturer he excelled. Allowing for contemporary hyperbole, it is clear that he was an impressive speaker in the style of his day, vocative, somewhat ornate, lengthy. He preferred to speak without notes. He might address his congregation for as long as an hour; that was not the rule. He was consistently described as 'elegant', 'eloquent' and 'powerful' in pulpit and on platform. Many of his addresses were published or reported *in extenso*. Some of his sermons appeared in booklet form. Perhaps the earliest description of his sermons appeared in the *Voice of Jacob* in September 1841: he 'instructed, corrected and comforted' the congregation. He became in his own way a one-man Jewish committee in Jewish public relations, as well as the pre-eminent purveyor in his time of Jewish adult education in England.

In the 1830s the population of Birmingham had continued to grow with the continuing expansion of the city's manufacture. Iron works and related industries prospered with the advantage of canal proximity. The need for additional factory labour attracted numbers from the countryside. Earlier popular unrest springing from unemployment and deprivation had been followed in the 1820s by comparative social calm. The first years of the 1830s was a time of rising middle-class prosperity in the city and a readiness for working-class radicals and middle-class radicals to work together for political reform. There developed a greater sense of social cohesion and civic pride.

From such circumstances flowed several particular consequences for Jews. The settlement of Jewish traders, of all levels, in the city was encouraged and facilitated thereby. The rise to varying degrees of commercial success on the part of Jewish petty dealers and shop-keepers formed part of the local advance of retailers generally. Further, there grew up a certain amount of fellowship between the Jewish middle-classes and their Christian counterparts, strengthened by the weight of the Nonconformist elements in the City's Christian society, which was itself to some degree a cause and a result of Birmingham's industrial and commercial progress.

It was against this background that Raphall, David Barnett, and other Jews in the city not only evinced a deeply felt civic pride but also enjoined upon themselves, as they perceived it, their duty as Jews and citizens, to cultivate close public relations with their Christian colleagues. The mutual regard was as much instinctive as considered. Raphall's addresses on Jewish themes to non-Jewish audiences, notably in and around Birmingham, were not far short in number of (and may indeed have exceeded) his addresses to Jewish audiences in and near Birmingham.

There were some Christians in the city, and more especially in the shires around, who did not welcome the Jewish advance in the city or in its counsels or in society generally, nor understand the enthusiasm of their fellow-Christians in associating prominently with Jewish personalities. It seemed to some of them to be at best a typical Nonconformist eccentricity, an unperceived error. Some conversionists were hopeful that cordial encounters with Jews would enhance the prospects of their cause. But to the critics that was generally assessed as a largely wasteful effort. Their overt hostility was directed at what they deemed the irretrievable particularity of the Jews, their ceaseless attachment to an international kinship, their national concerns and aspirations, and their unalterable adherence to their inward-looking (and 'anti-social') traditions and alleged usages.

Raphall applauded the capacity, as he believed, of the study of Hebrew literature and post-biblical Jewish history to enlighten Jews as to the continuing value of their traditions and achievements to the world, however ill-requited they may have been by the gentile world. But he was no less vocal or insistent upon their task of enlightening the gentiles about those traditions and achievements. He was both a Jewish educationalist and major Jewish 'apologist'. He was an epitome of his generation.

It is not surprising that he should have been in great demand – not only by the Jews. No Jewish minister was so frequently reported in the Jewish press in the 1840s or in the national or local newspapers in the Midlands and the North. On the second day of Passover in 1846, Christians attended the afternoon service in the Birmingham Synagogue to hear him preach, in addition to virtually all the Jewish adults of the city. He was a regular figure at major communal events outside Birmingham by invitation, and almost invariably was the principal speaker. He did not treat such occasions as suitable for casual or light lectures. His practice was to embark, as relevantly to the occasion as he could, on large issues – the attitude of Jews to the land of their birth or adoption, Jewish emancipation as the test of social progress, the nature of Jewish history, the significance of Hebrew prophecy, the many phases in the development of Hebrew poetry.

Sussex Hall was inaugurated in London in January 1844 as the foremost Jewish adult education institution. It was heralded as a communal event of the first importance, socially, educationally and in terms of Jewish public relations. It was natural that Raphall should be invited to deliver the inaugural address. It was reported that his courses of lectures at Sussex Hall on Jewish history and Hebrew poetry were the best attended at the institution. Christians came. One learned Christian wrote of him as 'one of the most eminent ... and zealous champions of the Hebrew race since Menasseh Ben Israel'. John Mills, the Methodist Calvinist conversionist, called him 'one of the finest minds of the age'. Even putting on one side the patronising tone of exaggeration, something remains of the ceaseless consistency of such remarks which testifies to his impact.

Pro-emancipation sentiment was not universal among the gentiles of Birmingham.[11] For instance, when Lord John Russell in December 1847 gave his famous notice of intention to introduce a Jewish Relief Bill, the Church of England Lay Association of Birmingham convened a meeting in Birmingham, attended by prominent local personalities, which unanimously resolved to petition the Queen and Parliament against the measure. Their main ground was that the admission of Jews would unChristianise Parliament. The local Jewish leaders, under Raphall's guidance, lost no time in securing from a general meeting of the Synagogue a

184

resolution repudiating the grounds of opposition, and procuring for the resolution the best publicity. There followed a somewhat acrimonious exchange of public letters between Raphall and the Lay Association. The whole episode was typical of the watch-dog attitude of Raphall. The predominant local feeling favoured the Bill; with the aid of Barnett, the Town Council unanimously resolved in its favour and submitted to Parliament an appropriate Petition. The bulk of the commercial classes in the city favoured the measure.

That sentiment contrasted with the feeling in the surrounding country areas. Charles Newdegate was a diehard Tory who gave frequent vent to his 'suspicion' of Jews and Roman Catholics. He represented North Warwickshire in Parliament and was among the most extreme of the opponents of the entry of Jews into Parliament. He regarded the Anglican settlement as the bulwark of English liberties. He contended that Jewish entry would imply or encourage support for its dissolution. He accepted the challenge of showing the anti-social nature of Judaism, including alleged Jewish practices. In June 1849 in the House of Commons he cited Raphall by name and quoted one of his addresses to demonstrate that the Jews are attached to rabbinic law even while they acknowledge the Talmud's moral imperfection. He revived ancient attacks on the morality of the Talmud, and attacked the absolutism of rabbinic jurisdiction as comparable only to that of the Pope. He repeated Cartwright's denunciations of some alleged Jewish practices. The extremity of Newdegate's onslaught, supported, it would have seemed to many, by a parade of learning (in which he was assisted by an anonymous Christian mentor) fed the already manifest prejudices in parts of the House, where the strenuous opposition to the measure continued until a late stage.

Raphall's reaction was instant. He publicly declared that he had been misquoted, and indeed Newdegate acknowledged as much, and declared that his own case did not rely on any statement by Raphall. On the substantive charges, Raphall prepared a Petition to be presented to the Speaker by Birmingham's Members of Parliament. The Speaker's office refused to accept the Petition on technical grounds relating to its form. Raphall thereupon published the Petition in the national press. Newdegate replied, and correspondence followed between Raphall and himself. Newdegate, believing that he had the better of the argument, published a

185

collection of speeches and documents, together with recent correspondence, in a 50-page book and including a letter from his mentor, who was probably a convert. At no stage of this encounter did Raphall consult any emancipationist activists or any of the communal leaders in London.

There was a sharp difference of opinion as to the utility to any Jewish cause of these public exchanges. When Raphall left England in October 1849 that issue was still under communal debate. The exchanges with Newdegate somehow rankled with the communal leadership in London. Not for the first time Raphall had acted on a major public issue independently and without consultation. In terms of the 'debate' between Raphall and Newdegate, there were differences of opinion about who came off the better. As an exercise in politics, one must have reservations as to whether it had any significant effect on behalf of the Jewish cause.

Birmingham was the home of a large variety of Dissenting bodies. The old popular antagonism against them as prevailed in the generation of the courageous Joseph Priestley, the famous local Quaker and Radical, had largely subsided. The city became well-known for the inventiveness of its industry, the extent of the spread of 'useful knowledge', and its elements of vocal radicalism, the most prominent unit of which was the Birmingham Political Union under the leadership of the local banker and Member of Parliament, Thomas Attwood. These features of local life were conducive to the increased participation of Jews in the public life of the city; Raphall quickly became a Birmingham personality. An illustration of his position in civic life was his association with the local movement in support of Hungarian independence. In August 1849 at a mass meeting in the Corn Exchange, the Mayor presiding, Raphall seconded the main resolution (moved by the city's senior MP) in a speech of sustained attack on Hapsburg and Romanoff 'tyranny'.

One of the compliments, as he saw it, often paid to him was that he was 'unsectarian'. He identified himself, or tacitly and consciously allowed himself to be identified, with the Birmingham congregation's tradition of independence. Like the Synagogues of Portsmouth, Brighton, and Southampton, and the Western Synagogue in London, that of Birmingham had not allowed the pronouncement in their midst of the Caution and Declaration

against the Reform seceders issued in 1842 by the Jewish 'ecclesiastical' and lay leaders in London. Although the Birmingham congregation had been represented at the Chief Rabbinate electoral
conference in 1844, it did not vote in the election. That did not
affect the outcome. The reason for the non-voting by the Birmingham representation, so it was stated, was that the Congregation
did not know enough about the rival candidates or about the
manoeuvres and motivations of the contending factions. They were
not prepared to add their names to the big battalions of the metropolitan City Synagogues. In this abstention, the Congregation was
joined by those of Newcastle and Bristol.

The Birmingham Jewish School, founded in 1840 and which
was entitled the Hebrew National School, was especially significant
for several reasons. It included pupils (girls as well as boys) from
all levels of society. Parents who could afford to pay did so, according to their means. For others the education was free. Free books,
footwear and other necessaries were provided to those in need, out
of a separately created fund. It was the first of the provincial Jewish

19. The Birmingham Hebrew National School, Hurst Street, 1843

187

day schools. The school-house, built in 1843, was opened in Hurst Street in great ceremony, which was treated in the city as a major civic event. It was the first purpose-built Jewish school in the provinces.

The classes were graded according to age. The curriculum included Bible, Jewish history, French, general history, as well as, for the younger grades, basic elementary education. Raphall taught the highest grade, in Jewish studies. The annual public examinations were said to be more extensive in time and more comprehensive in nature than at the Jews' Free School in London. The Birmingham school, very much smaller in numbers, was from time to time favourably compared to the larger school and was described by a contemporary as setting 'a shining example'. In Raphall's time, the number of pupils rarely exceeded eighty.

In 1845 at a local public meeting Raphall declared with some justice that 'the eyes of British Jews are on Birmingham'. What he had in mind were the standards and repute of the school, the educational impact upon adults attributed to his weekly sermons, and the systematic pursuit under his guidance of public and personal good relations between Jews and Christians in the city. In February 1846 the *Jewish Chronicle* referred to 'the sound state of Jewish feeling in Birmingham, Liverpool and Manchester' and attributed this to the 'efficiency' of the local Jewish day schools and the Jewish adult education 'afforded by regular sermons' in those cities. 'Our brethren in Birmingham', wrote the commentator at the time, 'are really men of spirit in works of education ... and benevolence.'

The new Chief Rabbi was shortly to introduce improvements at the Jews' Free School, through better grading, the institution of pupil teachers, and an expanded syllabus. Thereafter less was heard of the Hebrew National School of Birmingham as a model. Further-more, Raphall's numerous engagements in and out of the city, caused towards the end of his tenure less attention to be paid to standards at the school and to the recruitment of teachers. There were local murmurs of some decline in the School, which became more pronounced on his departure from Birmingham. He thought it necessary to write to the *Jewish Chronicle* to deny the charges of neglect, but the criticism was not bereft of some reality.

The great expense in building the school had been beyond the Congregation's means. The regular annual grant to the School by the Congregation was £100. The increased number of resident and 'casual' Jewish poor in the 1840s proved to be a substantial burden on its funds. The creation of a local Hebrew Philanthropic Society in 1838 did little to alleviate the pressure on the congregational purse. The finances of the School were greatly assisted by the sum of £1,800 derived from the concert given by Jenny Lind in 1847 in the freely provided Birmingham Town Hall. The noted Swedish singer was on her first tour of Britain and Raphall invited his 'fellow country-woman' to give this benefit-performance for the school as part of her tour. The concert was amply attended by country gentry and townsfolk, and the proceeds enabled the School to discharge its indebtedness.

To Raphall, it was the plain responsibility of the Jewish community to ensure that the Jewish poor were educated Jewishly and generally. In his outlook, which was highly class-conscious and one might say also minority-conscious, this was necessary not only for the moral elevation of the children of the poor and for the purpose of fitting them for employment, but also for the securer and prouder life of the Jewish Englishman. In this connection the interests of the rich Jews coincided with those of the poor, in his mind.

If he thus shared the spirit which was widely prevalent among the 'middle' and 'upper' strata of Jewish society in his day, he went further than they were generally ready to go in the degree of importance that he attached to the cultivation of Jewish education, including higher Jewish learning. The cultivation of serious adult education and Jewish private study were important practical aspirations to him. He often gave public utterance to the notion that the Jewish role in the development of western civilisation was of greater moment than that of any other people. He had an intense national pride as a Jew in the achievements of the Jewish people in the matter of teaching 'morality' to the world.

This was for him a continuing task. He had an enduring belief that its performance required Jews themselves to know and study the Bible, Hebrew literature, and the record of divine promises. He regarded the Jews as under an ancient duty to preserve the knowledge of their sources and expand the general appreciation of them preparatory to their own ultimate redemption for the good of mankind. Meanwhile in speeches he emphasised the non-political attachment of Jews to the land which he called Judaea. On these topics he had a growing Christian audience, to whom some aspects of what he said might have had a greater appeal than for some of his Jewish contemporaries.

The new Chief Rabbi's first provincial visit was to Birmingham. His weekend stay marked a new era in the Chief Rabbinate. It represented a wholly unaccustomed availability on its part, and a new kind of communal communication. The railways greatly facilitated his travels, and Raphall's. Adler used the occasion to state publicly that his recently published book of synagogal rules was hardly necessary in this city as its Synagogue already followed its pattern. This was regarded as a tribute as much to the lay heads of the local community as to Raphall. The community had an acknowledged high standing among provincial communities. By the time of Raphall's ministry it was more than a century old, and second in size only, to Liverpool. By the end of the 1840s it comprised about 750 souls.[12]

The location of Birmingham made it a natural headquarters or base for itinerant dealers, of whom many by that decade had settled to the life of shopkeepers in the city in an assortment of Jewish trades. Some were merchants of substance, notably David Barnett, jeweller and President of the Synagogue. Barnett, of Russian-Polish birth arrived in England in 1819 and settled in the city shortly thereafter. He became the principal founder of the School and was a close colleague and friend of Raphall throughout the latter's incumbency. Barnett was elected to the Town Council and took his seat thereon six years before professing Jews were in law entitled so to serve through the Act of 1845.

It was said of Raphall when he left England that he had 'awakened among Christians an interest and a consideration (in and for Jews) of a kind unknown in this country.' 'The achievements of such a man,' declared Marcus Bresslau, 'have conferred more lasting honour on his race than all the splendour of wealth, title, or position. ... Alas for the Jews of England (for letting him go). He should have been the Preacher of one of the largest congregations in Great Britain.' In a period when Christian 'interest in and consideration for the Jews' was at a premium in the minds of many who represented the Jewish community, it is reasonable to ask why Raphall was indeed allowed to go.[13]

The probable reasons are manifold. His scholarly interests were not a priority among many of those 'representatives', nor necessarily a commendation for advancement. He had no English background or connection, as was the case with Nathan Marcus Adler. Raphall was of robust independence in thought and deed; sometimes less subtle and more direct than circumstances might be thought by the leaders in London to warrant. He lacked the politician's flair, with perhaps a tendency to seek to win the debate when the question might rather be whether the debate was desirable. His polite and ever courteous personal manner may not always have concealed his intense intellectuality, which might well have given him his somewhat remote air in company. He did not show any marked organisational skill or interest, nor any administrative talent. There was an argumentative side to his otherwise equable temperament.

In August 1888, the *Jewish Messenger* (New York) in a review of leading figures in the history of the American Jewish pulpit, commented that Raphall, while 'esteemed' for his learning and oratory, 'lacked the soul and the resources for leadership'. In its obituary notice of Raphall on 26 June 1868, that journal referred to him as 'in appearance ... wrapt in his own affairs and in profound meditation to an extent that created a barrier between him and the unlearned – he was unquestionably British in his carriage and habits of social intercourse'. These expressions may to some extent reflect his comparatively early ageing, and perhaps also some sense of his (as may have been thought) 'British' form of reserve. His wife had died in 1858. Failing health led to his retirement (on full salary) in 1865. Yet one detects in his period in England signs of those qualities to which the above references draw attention in his American or late American period.

In 1860 Raphall's stature was recognised by the choice of this notable personality to deliver the traditional opening prayer at (the 36th) Congress of the United States. The event marked a recognition of the place of Jews in the life of America, and 'he was regarded as the foremost English-speaking rabbi in America'. Apparently to the surprise of many members of the Congress, Raphall pronounced the prayer 'in clear well-modulated tones which reached the uttermost ends of the legislative hall'. Opinions towards him changed somewhat in the northern States after his 'famous' sermon in 1861 in which he declared that there is nothing in the Bible which is inconsistent with the institution of slavery.[14] At a time of acute political tension on the issue of slavery and related matters, it was thought at best ill-considered to pronounce thus upon this issue in New York at that time. The memory of that 'indiscretion' may well have played a part in the somewhat restrained American obituaries in 1868, a few years after the Civil War.

By 1868 the Anglo-Jewish Ministry was different from that which Raphall knew. With all its limitations, it had advanced in the expectations reposed in it. Emancipation had been won. The Adlerian regime was nearing the height of its influence. New 'battles' in public relations remained to be fought. Jewish life was about to be transformed by the great immigration. By the end of the century, the long-deceased American Preacher aroused no special interest outside the dwindling numbers in England who remembered him. In his generation in England, Raphall had shone. For all his distinctive style and emphases which belong to the age in which he lived as much as to his personality, he deserves the tribute of remembrance and appraisal. His departure for America was seen by some at the time to be a reflection on the Anglo-Jewish community, and in particular on its lay and religious leadership in London. That judgement is not likely to be overturned.

NOTES

1. Cecil Roth, *History of the Great Synagogue*, 1950, Ch. XVI; A.M. Hyamson, *The Sephardim of England*, 1951, Ch. XV; A.J. Kershen and J. Romain, *Tradition and Change: A History of British Reform Judaism 1840–1994*, 1995.

2. Naphtali Hart Wessely (1725–1805), Hamburg-born Hebraist, philologist, and exegete, a prominent Haskalah figure in Germany. Raphall's assessment is over-effusive.

3. Amsterdam-born *chazan* of the Sephardi Synagogue in London (1818) and noted talmudist whose father-in-law Raphael Meldola was the rabbinic head of the Sephardi community. His edition of the Congregation's prayer-book (with his English translation thereof) continues in use.

4. *Essays in Jewish History*, (ed.) Cecil Roth, 1934, pp. 311–62. Written by Wolf around the time of Victoria's diamond jubilee in 1897.

5. Abraham de Sola, *Life of David Aaron de Sola*. The son had settled in Montreal and was the chief spokesman in Canada on behalf of Orthodoxy; R.D. Barnett, 'Haham Meldola and Hazan de Sola', *Trans.*, J.H.S.E., 21, 1968, pp. 1–38.

6. For the Haskalah in England, see Siegfried Stein, *The Beginnings of Hebrew Studies at University College London*, 1951; Raphael Loewe, 'Jewish Scholarship in England', *Three Centuries of Anglo-Jewish History*, (ed.) V.D. Lipman, 1961, pp. 125–48; R.D. Barnett, 'Anglo-Jewry in the Eighteenth Century', ibid., pp. 45–68; V.D. Lipman, 'The Age of Emancipation 1815–1880', ibid., pp. 69–106; Cecil Roth, 'The Haskalah in England', *Essays Presented to Israel Brodie, Chief Rabbi, on his 70th Birthday* (Jews' College), (eds) H.Z. Zimmels and others, 1967, Vol. 1, pp. 365–76; and Leonard Hyman, 'Hyman Hurwitz, the first Anglo-Jewish Professor', *Trans.*, J.H.S.E., 21, 1968, pp. 232–42. See also, Cecil Roth, *A History of the Jews in England* (1941), 3rd ed. 1964; and further for Michael Josephs, see James Picciotto, *Sketches of Anglo-Jewish History* (1875), 2nd ed. 1956 (Israel Finestein), pp. 308–9.

7. On Elkin, see Kershen and Romain, *supra*, and Israel Finestein, *Jewish Society in Victorian England*, 1993, pp. 105, 107.

8. Preface, 1st ed. *Pentateuch and Haftorahs*. See also J.H. Hertz, *Jewish Translations of the Bible in English*, published lecture, 1920. In undertaking their task, Raphall and de Sola were in their way responding to the frequent demand for a translation that would (according to their prospectus) 'in some measure supply the want of religious instruction in our synagogues', as well as counter the conversionists' presentations. Abraham Benisch's *Jewish School Family Bible* (1851–56) surpassed their work in popular use. Isaac Leeser, then of Philadelphia and later founder of the first Jewish Publication Society in America produced his English translation of the Bible in 1853, the first Jewish translation of it in English. In their prospectus, Raphall and de Sola characteristically observed: 'In a land whence the knowledge of the Bible goes forth to every part of the globe, British Jews offer the world the striking anomaly that they alone in the whole of Europe possess no Bible translation in the vernacular made by Jews for Jews.' When Benisch announced his intention of producing his own translation, he took the precaution of declaring that a pre-condition was the commitment of at least 500 subscribers. Leeser's translation was well received in Britain. Copies of the work of Raphall and de Sola long continued unsold.

9. Such unconsciously two-edged, and to later ears unctuous expressions, were typically found in the *Birmingham Journal* in July 1847 in support of Lionel de Rothschild's candidature for Parliament in the City of London. In terms reflective of Raphall's often repeated view, the editor wrote: 'It is easy to speak with contempt of the Jew when we have degraded him by centuries of persecution and forced him to adopt craft and cunning as the means of self-preservation. But the Jew, taken in the ideal abstract, has claims to respect not to be exceeded by any in the wide family of men ...'.

10. Levy (Levi) (1742–1801): translator of the daily and Festival liturgies; anti-conversionist polemicist; and defender of 'Old Testament' and biblical prophecy, notably in his much-noted public *Letters* to Tom Paine, 1797. Goodman (d. 1824): pioneer Jewish preacher (Liverpool and later Westminster (Western) Synagogue); and author of first English published sermon

193

(Liverpool, 1819), entitled *The Faith of Israel*; anti-conversionist polemicist. Hurwitz (1770–1840): headmaster and Hebraist – see note 6.

11. In 1847 Spooner, one of Birmingham's Members of Parliament and a member of a Christian conversionist society, was reported to have asked his Christian audience as follows: 'If when the Jews are restored to their native country – as I have no doubt whatever they will be – do you think they would permit a Christian to become a legislator among them?' David Barnett, in July 1847, on the approach to the Parliamentary elections of that year, at a public meeting, asked him to explain his position. Spooner, who did not deny that he had so spoken, affirmed that he could not support Jewish entry into Parliament since on principle he opposed entry for anyone who would not as a legislator act 'on Christian principles', and who thus by implication would threaten the Christian character of the legislature. His exclusionist opinion was shared by a body of local Tories. These exchanges were extensively reported in the local press and in the *Jewish Chronicle*.

12. See S.Y. Prais, 'The Development of Birmingham Jewry', *Jewish Monthly*, Vol. 2, No. 11, 1949 (Anglo-Jewish Association), pp. 665–79; Harry Levine, *Short History of Birmingham Hebrew Congregation*, 1956; Sharon Rothstein, 'Evolution of Birmingham Hebrew National School within the Context of Anglo-Jewish Education, 1841–70', abstract of Birmingham University BA dissertation, *Provincial Jewry in Victorian Britain*, (ed.) A.N. Newman, J.H.S.E., 1975, p. 5; Zoe Josephs (ed.), *Birmingham Jewry* (Vol. 1), 1749–1914 (Birmingham Jewish History Research Group), 1980, and Vol. 2, *More Aspects*, 1740–1930, 1984. For Raphall's American career, see Rabbi Israel Goldstein's history of the Bnai Jeshurun Congregation entitled *A Century of Judaism in New York* (1930) and Moshe Davis, *The Emergence of Conservative Judaism*, 1963.

13. On 26 June 1868 the New York journal *The Hebrew Leader*, edited by Jonas Bondi, reported that when Raphall arrived in America in October 1849 he embarked on an extensive lecture tour and that it was on his return to New York with a view to returning to Birmingham that the Bnai Jeshurun persuaded him to accept appointment as their preacher – on unusually favourable terms, including a provision that it should be a life appointment with pension rights in the event of incapacity. His tour had attracted great renown. He preached his farewell sermon in Birmingham on 12 October 1849, an event arousing considerable civic attention and described in some detail by Harry Levine in the *Birmingham Jewish Recorder* in October 1949. There is no indication of Raphall having visited America prior to his appointment at the Bnai Jeshurun or of any intention of returning to England. The *Hebrew Leader* was founded by Bondi in 1860; this Dresden-born scholar was a pupil of Nathan Marcus Adler before the latter became Chief Rabbi. Bondi was of the Conservative school of thought (as it later was termed as distinct from Orthodox), a trend which progressively marked the Bnai Jeshurun after Raphall's death. Bondi wrote that 'the foundation of Raphall's celebrity' was laid in 1844 when he effectively repulsed anti-Jewish insinuations by one Marsh, a senior Anglican cleric whose slanders and Raphall's replies (with Marsh's partial withdrawals)

gained much public attention through their publication in *The Times*. The American Jewish weekly, the *Asmonean*, reported (as cited by the *Jewish Chronicle* in February 1850) that in early June 1849 the New York congregation had appointed a committee 'to enquire into the expediency of appointing a preacher' and that while engaged in that enquiry the committee heard 'with delight' of Raphall's intended visit to America. The negotiations which Bnai Jeshurun eventually concluded with Raphall were followed by a unanimous formal decision to extend a 'call' to him. It is difficult to avoid the conclusion that Raphall knew of the vacancy and the 'enquiry' before he left for America. There is no indication of any intention or intimation on his part, on leaving England, that he would or might return.

14. In his address Raphall sought to distinguish the biblical concept of the slave as a person possessed of certain rights, in contrast to the institution of slavery as practised in America whereby the slave was held to be an object and rightless. The distinction did not curb the resentment of the abolitionists, and indeed did not wholly satisfy sections of retentionist opinion.

7

Matthew Arnold, Jews and Society

The appearance of *Culture and Anarchy* by Matthew Arnold (1822–88) in 1869 was a major publishing event. Its principal contents had first appeared in the form of periodic articles in the *Cornhill Magazine* in 1867 and 1868. They were widely noted, especially among the younger and socially more sensitive elements of the reading public. In a period of political flux and intellectual ferment, the book had a great impact. Succeeding editions maintained the influence of the work. It left its mark on the thinking of a generation as far as the educated sections of society were concerned.

If its high-mindedness of tone and principle was deliberate and self-conscious, it was not precocious, pretentious or patronising. It had a special appeal to well-read people, especially those in government or prospectively so, whether as politicians or civil servants nationally or locally who, while wanting to retain the system which had provided them with the advantages of their own standards of education, also wanted to raise the levels of education and culture among the 'mass' of society. The book offered an earnest and in some respects controversial philosophy for those who wanted change and reform without radicalism.

In a later age Arnold's literary style and his intellectual approach tended to give his writings a somewhat remote air. The mounting intensity of social and economic issues imposed an archaic look upon his categorisation of classes and his definitions of social problems. *Culture and Anarchy* is the quintessence of his work, not only in its distinctive cadences but also in its liberal inclusivist spirit and its concern for the states of mind of English people of his day and the next.

Like Alexis de Tocqueville and Thomas Carlyle, Arnold was acutely and ceaselessly aware of the central feature of the great social and political transformations which were in train in his lifetime. That feature was the emergence of the 'mass age'. In several respects he felt himself to be, in his words, 'a wanderer between two worlds ...'. His principal theme was that the nation should be educated in readiness, and suitably (according to his lights), for the coming of power and new opportunities to the 'masses'. The extension of the franchise in 1867, the expanding new means of travel, the progressive urbanisation of the population, and the changing industrial relations, set the context in which he wrote, and somehow added urgency to his words. The declining hold of religion, despite the prevailing public and social religiosity, added to his concern, notwithstanding his sense of its declining hold upon himself, and perhaps because of it.

Arnold was a political Liberal who made no shibboleth of individualism. He was not content with unfettering society from outmoded restraints. He favoured the positive ameliorating use of representative authority. He acknowledged the State's interventionist capacity and duty. He had neither the querulousness of de Tocqueville nor the temperamental pessimism of Carlyle in facing the new age. He regarded optimism as a Jewish trait. It was certainly one of his own.

A confident product of Winchester and Rugby, he took a degree in Classics at Balliol, became a Fellow of Oriel, and taught at Rugby. In 1847 he was appointed private secretary to Lord Lansdowne, the progressive Whig who as President of the Council in Lord John Russell's administration, was the Minister concerned with educational matters. For 35 years from 1851, Arnold was one of HM Inspectors of Schools. He was the eldest son of Dr Thomas Arnold, headmaster of Rugby and later Professor in Modern History at Oxford. Matthew Arnold's fruitful explorations and reports on foreign educational systems were famous in their day.

One of his sisters married W.E. Forster, who put through Parliament the Education Act of 1870, which provided for elementary education in Local Authority schools. In 1880 such education became compulsory. It was primarily in the field of education that Arnold believed and advocated that the State had a crucial role. As early as the 1860s he preached the need for a national system of education provided by the State, under the control of what he called a 'Minister for Education', based upon a reformed system of local government which would be party to the provision.

He was also ahead of his time in his plans for secondary education, and for University 'extension' teaching. Professor Dover Wilson, who in 1932 published an annotated edition of *Culture and Anarchy* (which edition was long in use in schools and Universities) described Arnold as 'the prophet of secondary education' in England. 'Culture,' wrote Arnold in the opening chapter of his seminal work, 'seeks to do away with classes; ... the men of culture are the true apostles of equality.' His particular appeal to wide areas of intelligent opinion, notably among the younger recruits to the Universities, sometimes centred on his definition of culture. It is set out in his preface, and was typical of the man. It is, he wrote, 'a pursuit of our total perfection by means of getting to know, on all matters which must concern us, the best which has been thought and said in the world; and through his knowledge, turning a stream of fresh and free thought upon our stock notions and habits which we now follow staunchly and mechanically, vainly imagining that there is a virtue in following them staunchly which makes up for the mischief of following them mechanically'. It was a point not lost in many circles, lay and clerical.

The lesson which he sought to teach in *Culture and Anarchy* was not only that the State had an important contribution to make to the moral health of society, but also that things should be seen as they are. He regarded the desire to see things as they are – that is divested of encrusting façades and confusing presumptions – as conducive to true progress, and he deplored the lack of that desire. It was his constant refrain. He also expounded the idea that religion was the best aid for the discovery of the better self. He remained attached to the Church of England, but was not in love with dogma. He accepted the higher critical approach to biblical study, and took for granted many of the conclusions of that school, notably in the work of the celebrated Ewald of Göttingen and Tübingen Universities. He continued to hold the Bible to be a work of outstanding social value, especially for instruction in ethics, philosophy, history and literature, and for instruction in the awareness that there is a divine scheme of things.

Arnold was profoundly interested in the history of the Jews and in Judaism. He held Jewish history in great respect, and had a high regard for what he deemed to be the distinctively Jewish elements in the Judaeo-Christian tradition. He found pleasure in the company of cultivated Jews. Unlike Carlyle, the gloomy sage of Chelsea, he took the trouble to try to understand the Jewish constituent in society. These sentiments were bred upon his love of the Old Testament, and nourished by a constant curiosity over the continuing Jewish role in the affairs of mankind. They were also encouraged by his regular encounters with the Jewish schools which he inspected, and with their managers and benefactors, especially the Rothschild ladies.

For the first 20 years of his inspectorate, Arnold was confined to non-Anglican schools, as inspection of Anglican schools was until 1871 restricted to clergymen. It was mainly through the Rothschilds that he came to meet leading Jewish figures of the time. The motivation for Jewish survival, and the techniques directed to that end, intrigued him. His friend and biographer, George Russell, referred to his 'affectionate and grateful feeling towards the Jewish race'.[1]

With many hosts Arnold formed mutually valued personal relationships. With some, the association was politically useful and socially interesting on both sides. Few of these relationships gave greater pleasure than his friendship with the household of Sir Anthony de Rothschild, the first President of the United Synagogue. His literary success led to his becoming a frequent visitor to the homes of leading families in politics and society, often in the country. In Louisa (1821–1910), Rothschild's wife, he found a woman of intellect and wide literary tastes. A genuine personal friendship developed between them. It was based upon his respect for her opinions and her admiration for his literary achievements and his stand on public issues.[2] She was the daughter of Abraham Montefiore the independent-minded and adventurous brother of Sir Moses.

In addition to his visits to Aston Clinton, the Buckinghamshire mansion of the Anthony de Rothschilds, Arnold was an occasional visitor to Mentmore, the neighbouring palatial residence of Sir Anthony's youngest brother, Mayer. Arnold was familiar with the social extremes in Anglo-Jewry, the *milieux* of the plutocracy on the one hand and the products of the lower middle classes and working classes on the other. He also had personal contact with members of diverse intermediate layers of the Jewish *bourgeoisie* through his meetings with the school committees.

In a significant passage in an obituary notice on Louisa de Rothschild, the *Jewish Chronicle* on 30 September, 1910, commented that 'she was an enthusiastic upholder of her ancestral faith, although she inclined to the views of her nephew Claude Goldsmid Montefiore'. That observation was a decorous over-statement of her attachment to traditional tenets. Montefiore was the principal founder of the Liberal Synagogue. Arnold died four years before his famous Hibbert Lectures on 'The Origin and Growth of Religion as illustrated by the Religion of the Ancient Hebrews', but he must already have been aware of Montefiore's modernist and reformist bent of mind and the implications of his approach. He made known to Louisa his own high opinion of the intellect of that wing of the Montefiore family.

'What women these Jewesses are', he wrote to his mother in October 1863, after a visit to Aston Clinton, where he also met some of the continental Rothschild ladies. They are possessed, he added, of 'a force which seems to triple that of the women of our western and northern races'. He did not cease to be impressed.

He was a welcome guest at anniversary dinners of Jewish schools in London. These were exercises in public relations as well as fundraising occasions. Arnold was struck by the degree of self-sufficiency in the Jewish community in respect of its charities, including the schools. He was especially moved by the size and multi-faceted influence of the Jews' Free School. He noted with approval the self-conscious aim of combining the inculcation of Judaism with basic secular education and civic pride and attachment. He rejected the contention that the standards of secular study were prejudiced by the amount of time devoted to Hebrew and related instruction. In any event he regarded the acquisition of a second language as a useful intellectual stimulus, which redounded to advantage in the area of secular instruction.

There was a remarkable contrast in relation to the Jews, between Arnold and his father. The contrast illustrates the nature and extent of the change in the intellectual climate in mid-Victorian England. More specifically, it demonstrates the growing secularity of society, and the effect of that process upon attitudes towards the Jews. Social attitudes towards them were inescapably involved in the wider changes. In some ways, they were the touchstone. Part of the interest in Matthew Arnold is that his thoughts in this field reflect both the developing status of the Jew in society, the opinions held about the Jews among the educated middle classes, and to some extent also the opinions held by the Jews about themselves and their own future.

Dr Thomas Arnold (1795–1842) was in many respects a man of liberal outlook. That fact increased the importance of his opposition to the civic and political emancipation of the Jews. Whether in the realm of education or of Bible criticism or the composition and character of the Established Church and its place in society, the elder Arnold represented departures from convention and tradition. So advanced were his opinions on Bible scholarship and church matters that when his friend Edward Stanley was appointed Bishop of Norwich in 1837, the Archbishop of Canterbury, William Howley, prohibited Dr Arnold from preaching at a consecration service. Arnold was much influenced by the German schools of Bible criticism. He was particularly impressed by the writings and personality of Bunsen, the Prussian diplomat, philosopher and Lutheran lay theologian who played a crucial part in procuring the Anglo-Prussian agreement for the creation in 1841 of the Anglican-Lutheran Bishopric of Jerusalem.

On the grounds of historical study, theological argument and civic considerations, Thomas Arnold wanted a widening of the qualifying ambit for the Church of England, and, in any event, a diminution of the privileges of that Church in relation to the Protestant Dissenters. He helped to rear a generation of public figures, especially ecclesiastics, who through his direct influence at Rugby or Oxford or by his indirect influence, shared his broad views. But he was equally firm upon the limits to this welcoming approach. He was no less resolute than, for example, Howley in opposing Jewish emancipation. The Archbishop repudiated Dr Arnold's broad-churchmanship, but shared his hostility to the Jewish claims.

It is noteworthy that Howley and some other prominent clerics, accompanied their opposition to Jewish emancipation with patently sincere utterances of respect for the Jews as a people who were deemed by them to be possessed of a continuing providential role.

These expressions were usually linked with the hope of conversion. Among laymen who adopted such tones the most prominent was Lord Shaftesbury. His reverence for the Jews as a people sprang from his belief in their once having been chosen for a high purpose, and his conviction that they had yet, in the inscrutable future, a particular part to play in the ultimate design, which was perhaps nigh. This Evangelical churchman, Tory politician and social reformer, could not bring himself, until the latest stage of the emancipationist campaign, to acquiesce in the admission of professing Jews to Parliament. 'A nation they are,' he declared in December 1847, while still in the House of Commons, 'and a nation they will continue to be to the end of time.' Whatever their role in the messianic era, he long felt that meanwhile they could have no legitimate place in the legislature of a Christian state.

Although Thomas Arnold had the due regard of a believing Christian for the Old Testament and gave much time to its study, there is a distinct absence in his language on the Jewish issue of the kinds of expression which came naturally to Howley and Shaftesbury. One of his pejorative terms for those of his own communion whose attention to ritualism was to his mind excessive, was 'judaizers'. In 1836 he wrote to a friend

> The world is made up of Christians and non-Christians; with all the former we should be one, with none of the latter ... the Jews have no claim whatever of political right ... the Jews are strangers in England, and have no more claim to legislate for it than a lodger has to share with the landlord in the management of his house. If we had brought them here by violence, and then kept them in an inferior position, they would have just cause to complain; even though when I think we might lawfully deal with them on the Liberia system, and remove them to a land where they might live by themselves independent; for England is the land of Englishmen, not of Jews.

From the views set out in this frequently cited passage, Dr Arnold never resiled, and often and in a variety of ways gave expression to them. In them, we can detect in part a medieval inheritance. The conception of 'church' and 'state' as but two capacities of the one unit, died hard. Indeed, the nation-state, for all its revolt against the medieval notion of a universal Christian society, adopted for its

202

own ends important strands of the older pattern. *Cujus regio ejus religio* is both medieval and modern, and as a principle or an ideal survived in varying forms at least into the nineteenth century: the religion of the governed is that of the governor. That was often the ethos of a principality or state. Thomas Arnold's views reflected a common belief – repudiated by the increasingly influential Benthamites – that the State owes to the Church the duty of legislating in a Christian spirit for Christian ends.

Furthermore, Dr Arnold associated the case for Jewish emancipation with what he called 'that low Jacobinical notion of citizenship', that is to say with such policies as 'counting heads' and with theories of natural rights. Residence, citizenship, the payment of taxes, may reciprocally involve the right to the protection of the law, but what had that to do with sharing in the legislative power of a Christian society?

Many of Dr Arnold's admirers developed his liberalism further than he contemplated. They perceived that once the Anglican establishment gave way to the Dissenters' claims for wider legal recognition and political and professional opportunity, and once the old biblical certainties lost their hold, the traditional relationship between the Church of England and the society comprising England, could not be sustained.[3] Degrees of pluralism engendered their own momentum, which could not be limited to Christians. What was to be the place of theists, deists and sceptics? In April 1853, five years before the admission of a professing Jew to the House of Commons, Richard Whately, the Archbishop of Dublin, startled the House of Lords in one of the many debates on that question, by declaring, with some exaggeration and oratorial licence, that 'the House of Commons is not Christian now – one half of them are deists'. The point was made, and could not easily be gainsaid by those who based their opposition on the risk of de-Christianising Parliament.

The effect of the slow dissolution of the old outlook was reinforced by many other considerations, as far as the attitudes to Jews were concerned. Matthew Arnold was far from alone in the world of English letters or socio-religious enquiry, to turn his mind to a study of the Jews and even to Jewish studies. He studied Hebrew to better understand and appreciate the biblical text, especially the prophetic passages. He produced his own English translation of

20. Matthew Arnold (1823–88)

Chapters 40–66 of Isaiah with their famous prophetic passages of Jewish–Christian controversial import. The mystery of Jewish survival, a respect for the sense of judgement conveyed in the Old Testament, the recognition of the untarnished loyalty of the Jews to the State, all contributed to various extents – in some cases combined with the hope of proselytisation – to make many a pupil of Dr Arnold an adherent of the campaign for Jewish emancipation.

Whether the interest in the Old Testament was that of curiosity over the remarkable history of the people whose distinctive survival was an historical improbability which had indeed come to pass, or whether the interest was cultivated for conversionist purposes or out of regard for what the Christians held to be the sacred precursor of the new dispensation, the fact was that the Old Testament was widely resorted to by scholar and layman in Arnold's generation. It was resorted to as history or for moral guidance or as a series of noteworthy manifestations of religious development.

The extraordinary interest aroused by Emanuel Deutsch's well-known article on the Talmud in the *Quarterly Review* of October 1867 made it look as though English men of letters had been awaiting such fresh English revelation of the methods, style and essential substance of the source books of the Jewish tradition. There was widespread curiosity about the nature of Judaism and about Jewish aspirations and self-assessment. It was fed from many quarters. There was the unabashed influence of Jewish families in the financial centres of Europe. There was the phenomenon of Disraeli, an avowed Christian who declared his belief in the superiority of the 'race' from which he sprang. And there were the Jewish emancipationists who consistently distanced themselves from any such idea. There was the striking contrast between Jewish affluence and influence on the one hand and the poverty, powerlessness and vulnerability of large segments of the Jewish people. There was further the riddle of the identity and outlook of the westernised Jew in a liberal and increasingly open society who remained a Jew, without necessarily any close adherence, if any at all, to the pieties or practices which were characteristic of the ancient faith. And there were the repeated and diverse pleas and proposals relating to Jewish settlement in Palestine, in which every sort of worldly and metaphysical motivation seemed to be involved.

Neither Deutsch nor Arnold nor any of his circle provided answers or explanations, nor were they expected to do so. But they felt impelled to explore the factors making for Jewish cohesion and distinctive survival under varying degrees of pressure everywhere, living on the strength of a faith which had transformed the world. Dr Thomas Arnold's antipathy sharpened his son's interest.

A striking demonstration of the practical importance attached to Jewish Scripture is found in the well-known sermon by John Keble entitled 'National Apostasy' delivered to the University of Oxford in 1833, which initiated the Oxford Movement. Keble, who was Arnold's godfather, was for all his high-churchmanship held in high esteem in Thomas Arnold's household. Their differences did not destroy their friendship. In that celebrated sermon, Keble, taking as his text 1 Samuel 12, 23, stated: 'We naturally turn to the Old Testament, when public duties, public errors, and public dangers, are in question.' He added: '... as regards reward and punishment, God dealt formerly with the Jewish people in a manner analogous to that in which he deals now, not so much with Christian nations, as with the souls of individual Christians ...'. The Old Testament, he declared, contains 'authoritative confirmation of the plain dictates of conscience in matters of civic wisdom and duty'. He went on to expound the opinion, with ample illustrative references to Samuel's generation, that the people of England were alienating themselves from the divine, and could escape the consequences only by a national retracing of steps. Higher critical study in England was not generally involved with antipathy to the Jews or to the Judaic contribution to western civilisation. The tendency was usually in the reverse direction.

One of the most influential of Thomas Arnold's pupils was Bishop Stanley's son, Arthur, Dean of Westminster and Regius Professor of Ecclesiastical History at Oxford. He was Dr Arnold's biographer, and a noted Judeophile. As with Dr Arnold, Dean Stanley's piety 'was practical and personal, not doctrinal nor speculative .... So much was in their opinion needed to fit the actual Church [of England] for its vocation, that in the eyes of many of their clerical brethren, their membership placed them in as false a position as if they had disbelieved half of its Articles.'[4] His mind was open to the new scholarship, but the essential historicity of the bulk of the biblical narrative remained for him intact. In 1856 there appeared his *Sinai and Palestine*, written after diligent travel in those regions, and close study of people and topography. It proved a popular work and was in tune with the spirit and emphasis of established mid-Victorian interests. By his well-known published *Lectures on the History of the Jewish Church* (1862–76), he gave a considerable impetus, as had Dean Milman's *The History of the Jews from the Earliest Period down to Modern Times* in the previous generation, to the study of the history of the Jewish people as part of the general education of educated laymen, 'a history to be judged with the same freedom as any other record of human character and action'.[5]

Connop Thirlwall, a follower of Dr Arnold was, like him, a supporter of the relaxation of the Anglican religious tests for University admission and degrees. In 1840 at Lord Melbourne's instance as Prime Minister, he was appointed Bishop of St David's, a highly controversial appointment. He was an influential advocate in the House of Lords of the Jewish case. Another significant member of Dr Arnold's school of thought was Richard Whately, Archbishop of Dublin from 1831 to 1863. Whately was older than Arnold but in some respects more forward-looking. In particular, he saw more clearly the present and future importance of religious dissent in state and society. Whately was the main ecclesiastical sponsor of the heterodox R.D. Hampden to the Regius Professorship of Divinity at Oxford in 1836. Hampden was a close associate of Dr Arnold and shared his critical scriptural opinions. His appointment at Oxford upon Melbourne's nomination created a stir, matched only by his elevation to a bishopric in 1847 at the instance of Lord John Russell. Whately's consistent advocacy in the House of Lords of the removal of Jewish disabilities carried increasing weight.

There was nothing in Matthew Arnold of the awesome expectancy of the older generation, which in that respect was so well represented by his father. 'My sense of the evils of the times,' declared Thomas Arnold, in his *Introductory Lectures on Modern History* (1842) 'is overwhelmingly bitter. All in the moral and physical world appears so exactly to announce the coming of the "great day of the Lord", [that is] a period of fearful visitation to terminate the existing state of things, whether to terminate the whole existence of the human race neither man nor angel knows.' This kind of foreboding was alien to the new generation.

Certainly there were limits to the extent to which Matthew Arnold shared the contemporary conviction that progress was assured through the presumed inevitable benefits of knowledge and science. He wanted to contribute to the improvement of the 'classes', all of them, whereby the standards of each would be conducive to healthier and less strained interdependence, and thus to a more stable society. A great deal of what he wrote was concerned with these tasks. But he was not depressed by the present state of society. He was not fearful of the many rapid changes. His concern was that they should be met and absorbed, and that the quality of life be enhanced and the social structure strengthened. In this state of mind, a widening democracy, greater accountability, more governmental intervention and a pluralist society held no terrors. He could see no reason why there should be any religious or ethnic test for the full rights of citizenship or civic and political participation. He took the creation of the first professing Jew as a Peer in 1885 as marking 'the total and final abandonment' of the old policy of exclusion. 'What have we not learned and gained', he wrote to Louisa de Rothschild 'from the people whom we have been excluding all these years'!

'Whoever treats religion', he wrote to a French clerical friend in October 1881, 'religious discussions, questions of churches and sects, as absorbing, is not in vital sympathy with the movement of men's minds at present.' It is a highly significant remark. In 1868, Campbell Tait, when Bishop of London, was appointed Archbishop of Canterbury. He was in the broad tradition of Dr Arnold, whom he had succeeded as headmaster of Rugby. He had been a tutor of Matthew Arnold and Benjamin Jowett at Oxford. His appointment to Canterbury, like Jowett's election as Master of Balliol in 1870, was indicative of the trend of prevailing opinion. By the early 1880s, writes one student of that era, 'the church was ... defensive and hesitant in intellectual controversy; religion had become almost without importance in this sphere'. Further, the generation of Tait, who died in 1882, 'was the last age in which bishops and the leaders of the schools of thought within the Church were figures of national importance. It marked the last serious attempt to make the Church of England the Church of the English.'[6]

It is against this background that one should see the growing support for the abolition of the disabilities of non-Anglicans, including non-Christians. Matthew Arnold favoured abolition, and at the same time hoped for a regeneration of the Church of England. These were not necessarily mutually exclusive. Wholly different criteria for social and political decisions had arisen. One notable feature in Arnold's assessment was that he detected in aspects of the Hebrew tradition, qualities which he thought might contribute towards the strengthening of Christianity. He attached even less importance to dogma than did his father.

Deutsch's article alighted upon a society already much interested in Jewish concerns, and that work greatly fanned the appeal. In a striking passage in a letter in August 1868, Arnold wrote that in 1868 Deutsch had told him that while writing the article, he was conscious 'that if it had not been for what I had done he could not have written that article in the *Quarterly*, and the British public could not have read it'.

It is likewise a notable fact that Spinoza became a fashionable subject of study. The reactions of his sceptical and critical mind could hardly fail to attract those who in the nineteenth century saw themselves involved in a revolt of their own against authority and convention. Wallis's English translation of his *Tractatus Theologico-*

Politicus in 1862 stimulated that study. Arnold's highly acclaimed paper on Spinoza and the Bible, which first appeared in 1863 and was two years later included in his widely read *Essays in Criticism*, was a major factor in heightening the interest in Spinoza. Works on that philosopher, wrote the *Jewish Chronicle* on 25 April 1884 – on the morrow of the publication of James Martineau's study (1883) and the English translations of Spinoza's *Ethics* by W.H. White (1883) and of works on Spinoza by R.H.M. Elwes (1883–84) – 'multiply daily, [yet] scarcely keep pace with the increasing enthusiasm for him'. White was a civil servant, Dissenting theologian and liberal philosopher, who was more popularly known as a novelist under his pen-name, Mark Rutherford. He was a friend of George Eliot, who herself fell under Spinoza's spell and tried her hand at translating him. Arnold began his reading of Spinoza well before the works of Spinoza aroused such wide attention. 'Smile as you will', he wrote to Arthur Clough in October 1850. 'I have been studying [Spinoza] lately with profit.'[7] Above all, it was his intensity, the zest of his argument, and his comprehensiveness which Arnold saw as Hebraic.

His study of Heine appeared first in 1863 and was incorporated in the *Essays in Criticism* in 1865. Arnold deplored Heine's moral laxity. What appealed to Arnold was Heine's 'intense modernism, his absolute freedom, his utter rejection of stock classicism and stock romanticism ...' He was 'that Paladin of the modern spirit'. 'By his perfection of literary form', he wrote, 'by his love of clearness, by his love of beauty Heine is Greek; by his intensity, his untameableness ... [by his] "longing which cannot be uttered" he is Hebrew.'

In his *Literature and Dogma* (1873) Arnold presented the clearest statement of his perception of the character and effect of the 'Old Testament', and indeed of the role of the Jew, as he saw it, in human history. It is set out in the chapter headed 'The True Greatness of the Old Testament'. It is essential to an understanding of his approach to what he termed Hebraism, as well as of his assessment of the Jewry which he knew in his day.

'Is it possible', he therein enquired, 'to imagine a grander testimony to the truth of the revelation committed to Israel? ... the whole history of the world to this day is in truth the continual establishment of the Old Testament revelation. ... Whether we consider this revelation in respect to human affairs at large or in respect to individual happiness, in either case its importance is so immense that the people to whom it was given and whose record is in the Bible deserve fully to be singled out as the Bible singles them. While other nations had the misleading idea that this or that, other than conduct, brings happiness, Israel had the true idea that righteousness is saving, [and] that to conduct belongs happiness. Nor let it be said that other nations too had at least something of this idea. They had, but they were not *possessed* with it [as the Jews were]; to feel it enough to make the world feel it was necessary to be possessed with it'.

Arnold acknowledged the considerable influence upon him of Spinoza. There appears clearly in the above passage an echo of that philosopher's reference to the divine intoxication of the Jews. To Arnold, that had been the secret of Jewish cohesion and survival. He read into it a continuing message in terms of the responsibilities on the part of society to all its members and the duties to one another of all individuals, subject to the interplay of that message with the aesthetic sense and intellectual development. Rigidity of ideas formed no part of his philosophy.

The most famous Chapter of *Culture and Anarchy* is entitled 'Hebraism and Hellenism'. He took the terminology and the idea from Heine. Arnold described Hebraism in terms of 'energy'. He described it thus: 'This energy driving at practice, this paramount sense of the obligation of duty, self-control, work, this earnestness in going manfully with the best light we have'. He described 'the uppermost idea with Hebraism' as 'conduct and obedience'. 'The governing idea of Hellenism', he added, 'is spontaneity of consciousness; that of Hebraism, strictness of conscience.' Each of these forces, he wrote, is a contribution to human development, and he wanted the best of both to merge.

In a passage of great interest, he wrote:

> Science has now made visible to everybody the great and pregnant elements which lie in race, and in how signal a manner they make the genius and history of an Indo-European people vary from those of a Semitic people. Hellenism is of Indo-European growth, Hebraism is of Semitic growth; and we English, a nation of Indo-European stock, seem to belong naturally to the movement of Hellenism. But nothing more strongly marks the essential unity of

man than the affinities which we can perceive, in this point or that, between members of one family of peoples and members of another and no affinity of this kind is more strongly marked than that likeness in the strength and prominence of the moral fibre, which notwithstanding immense elements of difference, knits in some special sort the genius and history of us English, and our American descendants across the Atlantic to the genius and history of the Hebrew people.

Whatever critique may be made of the assumptions and definitions implicit in such expressions,[8] Arnold had no doubt that western civilisation and Christianity had still much of advantage to derive from the moral impulse of the Hebraic tradition, enlightened, as he would say, by 'the thinking side of man' which for him was the vital element in Hellenism. He wanted the right balance. One of his reasons for welcoming Deutsch's article with such avidity, was that he considered it to be, if properly understood, an aid thereto. '… the long extracts from the Talmud itself', he wrote to Louisa de Rothschild in November 1867, 'were quite fresh to me and gave me huge satisfaction'. He went on, in an extraordinary and revealing passage: 'It is curious that though Indo-European, the English people is so constituted and trained that there is a thousand times more chance of bringing it to a more philosophical conception of religion than its present conception of Christianity as something utterly unique, isolated and self-sufficient, through Judaism and its phenomena than through Hellenism and its phenomena.' Commenting on that observation in 1895,[9] Joseph Jacobs described it as 'especially significant at present'. He regarded the statement as bearing upon the possible importance of Judaism as 'a means of reforming Christianity'.

When Jacobs wrote, Claude Montefiore and Oswald John Simon were developing their ideas for an assimilation between Judaism in a condition of advanced reform on the one hand and an undogmatic Christianity on the other. If, as I believe, it was to this that Jacobs referred, I think he read too much into Arnold's remark. It was not, however, a casual or unconsidered remark. What Arnold probably had in mind was a two-fold lesson which I believe he thought Christians might derive from Judaism. One was the desirability of emulating 'this energy driving at practice'. The other was by way of the unencumbered monotheism at the heart of Judaism.

Arnold saw the essential Jewish element as being action, intensity

211

of purpose, the creative spirit, all that was opposed to the contemplative life. He regarded 'righteousness' as an ingredient in or a concomitant of that element. He often presented the emphasis on 'righteousness' as the essential feature of what he called Hebraism. He developed the theme in *Culture and Anarchy*. The implication of his presentation seems to be that the hallmark of the Jewish element is action and effort, spurred by optimism. If this was the implication, it is an implication of a considerable truth.

By a variety of ways, history fashioned the Jews into such a mould. That process and those manifestations were evident before and after the fall of the actual or notional ghetto walls. Even the Jewish 'longing' was strenuous. Even study was a form of intense action. The sociological consequences of this deeply ingrained trait were substantial. Arnold saw this element in the Jews, even though his definitions of it were or became related to or were transmuted into other departments of life and thought.

His contrast between Hebraism and Hellenism, his criticisms of the Puritans and their Protestant successors for their alleged overemphasis on Hebraism, his insinuation that rabbinic Judaism tended by its nature to be out of accord with aesthetic values – all these are on the face of his work. Beneath, not always expressed, is the suggestion that what might be called the Jewish spirit has a restlessly creative quality which is distinctive of it.

In his memorable poem entitled 'Dover Beach', Arnold spoke of the ebbing of the 'sea of faith'. He was not immune to the predicaments of faith or to the personal sensation of loss at the departure of old certainties. Speaking of faith in his striking seashore metaphor, he says: 'But now I only hear its melancholy long withdrawing roar, retreating to the breath of the night-wind. And we are here as on a darkling plain swept with confused alarms of struggle and fight, where ignorant armies clash by night.' He was not thinking of any immediate military struggle, but he did not exclude in the licence of his poetic melancholy the feature of modern war.

He castigated commercialism when it was untouched by social responsibility. He was cautious about religious enthusiasms when untouched by reason and tolerance. Self-righteousness was his main target. He sometimes equated it with vulgarity. He deplored what he called the philistinism which he detected in the English middle classes. He regarded the landed aristocracy as even less accessible to ideas. He deemed the illiteracy and poverty of what he called 'the populace' as rendering them 'blind' to trends and vulnerable to destructive agitations. He was not content with the mixture of the 3 Rs and efficient mechanisation. Education should not be a privilege, and should not be left to chance or the cash nexus. His social reformism had a moral context, and a significant strand in that context were the principles of righteousness in action, the spirit and practice of which he sought in the Hebrew Scriptures.

The themes with which Arnold dealt, as even the titles of his books, may now seem somewhat old-fashioned. But his era is on analysis strangely near. The pace has altered, but some essential questions remain. Among them are the task of education, the place of religion in society, the impact of science on moral values, the interrelations of the 'classes', the role of the Jew, and the effect of what Arnold held to be the Hebraic spirit in the human drama. He had something to say about them all.

NOTES

Quotations from Thomas Arnold, save where otherwise stated, are from his letters contained in A.P. Stanley, *Life of Dr Arnold*, 1844: nos. 82 and 130. Matthew Arnold's letters are quoted from G.W.E. Russell, *Letters of Matthew Arnold*, 1895.

1. G.W.E. Russell, *Matthew Arnold*, 1904, p. 163. Russell was a nephew of Lord John Russell, the Parliamentary leader of the campaign for the removal of Jewish disabilities. For Arnold, see Lionel Trilling, *Matthew Arnold*, 1939; P.J. McCarthy, *Matthew Arnold and the Three Classes*, 1964; Joseph Carroll, *The Cultural Theory of Matthew Arnold*, 1982; and Nicholas Murray, *Matthew Arnold*, 1996.
2. There are occasional interesting references to Arnold in Lady Battersea, *Reminiscences*, 1922, and Lucy Cohen, *Lady de Rothschild and her Daughters (1821–1931)*, 1935. See also 'Lady de Rothschild and Matthew Arnold' in *Jewish Chronicle*, 7 October 1910, based on the letters.
3. '... before the 1851 Religious Census, few Englishmen realised quite how popular dissent was': D.L. Edwards, *Leaders of the Church of England (1828–1944)*, 1971, pp. 25–6.
4. R.E. Prothero, *Life and Letters of Dean Stanley*, 1893: Vol. 1, pp. 382–4.
5. Ibid., Vol. 2, p. 108.
6. P.T. Marsh, *The Victorian Church in Decline: Archbishop Tait and the Church of England (1868–82)*, 1969, pp. 9, 289.

7. *The Letters of Matthew Arnold to Arthur Hugh Clough*, ed. by H.F. Lowry, 1932. Reprinted 1968, p. 117.
8. For Arnold and race, see generally F.E. Faverty, *Matthew Arnold and the Ethnologist*, 1951: Arnold adopted some of the fashionable assumptions of his day. For a useful survey of 'European racist ideology 1850–1945', see Dr Michael Biddiss's Lister Lecture to the British Association for the Advancement of Science, delivered on 1 September 1975, and published in *Patterns of Prejudice*, Vol. 9, No. 5 (Institute of Jewish Affairs, London).
9. 'Matthew Arnold and the Jews', *Jewish Chronicle*, 29 November 1895. Jacobs wrote a much noted, at the time, obituary notice on Arnold in the *Athenaeum* (21 April 1888), published revised in his *Literary Studies* (1895).

8

Hermann Adler (1839–1911): Portrait of Jewish Victorian Extraordinary

In 1845 Nathan Marcus Adler arrived in London with his wife and children to take up his post as Chief Rabbi of the Ashkenazi Jews of Britain and her dependencies. This former senior rabbi of Hanover was born in that principality of which until 1837 the British monarch was hereditary ruler. He was a scion of a distinguished Frankfurt rabbinic line and married to a lady linked by family ties to elements in the Anglo-Jewish plutocracy.[1] He was a noted talmudist, staunchly Orthodox, university-educated, and familiar with the literature of the *Haskalah* as well as well-read in modern languages.

His second son, Hermann, was marked out from an early age as a prospective rabbi. From University College School he entered the University of London, where his course of study included English literature, history, philosophy, and Greek. His studies in Talmud and Bible had begun under his father and other tutors in London, including Barnett Abrahams, the Principal of Jews' College, whose son, Israel, became a prominent tutor at the College and was in the 1890s a leading member of the movement which led to the creation of the Liberal Synagogue. Hermann Adler was ordained as rabbi by the talmudic luminary and prominent *maskil*, Solomon Judah Leib Rapoport, in Prague, where he lived between 1860 and 1862 while a student at that rabbi's *yeshiva*.[2] Adler was to serve the College as tutor for many years in theology and homiletics successively. He followed his father as President of the College after long serving as Chairman of the Council.

Adler was a gifted student, serious-minded, with a deep sense of

21. Dr Hermann Adler (1839–1911), Chief Rabbi (1891–1911)

personal responsibility, which was reinforced by his life-long reverence for his father. He quickly made his name as a preacher, and in 1864 was appointed amid much fanfare as 'lecturer' or Minister-Preacher at the Bayswater Synagogue. The Great Synagogue in the City of London, adjoining the largest (albeit increasingly variegated) Jewish concentration in the land, retained its unique prestige. It was the synagogue of the Chief Rabbi, and the parent congregation of the Ashkenazi synagogues of Britain. But the lay power in the Jewish community steadily moved away from the older areas, in the wake of the fashionable migration of the governing and more affluent families, principally into central London and the West End. They exercised their sway in and from their new centres. During the tenures of Aaron Levy Green and Hermann Adler from the 1860s at the Central and Bayswater Synagogues respectively, those congregations established their pre-eminence; their lay heads constituted in practice the leadership of the Jewish community.

The young rabbi was sharply conscious of his status as the Chief

22. Aaron Asher Green (1860–1933)

Rabbi's son, and later as his perceived natural successor. He was compassionate without emotional excess, and markedly reserved in manner. He had a certain pride in the family connection with what had become the community's pluto-aristocracy; he tended to share that cadre's social outlook, while never understating his dismay over their lax standards of religious observance and the incidence of intermarriage. Devoid of pomposity and without any outward sign of personal self-importance, he yet evinced by language and public demeanour an unfailing awareness of, so to speak, the solemnity of his present and future office. His satisfaction with his role as a cultured English gentleman of Hanoverian birth and of eminent Frankfurt lineage was patent.

This sophisticated prelate-like figure was throughout his life treated almost universally with special deference. Yet history seemed with exceptional speed to antiquate him. There began on his death a lengthy communal debate on whether his office itself had had its day. In his closing years, the subject was discussed in tentative terms privately. Suddenly it became the major domestic communal issue, together with the questions as to what the criteria might be in the appointment of a successor for the new era, and what restructuring of the communal system might now be necessary.

The Jews in the East End of London, it was rightly said, were generally in no mood to accept any West-end-style successor, as was uneasily expected by the critics. Nor, it was reasonably thought, would the provincial rabbis. They were largely of Eastern European *yeshiva* training, and had come into greater prominence during Adler's tenure. They were considered unlikely to accept the chieftancy of any United Synagogue-dominated appointment at all, whatever might be the electoral formalities for provincial electoral representation.

In 1884 the *Jewish Chronicle* described the Chief Rabbinate as an institution which suited 'the temper of English Jews, with their moderate views and their love of union'. What was meant thereby was their presumed disinterest in theological or ideological dispute. 'The majority of English Jews', observed the editor, 'have no *shaaloth* to ask, at least of the kind usually connected by that word.' In an address at the St John's Wood Synagogue in 1905, in an already markedly different time, Adler frankly acknowledged the need for rabbis trained to respond to the expanding new Anglo-Jewish community. The impact of Eastern European *halachists* – usually influential members of the regional *batei din* – contributed to the raising of the query whether 'the Chief Rabbi's writ ran in the north'. A sharpening of divisions had also developed in London both on the religious 'right' and on the religious 'left' of the Chief Rabbinate, a condition which had increasingly preoccupied Adler whose pragmatic ambivalence satisfied the placid but not the critics.

Even the 'Jewish clergy', as the Adlerian ministers were characteristically called, who had long been demonstrably loyal to him, had become increasingly restive. Some were sceptical of the value of the centralisation of authority in the Chief Rabbinate. That office sometimes seemed to them to promote an unwelcome degree of inhibition against initiative. Some hoped to see the creation of formal machinery for more regular consultation. The new century seemed to add an acute contention and focus to an old-world complacency. In 1902, when the United Synagogue's proposals for the strengthening of Jewish life in the East End were under public scrutiny, Aaron Asher Green, the much-quoted Minister of the Hampstead Synagogue and nephew of Aaron Levy Green, amused some and embarrassed others by his public observation that there might well also be created 'a Whitechapel mission to convert the West End Jews to Judaism with a branch at Bayswater and Kensington, several in Hyde Park, and at least one in Hampstead'. It was a barbed comment on the lay milieu from which Adler drew much of his strength.

The new Principal of Jews' College, Dr Adolph Buchler, was aggrieved by Adler's advice to Lord Gorrell's recent Royal Commission on matrimonial law, that consideration should be given to the prosecution of rabbis who officiated at certain marriages[3] which were irregular in English law. Despite an increasing anxiety within the Jewish community over this practice, Buchler was far from alone in his dismay. He publicly chided the Chief Rabbi. Adler's view was thought to reveal less than a wholehearted respect for the *halacha*. Almost as important to some of the Orthodox critics was that Adler's action seemed to amount to an unseemly subservience to the lay heads of the United Synagogue and the Board of Deputies. The Board had often protested, in vain, against matrimonial unions, whether surreptitious or not, which would not be recognised by the law of the land. It was feared that certain lay attitudes on halachic

219

matters might impinge on the freedom of any new incumbent, in spite of and perhaps because of the fact that the Chief Rabbi was constitutionally the sole religious authority of the United Synagogue.

Some of the leading foreign-trained Talmudists were also Zionistically inclined. They doubted whether there would or could now be appointed any supporter of Zionism to this prestigious office. That doubt was shared by political Zionists of all schools of thought, secular or otherwise.

There emerged an unhappy feeling that the office had become a kind of dynasty. Now that there was no obvious successor, unlike the situation on the demise of Nathan Marcus Adler in 1890, it was thought that the future of the office was legitimately open to question. The new age bore little resemblance to the 1840s, and indeed considerable changes had further occurred since the 1880s in communal composition and aspirations. The death of Lionel Louis Cohen, the principal founder of the United Synagogue, in 1887 had deprived him of a mentor whose authority and communal skills might have assisted Adler in navigating the shoals of multiple controversy.

Adler was aware of the rapid and all-encompassing changes. He never reconciled himself to the nuances of the new age. He gave the impression to critics – and friends – of operating from a mixture of personal obduracy, an over-reliance on the say-so of the President of the United Synagogue, and an inhibiting concern over gentile opinion. He was a product of his own generation. He tended to equate duty with loyalty to his father's heritage; the communal interest with the retention of the status of his office; and prudence with the Anglicisation of those who had not been bred into its acceptance.

He became an English public figure, prominently associated with innumerable national public bodies, academic, philanthropic and social. Perhaps his successful nomination in 1890 by Dr Mandell Creighton, the Bishop of London, for membership of the Athenaeum, was in significance to him second only to his designation as Commander of the Royal Victorian Order, a title in the personal gift of the monarch.

His public relationships and friendships strengthened what in any event was an exceedingly strong influence upon him, namely the belief that the achievement of Jewish emancipation was a millennial episode, a desideratum of the ages. Its attainment in the

United Kingdom was held to be of particular importance because of British power and influence, and the hoped-for effect of its example. There was also, consequentially, the expectation of the greater influence of Anglo-Jewry in representations directed to improving the condition of Jewries abroad, in what was perceived to be their own slow and albeit sometimes painful journeys to an eventual like achievement. This long-term optimism gave way from time to time to mounting waves of genuine anxiety.

Anglicisation meanwhile came to be presented not only as expedient but also as a matter of moral principle. There was developed the idea that the inculcation of Judaism among Jews was a postulate of good citizenship. Irrespective of personal practice or attitude there was nurtured in some lay quarters the concept that public adherence to the faith of Judaism was a public duty and a requirement of self-esteem. Such themes carried weight within some families of longer residence. They were not, in any case, immune to the social fashion in some quarters of public religiosity.

Adler was a conscientious spokesman on behalf of these ideas and ideals. Some of his later critics dissented perhaps less from his conclusions than from his acceptance of the need to wear such philosophies on his sleeve. This self-consciousness involved a form of particularity which for him rested on the premise that more was indeed expected of the Jews than from others and that they had lessons to teach the wider society. These were conscious parts of his practical philosophy and inherent in his style of public relations.

The notion of having reached an historical goal affected everything. It was deemed self-evidently good and was not to be allowed to be endangered by what Adler construed as the mis-conceived pessimism of political Zionism. A classic example of the old optimism was that expressed by Frederic David Mocatta, the noted philanthropist in 1871. 'There is little doubt', he said 'that as civilization advances generally in Russia, the Jews will acquire an extension of their rights and that before the end of the century they will be on a perfect equality with their fellow-citizens.' Citing that passage to the Jewish Historical Society his junior kinsman Sir Alan Mocatta referred to the older Mocatta's sharp disillusion-ment in the 1880s (*Trans.*, J.H.S.E., 23, 1971, p. 6). Yet the accepted implications of the emancipation were not dislodged.

For Adler, a plain corollary continued to be the exercise of the

Jewish mission. He urged the importance not only of public Jewish acceptance of the mission but also of encouraging the express gentile acknowledgement of it. It was defined as nothing less than to raise the moral standards of mankind. If he thus reflected an old Jewish aspiration, it was also a prudential statement and an explanation. The doctrine was presented as justification for those forms of separation practised by Jews notwithstanding the call of the emancipationists to be seen as Englishmen. The doctrine of mission also provided a high-minded and seriously entertained reason for separateness when such was no longer postulated on any ground of nationality or by any material differences in the ways of everyday life.[4] Linked with these considerations was the moral imperative, as it was perceived to be, of pursuing as a communal priority the process of Anglicisation. This combined public philosophy lay behind many movements of opinion within the Jewish community and was at the root of many strains within Anglo-Jewish life, ranging from the long opposition to the establishment of a Jewish hospital to the yet wider opposition to political Zionism.[5]

The practical policy of being seen to encourage Anglicisation and westernisation went back at least to the 1840s. It included the promotion of secular education, the teaching of English and the positive discouragement of the use of Yiddish; the training in and the diversification of manual skills; and the fostering of a heightened sense of loyalty and gratitude to Britain. In 1897, in a typical address, Adler, in this instance perforce speaking in Yiddish, urged his audience, namely the Artillery Lane congregation in their conventicle off Bishopsgate in the immediate vicinity of the East End of London, and through them their resident fellow-foreigners, that they should 'lose no occasion of showing gratitude to the Government and people of this tolerant country'.

In the 1840s and for some time thereafter the object had been to demonstrate the justice of the emancipationist cause and the worthiness for it on the part both of the long-settled Jewish community and the more recent arrivals. In 1845 municipal office was opened to professing Jews and in 1858 likewise the House of Commons. Thereafter the aim was extended so as to prove by the Jewish responses thereto, that the emancipatory legislation had been in the public interest. In and from the 1880s the objects of the visible efforts towards Anglicisation were further extended to include, more strenuously than before, the disarming, so far as that could be done, of those at whatever level in society, who were hostile to the new immigration and critical of the newcomers, and who used these issues in their condemnatory campaigns against Jews generally. In and from the 1890s these objectives were joined by the aim of preserving the visibility of the Englishness of the Jews as against the peril of being regarded as caught up in political Zionistic affiliations. From time to time Adler invited rabbis abroad, in some areas from which immigrants were coming, to discourage departure for Britain because of pressure on housing and employment and the anti-Jewish agitation.

There was a certain inertia among Jews against proclaiming or publicly making explicit their sense of mission. This sprang in part from the evident particularist nature of thus exhibiting or declaring that element in the character and objectives of the Jewish Englishman. It evoked an historico-national, albeit also religious, separateness. In a long editorial (signed 'H', possibly the Rev. Isidore Harris) in the *Jewish Chronicle* in April 1886, the writer observed that 'Judaism is prone to shirk its mission … rather than assert it'. He described Jewish faith as having become 'a silent witness of the Revelation of which it is the human vehicle rather than its firm-voiced champion'. Many adhered to Judaism, the writer commented, 'through habit only', thereby (he averred) occasioning 'apathy'. There is, he added, 'a fear of being outspoken'. Adler knew of and understood this reticence and wanted an end to the apathy. He became the major exponent of the doctrine of mission and cultivated effectively the widening of the fashionableness of its public expression. The religiosity of its expression, the advocacy of good citizenship as part of the exercise of the mission, and the Anglicisation which was deemed a vital element in good citizenship (on the part of the anglicisers and those anglicised), all hung together. Each facet was typically Victorian in its identification of the public good with religiously motivated action and purpose. The Jewish Englishman was an acutely self-conscious Jew (whatever the degree or limits of his Jewish observance) and an even more sharply self-conscious Englishman. In this state of mind, it was inevitable that Jewish public relations should dominate communal policy, where the pursuit of image was often the substance.

It was against such a background that Adler's interest in

projecting Judaism to the wider society deepened. His avowed purpose was to present it as a faith which, when properly understood, placed it in the van of progress, a continuing civilising force entirely compatible with modern sophistication. This presentation was in his eyes a prime task of the 'pastorate'. In his installation address, significantly entitled 'The Ideal Jewish Pastor', this was his underlying theme.[5] Certainly the pastor should 'rally round the poor and uncultured [in the Jewish community], sympathise with them in their struggles, mitigating their troubles and advising them in their perplexities ...'. Virtually every phrase in that passage catches Adler's instinctive social outlook and characterises the man and his office in his day. In addition to these duties, Adler never ceased to dwell throughout his incumbency upon the importance of the public relations side of the ministerial task. At the Central Synagogue in October 1902, in a sermon later published, he urged the ministers 'to show that Judaism is in harmony with the best and healthiest aspirations of the day'. Their *esprit de corps*, which he did much to advance, was an instrument for the purpose of instilling in them an adequate regard for and skills in the presentation of Judaism to society, as well as enhancing the extent of the general ministerial engagement in the special tasks of day-to-day pastoral work.

He attached great value to what he called 'the visitation of the poor and infirm'. It was said of him that when at Bayswater he turned 'visitation into a fine art'. Before his appointment as Chief Rabbi he had organised cadres of elected men and women for the task. His references to this work in his installation address were not a pious formality. He organised visitation on a substantial scale and publicly laid down the rules and procedures. Domicillary visits were not to be made in order to look pious. The 'visitors' were to counsel and assist with the aid of the main welfare and educational bodies, to whom they should report. Yet without derogating from his humanitarian impulse, other practical considerations weighed with him, as may be gathered from his periodic public comments. 'Visitations' would have the following additional advantages. They would encourage self-help by facilitating industrial training with the help of the Jewish schools and the Board of Guardians; encourage regular attendance at those schools or the Local Authority Schools; preclude disenchantment with the synagogues; deter any temptation to socialism (or, even worse, 'anarchy'); forestall Christian conversionists; enable ministers and others to be seen to be engaged in organised efforts to anglicise newcomers; and help to bridge communal and social divisions. His observations throw much light both upon his era and his priorities.

Gentile examples were eagerly followed. These ranged from setting up the Jewish Lads Brigade[6] on the model of the Church Lads Brigade, to the foundation of Jewish Working Men's Clubs on the national pattern. There were proposals (such as by Norman Bentwich in 1904) for a Jewish Toynbee Hall in the East End of London, and for 'settlements' in the foreign Jewish areas of the capital by Jewish University graduates on the model of their Christian counterparts in areas of poverty and depression.

In such a spirit Adler addressed Jewish students at Cambridge in their Synagogue in February 1895. He pointedly entitled his sermon 'Israel's Deathless Mission'.[7] The following two passages enshrined his deepest convictions, fears and hopes.

> How can it be maintained that the mission of Israel is ended? While misery and ignorance still prevail on earth; while the deification of nature and of natural instincts is regarded as the sign of culture; while the fabric of social order is being gravely endangered by the dissemination of anarchist, communist, and revolutionary doctrines; while religious persecution, fanaticism, and intolerance prevail in their most hideous aspects, it surely cannot be maintained that Israel need no longer preach his message.

He declared, in what clearly was for him the heart of the matter,

> I ardently hope that when your academic career terminates, when you enter upon the several professions you have chosen, you will devote some time and thought to our brethren who toil in East London; that you will aid in bringing beauty and brightness ... knowledge and hope, to the poor overdriven workers; that you will help to mould and influence the minds of the young for purity and uprightness, for loyal allegiance to their faith. For be assured, ... the credit and honour of Anglo-Judaism are indissolubly bound up with the conduct and bearing of the industrial section of our population. By labouring in this field you prove that you are members of the kingdom of priests, you help in accomplishing the mission and proclaiming the message of Judaism.

Adler became the premier exponent of the entire philosophy of Victorian Jewishness. He presented his thoughts over the whole range of communal issues, with the knowledge that many of his addresses would be extensively reported, if not also separately published. His addresses were hortatory in tone, Anglican in their cadences, and directed to the enlightenment of the Jewish reading public on communal policy as he judged occasion required. His finely chiselled sermons were almost as likely to contain English or classical literary allusions as rabbinic or biblical citations. They were devotional, intellectually undemanding, usually topical. His esteem as a preacher endured. His style set examples. His slight lisp did not mar his impact. He characteristically declared on his appointments in 1891 that he had 'endeavoured to draw my mental nurture from the rich stores of our dear England's thought and learning'.

In his *Sketches of Anglo-Jewish History* (1875) James Picciotto, a pioneer Anglo-Jewish historian, wrote that 'the present generation has scarcely witnessed in its midst any stirring events. ... Social prejudices against Israelites are fast vanishing, and the Jews have rendered themselves completely worthy of their influential position.' These expressions of contentment on the part of a member of the Sephardi wing of the Jewish middle classes were soon belied by events, and indeed had begun to be so by the time Picciotto wrote. The new types of anti-Jewish agitation which came to the fore, were associated on the continent of Europe with heightened nationalism, inflamed political, social and economic tensions, and a sharp reaction against the advancement of Jews in society. Issues which in Adler's youth had been debated in Britain largely in the realm of prospects (especially in connection with opposition to the successive Bills in Parliament in the 1840s and 1850s for the opening of municipal office and Parliament to professing Jews) now assumed greater and practical prominence in public life. After 1881, and markedly in the 1890s, these subjects came into the sharpest prominence in the context of the campaigns against the immigration.

The resulting acute Jewish self-consciousness in public relations involved frequent advice by Adler to his ministers to preach the merits of a low profile for Jews. One of Adler's longest synagogal speeches was delivered at the consecration of the newly built synagogue for the West Ham Jewish community in Earlham Grove in 1909. The congregation had been established in 1907 as one of the outlying affiliated units of the United Synagogue in the eastern regions of London, with the object of encouraging the movement of Jews out of the crowded areas of the East End. It consisted largely of small shopkeepers and workers in traditional Jewish trades. The question which the Chief Rabbi posed to the assembled congregation was how 'to silence hostile criticism' of the Jews.

Adler's direct and simplistic remedy was through what he called 'righteousness'. He devoted the major part of his address to its definition. The speech constitutes a vignette of the times as seen through his eyes, and of himself. The definition included loyalty to faith and country, and honest dealing with fellow-citizens. He went on: 'You must be on guard against making yourselves conspicuous in the streets, at places of entertainment, or at the open windows, by a loud tone of voice, by showiness of dress, by violent gesticulations and the absence of quiet and reserve ...'. Yet this eloquent mixture of rabbinic anxiety and patronising condescension may not have seemed out of place to many in his captive and respectful audience.

Adler made many public declarations against Jewish involvement in usury and against bad landlords. This was part of what he regarded as the public duty which devolved upon Jewish spokesmen to make manifest the character of Judaism and indeed the purpose of Jews in society. A series of law cases involving Jewish moneylenders and allegations of unconscionable interest had attracted wide publicity. It was not until the Moneylenders Act of 1900 that any serious restraint began to be imposed upon the trade. The practice was far from limited to Jews but they had a disproportionate and prominent presence in the business and they dominated the public vision of the subject.

It is noteworthy that in his traditional 'ethical will', Adler's father had included an injunction against excessive rates of interest. When *The Times* reported on his will in 1891, the only specific provision which it cited was this injunction, together with the deceased's description of usury as an evil which 'still constitutes the malignant cancer' among Jews. The Adlers were not speaking of banking or merchant finance. Hermann Adler's frequent attacks on the charging of excessive rents belong to the same area of thought, as also did his regular public identification of Judaism with social reformism.

In addition to his humanitarianism, he deemed it important in the context of the new freedoms enjoyed by Jews and their advance in public life, that they should be seen to be engaged in works of social amelioration, Jewish and general. This, he considered, would testify to the outward-lookingness of the modern Jew, his civic attachment, his abandonment of the ghetto in spirit, and, in particular, his eagerness to set moral and social standards.

Within the Anglo-Jewish leadership there was a puzzled unease over the new kinds of antisemitism at home and in Europe. In spite of the prevailing sense of the considerable success of Jews individually in society and in business, spectres were raised which Adler had long sought to dissolve without success, but which now had about them a new air of confidence and an unsettling expansion in impact. The achievement of emancipation had been gained on the basis of the Jews as a community of faith, a religious communion. Any form of secular Jewishness would have seemed to Adler's generation a contradiction, and in any case a challenge to the 'terms', so to speak, on which the Jews had entered western society. What would be the purpose of any forms of distinctiveness if the grounds thereof were not of a religious nature? To some, the political Zionist movement seemed bound to raise the issue.[8] It was represented as offering to enemies of the Jews evidence of alleged international Jewish designs and lack of patriotism. Adler was acutely sensitive to these considerations. Likewise his fear of and his repeatedly expressed hostility to socialism were compounded as far as Jewish socialists were concerned, by his no less sharp concern lest their secularity might add some colour to the image of the rootless international Jew, the antithesis of the ideal which he strove to mould, to serve, and to delineate in the actuality of Jewish life.

The Tory champions of restriction on alien immigration always had amongst them a leaven of crude, irrational antisemitism. But the restrictionist campaigns also reflected a continuing puzzlement over the nature of Jewish kinship and the objectives of Jewish separateness. The aliens question in one way and another sharpened the persistent public debate on those subjects, at a time when it had been assumed that the debate was largely at an end.

Had not Mr Gladstone himself been heard to decry Disraeli's 'Judaic sympathies'? Was not Professor Goldwin Smith a prominent

228

Liberal as well as the most literary of English antisemites? How was one to react to Goldwin Smith's Zionist proposals? Were his suggestion that the Jews deserved their own independent country and his comparison of them in that regard to the Greeks and the Italians, to be welcomed or denounced? To the nineteenth-century mind, the insinuations were immense. What of Henry Labouchere, the radical journalist? How far did his vocal anti-Jewish prejudice reflect popular and intelligent opinion? Many a trade unionist was as opposed to the immigrant competitors for jobs as to the influence of the 'Randlords' and capitalists, including Jewish 'Randlords' and capitalists.

International Jewish kinship was a fact. The forms of its expression could be distorted by the unfriendly and sometimes misunderstood by the friendly. Even the messianism which figured on every page of the Jewish liturgy had to be explained so as to divest it of any breath of excessive particularism.

Adler was for long much troubled in particular by Goldwin Smith's repeated refrain that 'Israel ... is a power and an interest apart from the nations'. In repudiating Smith's surgical solicitude Adler deemed it essential to deal with his specific charge of 'tribalism'. Adler's efforts to display Judaism as a proselytising creed in distant times was in part directed against this attribution. His plea had an empty ring in his contemporary scene wherein any such idea was plainly incongruous. Adler likewise strove to explain the Jewish attitude to inter-marriage to which Smith and others made frequent reference, denying that it sprang from any racial or national spirit. He related it to the essentiality in his philosophy of being able to preserve and transmit Jewish faith and practice, if the Jews were to be true to their trust, in the interests of all.

Gentile observers were not alone in gleefully pointing out inconsistencies between the rejection of the Jewish national idea and the forms of liturgy in the prayer book issued under his father's and his authority. Zangwill ironically called for a revision of the Adlerian 'authorised daily prayer book', edited by Simeon Singer, the influential minister of the New West End Synagogue. Singer had at first given Herzl his personal encouragement, but his interest markedly waned when faced with the plans for the first Zionist Congress. Adler made his own position clear, never more so than in his public statement in April 1909 that 'since the destruction of the Temple, we no longer constitute a nation; we are a religious communion'.

Smith's barbed articles in prestigious journals gave a certain intellectual respectability to pejorative assessments of the roles of Jews in modern society. Jewish integration, zealously fostered by Adler within the limits of retaining and seeking to transmit his brand of Judaism, did not allay the continuing presentation in English literature of the Jews as foreign if not also intrinsically sinister.

Adler sought to dispel the idea that Judaism was a legalistic creed with little humanising content. That idea was not restricted to opponents of Jewish emancipation. In this context criticism of the practice of *shechita* became a special target of his attention. The modern Jewish defence of *shechita* in England began in the 1870s and 1880s. It took the form of a series of papers in the medical journals by Dr Ernest Hart, the joint editor of the *British Medical Journal* and chairman of the National Health Authority. His principal collaborator was Dr Henry Behrend, a prominent member of the Council of Jews' College and a close friend of Adler.

These papers were followed by a long address by Adler in November 1893 (later published and widely circulated) to the national conference convened at Church House, Westminster by the Church of England Sanitary Association. His paper, entitled 'Sanitation as Taught by the Mosaic Law', dealt with various sections of biblical law, including the dietary laws, and the rabbinic require-ments relating to *shechita*. He stressed the 'moral' and 'disciplinary' sides of the argument, as well as presenting a meta-historical context for the ordinances. The favourable response to his speech was assisted by the literal acceptance of the words of scripture by many in that audience.

'It is a great mistake,' Adler later declared, 'to suppose that religion concerns itself exclusively with the intellectual, moral and spiritual nature of man and that its single purpose is to obtain salvation for the soul hereafter.' He thereby indicated his own and the general Jewish dissociation from those strands of Christian thinking which traditionally concentrated on ways of earning salvation or of testing or manifesting the receipt of 'divine grace'. Some critics had fathered these ideas on Judaism. Adler sought to redress the balance.

His example and exhortations greatly encouraged the already

expanding practice of addresses by Jewish scholars of all grades, including widely-read laymen, to all kinds of gentile bodies on Jewish subjects, especially historical and religious. They were often lengthily reported, particularly in the local press. The *Jewish Chronicle* frequently commented upon the effects of these encounters. They tend, observed the editor, 'materially to increase the estimation in which the Jews are held by members of other denominations'. Such laudation reflects much of the spirit of the Jewish middle classes in the Victorian age.

Adler never entirely abandoned the Victorian idea that knowledge was likely to induce virtue and rationality, nor the related assumption that technological advance was likely to be conducive to wider happiness. The power of the spoken and written word to dispel prejudice was widely believed in.

In April 1887 at a meeting of Ministers in London under his jurisdiction, convened by Adler, he invited them to consider the preparation and publication of 'a hymnal' for the synagogues. His practical interest in music for the synagogue was in part genuinely based on aesthetic considerations. He was no less motivated by his wish to enhance the impact of the synagogal service upon the devotional inclinations of the congregants. The state of devotion was a ceaseless subject of widespread criticism, notably in the Jewish press. Adler believed, as did his father, that the level of congregational openness to influence through the service would be raised by the encouragement of a degree of solemnity and uniformity. He saw in synagogal music a means of establishing these qualities. He was impressed by the results of Sephardi precedents and also by the fame of Charles Kensington Salaman's liturgical compositions for the Reform congregation. In addition he was aware of the increasing use in Cathedrals and churches of new compositions or revised renderings of the Christian hymnal, which were purposefully directed to enhancing the dignity and deepening the effect of the religious services.

Arising out of the deliberations of the meeting of April 1887 and under the expert guidance of Francis Lyon Cohen,[9] there emerged two volumes of liturgical scores of which Cohen was the senior editor and which were published under Adler's authority. At the service in the Great Synagogue on 19 June 1887 to mark the Queen's golden jubilee there was an organ prelude and orchestral

23. Francis Lyon Cohen (1862–1934)

accompaniment composed by the Chazan of the Synagogue, Marcus Hast, Cohen's father-in-law. Anglican-style solemnity and formality were unmistakable features of the system which Adler strove to evoke. At his request the organ was used at the synagogue service on the occasion of his installation in 1891. *The Times* in a somewhat reverential report of the proceedings, significally noted the reservations of some of the Orthodox of an older school in regard to that instrumental aid whose use was deemed by them to be pursuant to Christian example. Early in his tenure at the Bayswater Synagogue Adler had disallowed the use of an organ in the synagogue.

Adler would refer to the Jewish community as 'our communion'. At the Chief Rabbinical electoral conference in 1891, Adler's nominator in an unopposed election was Benjamin Cohen, brother of the principal founder of the United Synagogue. He referred to the Chief Rabbi as 'the head of our Church'. Adler's reaction is not recorded. These English expressions jarred or puzzled some critical observers. It is no accident that it was during his tenure – certainly by 1905 – that the Great Synagogue began to be referred to by Jews, without any sense of anomaly, as the Cathedral Synagogue.

On Sunday, 20 June 1897, there was a special service at the Great Synagogue to mark the Queen's diamond jubilee. It featured a mixed choir of men and women. The *Jewish Chronicle* doubted whether 'the introduction of female voices added to the impressiveness of the Service', and added more grimly that 'the innovation ... has caused great heartburning among a large section of the ordinary worshippers at the synagogue ...'. It became clear that the Chief Rabbi, who addressed the congregation, was perturbed by the innovation. His authority, commented the editor on 2 July 1897, had been 'flouted' both by the introduction of a mixed choir and by the closure of the synagogue on the preceding Sabbath to enable decorations to be put in place on that day. Following 'plain speaking' by the Chief Rabbi, the warden, Abraham Rosenfeld, who assumed responsibility for the arrangement of the service, resigned, later resuming office. His controversial decisions were said to be against the wishes of the congregation (*Jewish World*, 9 July 1897). Adler's views were not shared by a significant section of the United Synagogue's lay leadership. At comparable special services at the Central and New West End Synagogues, there were mixed choirs, as well as at the North London and East Synagogues, and in Brighton and Portsmouth. What the *Jewish Chronicle* described as 'bickerings' over the issue at the Great Synagogue, were symptomatic not only of the more 'advanced' opinions held by Rosenfeld and in other influential lay quarters, but also of the readiness to exercise in specific matters an instinctive sense of *de facto* primacy by the lay heads over the religious. Mixed choirs had for some time been and continued to be a divisive issue whose significance went beyond the choristers' enclosure.[10]

On 18 June 1897, the *Jewish Chronicle* wrote: '... in every sphere of life English Jews are able to go in and out among other Englishmen without feeling or arousing any estrangement on account of their race or religion. It is only in England and in the England of our days that this has been possible. ... We have become Englishmen ... our constant effort is to anglicise our community. ... without damage to our religion.' While Adler would have shared these sentiments and aspirations, the practical implications which he drew therefrom fell short of those which were drawn instinctively or as a matter of policy by his principal lay colleagues. Yet by those who regarded him and them as excessively 'assimilated', he was viewed as their compliant representative.

In 1897 Lucien Wolf wrote his celebrated paper on 'The Queen's Jewry'. In that work, which long contributed to the received wisdom of his many Anglo-Jewish acolytes, Wolf did more than reflect the spirit in which the Jewish emancipationists and their children remembered the campaign for emancipation and the years which immediately followed. He preserved for those who wished it, that body of hopes and priorities by which later representatives of that layer of communal opinion ordered their communal affairs. The paper is both a record of history and in itself an historical record.

Writing therein on the mid-century religious divisions, Wolf comments that now 'in all essentials – the Anglo-Jewish community is absolutely united'. Neither the fathers of the Federation of Synagogues (founded in 1887) nor the members of the *Machzike Hadath* (founded in 1891) nor any of their immediate institutional predecessors would have taken that view. Nor would every member of the United Synagogue or of the West London Synagogue of British Jews have regarded Wolf as entitled to carry poetic licence as far as that. There were divisions. Wolf's point was that the old antagonisms had become blunted under the impact of the social bonds between the established 'right' and the no less socially established 'left'. Adler's westernised orthodoxy, and English Reform, shared a common English placidity and the common English predilection for the avoidance of sharp ideological debate. In his term 'The Anglo-Jewish community', Wolf did not include the newer and growing foreign element.

A point of criticism against Adler was his reluctance to institute facilities for the training and ordination of rabbis. Jews' College formally adopted the right of awarding the rabbinical diploma in 1883. Yet his reticence remained. The presumed formal right of Ministers of all ranks to call themselves 'The Reverend' undifferentially, compounded the Chief Rabbi's failure to show enthusiasm for the hard-fought innovation of 1883. Indeed he sometimes formally conferred the title of 'Reverend' on Ministers as he did with A.A. Green and Moses Hyamson on their first ministerial appointments at Sheffield and Swansea respectively in 1884.

The 'foreign' Rabbis regarded the official negative communal attitude towards the provision of Talmudic education, as at best an Anglo-Jewish eccentricity. Jews' College did not meet their requirements. It suffered from two weaknesses. The first was that whatever communal differences arose over educational policy or ministerial training, the College was the instant object of criticism from one side or the other. Sometimes those differences related to the kind of community which it was felt should be nurtured. Secondly, the College became and, as though by a settled tradition, remained a Cinderella in terms of the financial resources made available to it. There was a deeply-rooted habit of thought within the Anglo-Jewish leadership that higher Jewish study was not a priority, nor meritorious of major endowment, least of all rabbinic study. These factors long reacted upon one another as mutual cause and effect. Debates at the Council of the United Synagogue on the nature and extent of that body's subventions and financial commitment to the recruitment and training of the ministry at the College, consistently revealed a degree of financial 'prudence' which in practice differed little from an uncomprehending meanness.

A writer in *The Times* on 13 January 1912 described 'the Chief Rabbinate clauses' in the United Synagogue's Deed of Foundation and Trust as having established 'an absolute autocracy'. Adler's reluctance was fortified by his conviction that the ordination of rabbis was within his personal province – it was a prerogative which he used sparingly. Simeon Singer, who had received the rabbinical diploma from renowned rabbinic hands at the Vienna *Beth Hamedrash*, chose, out of deference to Adler and the prevailing system, not to make public use of the title. His son-in-law, Israel Abrahams, wrote in his *Memoir* of Singer (1908), that his receipt of the rabbinical diploma 'did much to oust the nondescript "Reverend" for Rabbi'.[11]

The public provision of elementary and secondary education, following upon the Education Acts of 1870 and 1902 respectively, was bound to affect Jewish policy. One of the main fields affected was that of Jewish day school education. By an instinctive reaction – as well as through the impact of the education legislation – it became Jewish communal policy not to plan for more Jewish day schools. The clearest formulation of the attitude was offered by Sir Samuel Montagu, later the founder and long-term President of

24. Israel Abrahams (1859–1925), Liberal Theologian and
Reader in Rabbinics at Cambridge

the Federation of Synagogues, on a public occasion at the New West Synagogue in November 1884, of which he was a prominent member. 'Let [the children]', he declared, 'be taught Hebrew and the elements of Judaism at home or in religion classes'. The revealing phrase 'religion class' was coming into vogue in its modern connotation, namely in reference to part-time classes attached to synagogues, notably in the newer and more salubrious localities where Jews were to be found in London. Between 1883 and 1885 the first such classes were opened within the United Synagogue, the North London and the St John's Wood Synagogues being among the first.

The children, added Montagu, would then have 'sufficient intercourse' with their Christian friends, and that would mean, he stated, that 'narrow-mindedness would be "prevented"'. 'I am entirely opposed', announced this leading Orthodox spokesman, 'to general Jewish day schools except where there was a concentration of foreign Jewish poor.' Adler was not behind in advocating and elaborating upon the new policy,[12] which was out of tune with his father's earlier plans for middle-class Jewish day school education, and out of accord with later Zionist assumptions, preferences and efforts concerning Jewish day school education.

If Adler was unable to break through the inhibitions of those upon whom the finances for ministerial training depended, it has to be said that his own public emphases on what he deemed to be the ministers' prime tasks were not conducive to any encouragement of an extended curriculum or high scholarly aspirations such as might have satisfied the critics of prevailing standards. In the East End, and not only there, he was seen as a temporiser. In particular, the *Jewish Review*, founded in 1910 and edited by Norman Bentwich and Joseph Hochman (formerly Minister of the New West End Synagogue) was robust in its critical assessments of standards and the Adlerian system generally. It soon became an organ of the younger intellectuals.[13]

Augustus Khan was a notable educationist and a highly esteemed Inspector of Schools. In the *Jewish Review* in April 1911, in commenting on the Ministry, he pointedly observed that men of commanding personality who attained positions with real influence were the exceptions. The Council of the United Synagogue had recently adopted a report which stipulated that 'other requirements should not be sacrificed to the attainment of profound scholarship'. By 'other requirements' were meant in particular public relations, secretarial duties and acting as Reader. 'The combination', he wrote, 'of the offices of Preacher, Second Reader, and Secretary is quite peculiar to this country and at the same time Anglo-Jewry is distinguished unenviably by the low standards of qualifications of its Ministers and the non-existence [except in the case of Chevras and congregations of foreign Jews] of Rabbis.' Allowing for some exaggeration – there were by now a few Rabbis in the Ministry who were so called – Khan's point was difficult to controvert.

When in the following issue A.A. Green ventured to reply, he added a dramatic admission: 'One of the bitter regrets of the lives of the older generation of ministers', is 'that a fuller theological training was not provided. ... The centralisation of rabbinical functions in the Chief Rabbi was wrong to start with.' By 'theological' he meant 'rabbinic'.

Adler made his own thoughts sharply clear on 12 June 1911 at the second Anglo-Jewish Preachers Conference. He knew that he was close to the end of his life. 'A point that must press itself', he frankly observed, 'on every thoughtful mind is that a measure of decentralisation has become requisite.' It was an acknowledgement of the widespread support in his audience and beyond for a scheme for the 'district organisation' of provincial congregations which had been presented to the Conference by its standing committee. It envisaged in practice the creation or recognition of local *batei din*, a consequential increase in the number of rabbis in the ranks of Adler's body of Ministers, and a wider acceptance of the authority of the 'foreign' rabbis. J.F. Stern had long been a public advocate of decentralisation in the exercise of 'religious authority'. Adler, in expressing his approval in principle, had at first related the need to his inability through ill-health to engage in lengthy travel and 'prolonged' pastoral visits as hitherto, and to the growing number of Jewish communities and their diversity. He now went beyond such reasons.

Stern had already gone beyond those particular reasons in advancing the case. He called for a 'more democratic method' for meeting the 'necessities of the times'. Nor was he thinking of the provincial communities only. In reference to the United Synagogue, he added: 'I fail to see how it is possible for the union, such as it is, to hold together if a greater latitude and a wider scope for local option with regard to ritual than have hitherto been allowed, be not included in the changes that are inevitable when the question of the future constitution of the Rabbinate is under consideration.' He asked whether it was 'advisable in the interests of the community' and of the Rabbinate that 'the present autocracy should survive ...'. The proposals exceeded those of the Chief Rabbi. Opinions at the Conference on these issues were mixed, ranging from those of Dr Samuel Daiches, a senior lecturer at Jews' College, who advocated the 'abolition' of the Chief Rabbinate, to those who while favouring 'judicious' changes feared 'anarchy' if the more extended proposals were implemented.

Stern formally moved the adoption of the series of devolutionary and related recommendations made by the Conference's standing committee in January 1911. Parts of his address went beyond those recommendations. The Conference largely accepted those recommendations, falling short of Stern's own added proposals. The Conference declared that it regarded as 'of extreme urgency' the 'problem' of 'the future ecclesiastical administration of the community'. The standing committee was expressly authorised to confer with the 'lay leaders of the community' in order 'to secure early and adequate consideration of the question'.

Adler's death shortly after these proceedings delayed such a course. In any event the leaders of the United were not attracted to any scheme which either raised the prospect of the abolition of the Chief Rabbinate or weakened its authority. They understood, as well as Adler had done, the need on practical grounds to give public recognition to local *batei din*. The discussion was concerned with more than questions of jurisdiction. It touched on issues relating to communal structure, ministerial status, the standing of provincial communities, Jewish educational standards, local initiatives, and local options. If these questions did not impinge directly upon the constitutional role of the Chief Rabbinate within the United Synagogue, they did seem to its leaders to have a bearing upon the wider authority of that office and, possibly, if indirectly, upon the efficacy of the office in the metropolitan scene. Adler's illness, aggravated by the deaths of his elder brother, Marcus, and his own son, Alfred (of whom he had high hopes for a senior rabbinic

25. 'Jewish immigrants just landed', 1902

position), had not diminished the public discussion, respectful in personal terms though it largely was.

In 1880 the Jewish population in Britain stood at about 60,000. By 1910 this number had more than quadrupled, largely through Eastern European immigration. The community in Manchester rose from a few thousand to 30,000. The local Sephardi community (settled in Manchester since the 1860s) was the only Sephardi body outside London save for the small community in Ramsgate. The Jewish community in Leeds rose from about 3,000 to about 20,000. The third largest Jewish community outside London was that of Glasgow, which by 1910 totalled 11,000. By that date about 110,000 Jews lived in more than 60 communities outside the capital, many with their respective traditions, *esprits de corps*, and local needs. At that time the metropolitan Jewish community approached 150,000.

The growth of provincial centres was accompanied by an ever increasing emancipation of the larger communities from any subordination to lay leaders in London. Relations between the provincial communities and London were under constant scrutiny. Inadequate provision for collaboration was a standing cause for concern. The provincial tours of the Adlers did little to satisfy long-term requirements in the fields of education and the relief of the Jewish poor. The provincial communities themselves were in any event jealous of their independence, often in relation to one another as much as in relation to London. The Anglo-Jewish community was becoming a community of communities, and within each of them there were social and economic divisions, religious dissensions, and polemics over Zionism which were, at times, especially heated in London, but were no less familiar in provincial communities. A larger proportion of the Jews of Leeds belonged to the working class (mainly employed in the clothing trades) than in Manchester, with the longer residential record of its community, including in particular a prosperous Sephardi middle class (sections of which were engaged in trade with the Levant). The prominence of individual Jews in local government and philanthropy enhanced the sense of independence on the part of a number of provincial communities.

In 1904 Jacob Samuel Fox founded a pioneer Hebrew-speaking day school in Liverpool. The Bialystok-born Fox, between 1891 and 1904, edited the European Hebrew weekly, *Hamaggid*. The

26. Jacob Moser of Bradford (1839–1922)

school offered primary secular education and Zionist-inspired religiously Orthodox training for boys and girls. It belonged to the same genre of education as emerged in the larger Hebrew-speaking Talmud Torah founded by J.K. Goldbloom in the East End of London. The first English Zionist journal (*The Zionist Banner*) appeared in Manchester in 1910. The local Zionist society was founded in Manchester in 1896, the local Zionists later becoming the main Zionist group outside London. Likewise in Leeds, Bradford and elsewhere prominent Zionists were leading figures in local Jewish life and often exercised influence beyond their local confines.[14]

The provincial communities exhibited distinctive enthusiasms of their own. In Leeds in 1896 there was founded *The Express*, a Yiddish weekly whose local and nation-wide circulation grew. It was transferred to London in 1899. The first provincial Yeshiva was that of Sunderland (1905), founded a year after the Etz Chaim Yeshiva in the East End of London. Comparable institutions were to follow in Manchester (1911), Liverpool and elsewhere. In provincial eyes the Chief Rabbi was essentially a London personality with predominantly London interests. The German-Jewish textile merchants who founded the Jewish community of Bradford appointed as the Rabbi of their Reform Synagogue in 1873 a German-Jewish scholar, Joseph Strauss, who was to serve that congregation for half a century. Strauss became a vocal and influential Herzlian Zionist. A fellow Zionist and member of his Synagogue was Jacob Moser, industrialist, philanthropist, and Mayor of Bradford.

In the tense and often strident exchanges between Jewish employers and Jewish employees in London and Leeds in the competitive garment and textile trades,[15] Adler was seen by the workers (whatever might have been his personal sympathy with their conditions of labour and terms of employment – and unemployment) as, virtually by definition, remote from their concerns. In this sphere (not only among workers who were socialists), as in other areas of discord, he seemed an arch-representative of established authority, an appearance which served to aggravate the sense of disenchantment with his title and his office.

Everywhere there was an expanding diversity. Everywhere new and independent institutions – synagogal, educational, charitable, political – had come into being. The old framework within which Adler had grown up belonged to a comparatively compact community and had served ends and priorities which were now everywhere under enquiry. Many of the new institutions, ranging from the Jewish trades unions to the Federation of Synagogues, represented outlooks and objectives which were less attuned to satisfying the fashions and the condescensions of the West End. Adler could not easily feel at home with them, nor they with him. In particular there was posed with growing acuteness the question whether the old structure could be made to respond at one and the same time to the pressures from the religious 'right' (mainly but not entirely from outside the United Synagogues) and the religious 'left' (to some extent found also within the United Synagogue).

Adler believed that the degree of unity secured by his office, although in some respects formal only, facilitated, if it did not guarantee, the continuity of his brand and style of Orthodoxy. He was disturbed by the waning of interest among the younger echelons of the more affluent sections of Jewish society, including the families of his father's associates who had founded the United Synagogue. He was keenly aware of the declining hold of religion in those quarters. It is ironic that the distinctively English and accommo-dating Judaism which he was regarded as personifying, satisfied neither the rigid right nor the 'ideological' left, and was losing something of its appeal among potential successors to the leading lights of his own power base.

It did not occur to him that his patronising speech and habits or those of the lay and of parts of the religious leadership generally, could be thought offensive. Communal government by the old families continued to strike him as self-evidently desirable. The ceaseless public presentation of the Jews as loyal citizens was to him natural, wise and obligatory. He regarded his frequent deprecation of the use of Yiddish as a necessary warning of the social mischief which he, like Lord Rothschild, the President of the United Synagogue, thought would flow from what they held to be an outlandish and segregationist barrier to integration.

All these and related features of his thinking were connected with his conviction that his community had been and was provi-dentially fortunate in its particular evolution. Its many-sided English characteristics comforted him, including what he saw as an aversion to extremism and the presumed tradition of respect for establishments generally. Under him the Chief Rabbinate became

27. Sir Leon Simon (1881–1965) as a young man in Manchester

28. Selig Brodetsky (1888–1954) as Senior Wrangler, 1908

an English institution as well as a Jewish office. The continuing and widening disillusionment with the office within sections of the Jewish community (which became increasingly evident during the turbulent interregnum after his demise), was stayed by his successor and by the outbreak of the First World War. But some of the disenchantment remained a communal feature. Adler was remembered by some with veneration, but by others with a combination of respectful mirth and some incredulity. Neither estimate does him justice.

The *Jewish Review* showed great interest in the Leeds conference of Orthodox Rabbis from the north and from London outside the United Synagogue, in 1911. The conference, which had a vocal Zionist element, came out strongly in favour of Jewish day school education and of raising educational standards generally in the community. Somewhat paradoxically the rabbis had some vocal allies in the younger generation of Anglo-Jewish *litterati*. That growing element of university-trained Jews, often children of comparatively recent immigrants, were affected by the Hebrew revival of the day. They were impressed by the intensity of Jewish enthusiasms in the East End and were concerned at the comparative placidity and Jewish educational minimalism among many of the Jewish middle-class families in the newer areas of residence. They had rallied to the banner of political Zionism. Men such as Leon Simon and his brother Maurice, Herbert Bentwich and his son Norman, Israel Zangwill, Harry Sacher, Leonard Stein and Selig Brodetsky, looked upon the system of communal government of which Adler was the centre, as exercising an enervating influence both on Anglo-Jewish intellectual life and on the future of the Jewish quality of the community. They deplored the widening rift between the outlook of the communal leadership and the preferences of the new community in terms of the Zionist impulse and the growing distaste over the oligarchic system. They saw Adler as both a victim and an executant of an outmoded system.

Adler could not fail to be affected by the vocality and standing, current and potential, of this intellectual 'opposition'. When towards the end of his life he advised the leaders of the United Synagogue to cause to be appointed a successor who could unite East End and West End, it was indirectly a plea motivated in part, if not mainly, by his anxiety that these newer forces should not be lost to the future leadership of the community at large. They were potentially a significant element in the task of consolidating a disparate community. Adler had come to acknowledge that he had outlived his epoch.

NOTES

1. Adler's first wife, Henrietta, Hermann Adler's mother, was a member of the Worms family, whereby Hermann was a cousin of Henry de Worms, the first Lord Pirbright and thus related indirectly to the Rothschilds. A more direct connection with an Anglo-Jewish lineage is that Nathan Marcus Adler was the great-nephew of David Tevele Schiff, Rabbi of the Great Synagogue from 1765 to 1792.
2. A. Schischa, 'Hermann Adler, Yeshiva Bahur, Prague 1860–62', (ed.) J.M. Shaftesley, *Remember the Days*, 1966, pp. 241–78.
3. David Englander, '"Quiet Marriage" among Jewish immigrants in Britain', *Jewish Journal of Sociology*, Vol. 34, 1992.
4. See Israel Finestein, 'Post-Emancipation Jewry: The Anglo-Jewish Experience', in his *Jewish Society in Victorian England*, 1993, pp. 154–81.
5. In one of his last major public addresses, delivered to the second Conference of Anglo-Jewish Preachers on 12 June 1911, Adler stated that 'all my thoughts on this theme have been concentrated in my [inaugural] sermon'. Although on that occasion in 1911 he was speaking of the qualities required of the 'spiritual head of our community' (namely the incumbent of his own office), it is clear that he was in effect commending his original formulation of the necessary attributes of 'ideal Jewish pastors'. Without expressly saying so, Adler endeavoured to present his own emphases and choices in thought and action as the model.
6. Sharman Kadish's centenary history of the Brigade was published in 1996.
7. Hermann Adler included this address in his published volume of speeches, *Anglo-Jewish Memories*, 1909.
8. In some anti-Zionist circles there was developed the concept that Jewish civil emancipation was or was to be deemed to be part of a reciprocal arrangement whereby the Jews thereafter were to be 'entirely English in thought', and that this precluded any attachment to political Zionism. Sir Philip Magnus (prominent educationist, former Reform minister and later Member of Parliament) gave characteristic expression to this outlook in his pamphlet (which had already been substantially published in the *Jewish Chronicle*) in 1909 in reply to a Zionist declaration made in that year by Jewish graduates of the Universities of Oxford, Cambridge and London. The Jews, he declared, should be as English in aspiration as those 'descended from ancestors who have mingled their blood with other Englishmen for generations'. While Adler would not have adopted Magnus's style of language or imagery, in substance

he differed little from that formulation. Zionist critics declared such notions to be influenced by what they dismissively called the 'contract theory' of emancipation. Claude Montefiore in his presidential address to the Jewish Historical Society in December 1899 (*Trans.*, Vol. 4) spoke approvingly of Adler's statements in *The Nineteenth Century* (July 1878 and December 1881), citing in particular Adler's comment that 'we are simply Englishmen or Frenchmen or Germans as the case might be ... . We regard all mankind as brethren ...'. Prominent among those who repudiated the idea of any 'contract' and rejected the suggestion that the emancipation was inconsistent with the Jewish national idea, were (in addition to some Orthodox rabbis outside the United Synagogue) Harry Sacher and Leopold Greenberg (the editor of the *Jewish Chronicle* from 1907 to 1930, who had been Herzl's representative in London).

9. Cohen (1862–1934) received his rabbinical diploma at Jews' College after holding a series of ministerial appointments in Dublin and London. His paper on 'The Rise and Development of Synagogal Music' on the occasion of the Anglo-Jewish Historical Exhibition in 1887 (published in *Papers Read* to the Exhibition, 1888) attracted much attention. He became Chief Minister at the Great Synagogue in Sydney in 1905. The current holder of that office, Rabbi Raymond Apple, has published a biography of Cohen (1994).

10. Adler, on grounds of *halacha*, disallowed the introduction of ladies into the choral singing at the foundation and consecration services of the Hampstead Synagogue, founded in 1892, but thereafter abided by that congregation's decision to engage mixed choirs at their regular services. He did so in order to secure and retain that congregation within the United Synagogue. He ruled against the appointment of Morris Joseph as Minister thereat because of his negative public expressions concerning the 'sacrifice' sections of the liturgy but accepted leading members of Reform (where Joseph became Senior Minister) in prominent positions on educational bodies under his authority. His denunciation of the Jewish Religious Union, the precursor of the Liberal Synagogue which he also publicly criticised, did not lead him to seek the withdrawal of such of those on the educational bodies as had moved into the Union or into the Liberal Synagogue. On the 'right' and on the 'left', these 'decisions' were seen as unsatisfactory tergiversations. Israel Abrahams retired from his teaching post at Jews' College on the establishment of the Liberal Synagogue of which he was a prominent supporter. 'To both East and West,' Adler declared in 1891, 'I appeal, let not your divergences of opinion lead to schisms ... discord and disruption.' His tenure was beset not only by what he called the 'extremes of the religious thermometer' but also by social, cultural and political divisions. In 1854 there was published a recent sermon by Adler's father entitled 'Solomon's Judgment', concerning the Orthodox–Reform disputes of that time. The elder Adler said, where the breach cannot be healed, 'let us agree to differ and let us have peace in our own camp. Why should you diminish your own strength ... your own vitality, without any real benefit to either party ...'. He said it would be better to improve schools and charities and 'put away anger and ill-feeling and be kindly affectioned to one another'.

The elder Adler at times found it a difficult prescription. So did his son in yet more turbulent times.

11. Hermann Gollancz, Adler's successor at Bayswater, felt obliged by the current situation to resort to rabbinic authorities in Galicia for his rabbinic diploma in 1897. Adler's failure to acknowledge the title was followed after public dispute, by Adler's acceptance and recognition. It proved to be a significant breach in the old system. In 1902 Gollancz succeeded Schechter as Goldsmid Professor in Hebrew at University College London and was knighted in 1923, the first rabbi to receive that award. His brother, Israel, was appointed Professor in English Language and Literature at King's College London and was knighted in 1930. Israel Gollancz was the principal public advocate for the recognition of his brother's title, which support proved to be a weighty factor in the persuasion of Adler.

12. The policy was defended less on educational grounds than on public policy. It was not only that Jews contributed to the rates and taxes by which the new Local Authority (Board) schools were sustained and which they were entitled to use, but it was seen as a kind of moral duty to use them. It would demonstrate the openness of the Jewish community in the new age, and show that the Jews wanted their children to know and be known by their peers in society. Whereas in 1895 the number of children at the Jewish schools in London (8,100) exceeded the number at Board schools (7,800), ten years later the respective numbers were 7,500 and in excess of 20,000. The changing proportions reflected in part the continuous migration from the East End, but also in part marked the growing preference for Board School education supplemented by part-time Jewish education. In 1905 more than 10,000 children in Board Schools in London received such education during school hours, as well as the many who attended classes after school hours on the school premises and a smaller number at Sabbath classes. These forms of supplemental education were provided by the Jewish Religious Education Board under the Chief Rabbi's authority. Adler shared the Jewish West End's anxiety over alleged insanitary premises which houses the *chedarim* and Talmud Torah centres favoured by some in the East End – as well as the alleged oppressive effect caused by the intensity of study after school hours. He was well aware of the inadequacies of the 'synagogue classes' which were arising in the newer areas of Jewish residence and the limitations of the Jewish tuition at some of the Board Schools. Efforts to improve standards were constrained by the lack of trained teachers and resources. The appeal of the J.R.E.B. in 1897 after its first full year since its reorganisation, reached only one half of its target. An example of the limited horizons of the day – set though they were around high ideals – was the Board's aim as defined by its President, Henry Lucas, a leading figure in the United Synagogue. The object, he stated at that time, was 'to prevent children from becoming converted to other religions or growing up atheists'. Jewish educationists in the East End had no confidence in the standards purveyed by the Board. It is noteworthy that a major reason for the secession from the Great Garden Street Talmud Torah in Whitechapel in 1895 was the use of English there as a language of instruction. Yiddish was preferred.

Out of that secession arose the Brick Lane Talmud Torah in the same locality which by 1900 was attended by 1,000 boys. In his presidential address at the annual meeting of subscribers to the latter in 1897, Chaim Zundel Maccoby, the leading religious spokesman of the Federation of Synagogues, stoutly defended the Talmud Torah system of education with its emphases on Talmud and *dinim*. He severely rebuked the J.R.E.B. to whom, he stated the East End would 'not entrust' its children. He referred to the J.R.E.B. as being composed of 'avowed Reformers and so-called Orthodox'. Claude Montefiore was prominent in its counsels. Ironically the Federation was at the time a contributor to the funds of the J.R.E.B. David Fay, Minister of the Central Synagogue in the West Central area of London and often the public champion of the causes and institutions sanctioned by or under the authority of the Chief Rabbi (including the J.R.E.B.), publicly upbraided Maccoby on the score of divisiveness. In significant terms he added that Maccoby had lived in England long enough (since 1890) to know that there had been a continuous effort on the part of 'English Jews' to avoid emphasis on differences. Clearly what to Fay was a vice was to others a virtue and a duty.

13. The *Jewish World*, founded in 1873 by George Lewis Lyon, had likewise been a consistent critic of the centralisation represented by the Chief Rabbinate. Among its sponsored causes was that of liturgical reform. In 1895 it conducted in vain a campaign for the amalgamation of the United Synagogue and the Federation of Synagogues, lest 'obstruction paralyse all the beneficial action for the improvement of our foreign brethren ...'. The deaths of Jacob Reinowitz (1893) and Bernard Spiers (1901) – Polish-born dayanim who had been useful links with the immigrants – had weakened Adler's authority among them. His decision, long urged by the *Jewish Chronicle*, to take up residence in Finsbury Square at weekends so as to be close by, was of limited effect. The *Jewish World* (and the *Jewish Chronicle*, especially under Greenberg) urged the need for some kind of federation or official association between the metropolitan synagogal bodies and provincial communities, particularly to promote Jewish education. Prominent among the advocates of such proposals was George Emanuel, the Minister of the Birmingham Hebrew Congregation. Adler's active interest in such proposals was limited (personalities and organisational *amour propre* apart) by the insufficiency of resources and the then lack of enthusiasm for such undertakings on the part of the successors of Lionel Louis Cohen, who died in 1887, within the leadership of the United Synagogue. Reinowitz came to be recognised as the 'halachic authority' of the Beth Din, of which he became a member in 1876. The number of *she'elot* submitted to him 'was exceedingly great': Eugene Newman, 'The Responsa of Dayan Jacob Reinowitz', *Trans.*, J.H.S.E., 23, 1971, pp. 22–33.

14. In January 1911 there was held in London a combined meeting of the Zionist Societies of the Universities of Oxford, Cambridge and London, addressed among others by Selig Brodetsky and Chaim Weizmann. Among those present were students and graduates who were or would become leading figures in their respective Jewish communities in London and in provincial cities. Adler had from time to time published speeches made by him on the subject of

'religious Zionism', as he called it, as distinct from any form of political Zionism. Brodetsky and his colleagues, like Weizmann, regarded Adler as an inflexible anti-Zionist. They did not regard his concern for bringing succour to Jewish residents in Palestine as Zionism. Adler had made a well-publicised visit to the land in 1885 when he distributed aid to recent Russian-Jewish immigrants on behalf of the philanthropic Russo-Jewish Committee in London, and toured the country: Shaul Sapir, 'From London to Jerusalem: Journeys of the Adler Brothers in the 1880s', in (eds) Yehoshua Ben-Arieh and Moshe Davis, *With Eyes Towards Zion*, Vol. 4, Praeger, 1997, pp. 58–73. For characteristic presentation by Adler, see his published address (at the North London Synagogue) entitled *Religious versus Political Zionism*, November 1898. For an appraisal of Adler's 'religious Zionism', see Rav (now Lord) Immanuel Jakobovits, 'If only my people ...', 1984, Ch. 15 ('The Attitude to Zionism of Britain's Chief Rabbis as Reflected in their Writings').

15. Peter Elman, 'The Beginnings of the Jewish Trade Union Movement in England', *Trans.*, J.H.S.E., 17, 1953, pp. 53–62; L.P. Gartner, *The Jewish Immigrant in England 1870–1914* (2nd ed.), 1973; W.J. Fishman, *East End Jewish Radicals 1875–1914*, 1975, and *East End, 1888*, 1988; Geoffrey Alderman, *The Jewish Community in British Politics*, 1983, in particular Ch. 4; and J. Buckman, *Immigrants and the Class Struggle: The Immigrants in Leeds 1880–1914*, 1983.

Glossary

aggada: 'narration', comprising folklore and ethical parable.

Ashkenazi(m): Jew(s) of central or eastern European origin.

Beth Din (batei din): Jewish religious three-judge court.

chazan: Cantor (often called Reader). Conducts synagogue service. Sometimes combined with office of preacher.

cheder (chedarim): 'room(s)'; old-style religion classes, sometimes in makeshift premises.

chevra (chevrot): chaver, 'friend' or 'associate'; small congregation, often arising from society founded for religious study, sometimes motivated by shared local origins.

Damascus Affair: Jews falsely charged in Damascus (1840) with ritual murder of a monk, followed by anti-Jewish violence and Jewish deaths. Mission by Sir Moses Montefiore (in association with French/Jewish leader, Isaac Adolphe Crémieux) to independent 'viceroy' of Egypt (then in control of Damascus) and to the Sultan (who later resumed control of the City), resulted in release of imprisoned Jews and the Sultan's public repudiation of all such charges against the Jews.

Dayan(im): Judge(s) of a Beth Din.

Haham: 'sage'; rabbinic authority of Sephardi community.

halacha: the corpus of Jewish law.

Haskalah: 'enlightenment'; the new Jewish learning cultivated among westernised Jewish scholars in the eighteenth and nineteenth centuries, of which Moses Mendelssohn is usually deemed the principal initiator.

kosher: of food, 'fit' to consume according to the laws of *kashrut* in Halachah.

maggid: 'preacher', usually of aggadic material, notable for length and emotional content and style of presentation. Mostly in Yiddish.

Machzike Hadath: 'upholders or strengtheners of the law'; an independent Orthodox society (later a congregation) founded in Whitechapel in 1891 mainly through dissatisfaction with perceived standards of *kashrut* observed under jurisdiction of the Chief Rabbi. The congregation, under whose auspices the large Brick Lane Talmud Torah operated, joined the Federation of Synagogues in 1905.

Mahamad: Executive Committee of Spanish and Portuguese Synagogue.

maskil(im): Exponent(s) of Haskalah.

matzo: Unleavened bread required for the Passover.

Mishna: see Talmud.

misheberach: opening phrase of prayer for welfare of persons 'called up' to the Reading of the Law in Synagogue, sometimes accompanied by announcements of donations respectively made by them to the congregation and other causes.

Sephardi(m): 'Sepharad', Spain; Jew(s) of Iberian, North African or Middle Eastern descent.

Shabbat Hagadol: 'the great Sabbath'; the Sabbath before the Passover.

Shabbat Shuva: 'the Sabbath of "Return" or Repentance'; the Sabbath between Rosh Hashanah (New Year) and Yom Kippur (Day of Atonement).

she'elah (she'elot/shaaloth): 'question(s)'; request to rabbi for ruling or guidance on Jewish religious practice.

shechita: Halachically correct method of animal and bird slaughter for food.

Talmud: 'study', 'teaching'; record of centuries of debates and laws laid down in the academies of Palestine and Babylonia, completed about 500 CE, the basic text of which was the *Mishna* ('teaching'), namely rabbinic enactments, based on biblical injunctions and evolved over many generations, and completed in the academies of Palestine by about 200CE.

Talmud Torah: 'study of the law'; institute for Jewish religious instruction, usually larger and more formally organised than the *cheder*.

Yeshiva: 'sitting'; institute for rabbinic study, mostly of Talmud.

Select Bibliography
(exclusive of works named in Notes to text)

Israel Abrahams, *Simeon Singer* (a memoir), 1908.

Geoffrey Alderman, *The Jewish Community in British Politics*, 1983.

—— 'The British Chief Rabbinate; a Most Peculiar Practice', *European Judaism*, 23, No. 2, 45–58, 1995.

Noel (Lord) Annan, *Leslie Stephen: the Godless Victorian*, 1984.

J. and B. Baum, *'A light unto my path': The Story of H.N. Soloman*, Edmonton Hundred Historical Society, 1981.

Norman Bentwich, *Solomon Schechter*, 1938.

—— 'The Social Transformation of Anglo-Jewry, 1883–1960', *Jewish Journal of Sociology (J.J.S.)*, 2, 16–24, 1960.

Chaim Bermant, *The Cousinhood*, 1971.

—— *Point of Arrival*, 1975.

Eugene C. Black, *The Social Politics of Anglo-Jewry 1880–1920*, 1988.

Gerry Black, 'The Struggle to Establish the London Jewish Hospital', *Transactions*, Jewish Historical Society of England (J.H.S.E.), 32, 337–53, 1993.

David Cesarani (ed.), *The Making of Modern Anglo-Jewry*, 1990.

Bryan Cheyette, *Constructions of 'The Jew' in English Literature and Society: Racial Representations, 1875–1945*, 1993.

Kenneth E. Collins, 'Jews in the Scottish Universities in the Age of the Enlightenment', *Bulletin of Society for the Social History of Medicine*, 38, 14–16, 1986.

—— 'Jewish Medical Students and Graduates in Scotland 1739–1862', *Transactions*, J.H.S.E., 29, 1988.

—— *Second City Jewry: The Jews of Glasgow in the Age of Expansion 1790–1919*, 1990.

Peter Elman, 'The Beginnings of the Jewish Trade Union Movement in England', *Transactions*, J.H.S.E., 17, 19, 53–62.

Todd Endelman, 'Communal Solidarity among the Jewish Elite of Victorian London', *Victorian Studies*, 28, 3, 491–526, 1985.

David Englander, 'Anglicised not Anglican: Jews and Judaism in Victorian Britain' in G. Parsond (ed.), *Religion in Victorian Britain*, 1, 235–73, 1988.

David Feldman, *Englishmen and Jews: Social Relations and Political Culture 1840–1914*, 1994.

W.J. Fishman, *East End Jewish Radicals 1875–1914*, 1975.

—— *The East End 1988: A Year in a London Borough Among the Labouring Poor*, 1988.

L.P. Gartner, 'Urban History and the Pattern of Provincial Jewish Settlement in Victorian England', *J.J.S.*, 23, 1, 37–55, 1981.

—— 'Emancipation, Social Change and Communal Reconstruction in Anglo-Jewry 1789–1881', *Proceedings of American Academy for Jewish Research*, 54, 73–116, 1978.

—— 'Eastern European Immigrants in England: A Quarter-Century's View', *Transactions*, J.H.S.E., 29, 297–309, 1988.

Bernard Harris, *Anti-Alienism, Health and Social Reform in Late Victorian and Edwardian Britain*, 1993.

Ursula Henriques (ed.), *The Jews of S. Wales: Historical Studies, Patterns of Prejudice*, 31, 4, 3–34, 1977.

Colin Holmes, *Anti-Semitism in British Society 1876–1939*, 1980.

Bernard Homa, *A Fortress in Anglo-Jewry: The Story of the Machzike Hadath*, 1953.

—— *Orthodoxy in Anglo-Jewry 1880–1940*, 1969.

A.M. Hyamson, *Israel Abrahams: a Memoir*, 1940.

Louis Hyman, *The Jews of Ireland to the Year 1910*, 1972.

David S. Katz, *The Jews in the History of England 1485–1850*, 1994.

A.J. Kershen, *Uniting the Tailors: Trade Unionism and the Tailoring Workers of London and Leeds 1870–1939*, 1995.

B.A. Kosmin, 'Localism and Pluralism in British Jewry 1900 to 1980', *Transactions*, J.H.S.E., 28, 111–25, 1984.

Ernest Krausz, *Leeds Jewry: Its History and Social Structure*, 1964.

Tony Kushner (ed.), *The Jewish Heritage in British History*, 1992.

Ruth P. Lehmann, *Hermann Adler, Chief Rabbi of the United Hebrew*

Congregations of the British Empire 1891–1911: A Bibliography of His Published Works. Reprint from *Studies in the Cultural Life of the Jews in England*, Vol. V (Folklore Research Center Studies, 1975).

S.S. Levin, *A Century of Jewish Life*, 1971.

Vivian D. Lipman, *The Anglo-Jewish Community in Victorian Society*. Reprint from *Studies in the Cultural Life of the Jews in England*, Vol. V (Folklore Research Center Studies, 1975).

H.C.G. Matthew, *Gladstone 1809–98*, 1997.

A.N. Newman, (ed.), *Migration and Settlement*, 1971.

—— (ed.), *Provincial Jewry in Victorian Britain*, 1975.

—— (ed.), *The Jewish East End 1840–1939*, 1981.

—— (ed.), *The United Synagogue*, 1977.

—— 'The Chief Rabbinate and the Provinces 1840–1914' in Jonathan E. Sacks (ed.), *Tradition and Transition*, 1986, pp. 217–26.

Louis Olsover, *The Jewish Communities of N.E. England, 1755–1980*, 1980.

Harold Pollins, *Economic History of the Jews in England*, 1982.

Cecil Roth, 'Educational Abuses and Reforms in Hanoverian England', in his *Essays and Portraits in Anglo-Jewish History*, 1962.

—— 'The Chief Rabbinate of England' in I. Epstein, E. Levine and C. Roth (eds), *Essays Presented to the Chief Rabbi, Dr. J.H. Hertz*, 1942, pp. 371–84.

W.D. Rubinstein, *History of the Jews in the English-speaking World: Great Britain*, 1995.

Bill Williams, 'The Anti-semitism of Tolerance: Middle-class Manchester and the Jews 1870–1900' in A.J. Kidd and K.R.V. Roberts (eds), *City, Class and Culture*, 1985.

Index

Sephardic community, 28, 45, 58–60,
226; divisions, 15–16; rabbinate, 65,
67; records, 29; services, 53–4, 63
sermons, 53–7, 66–7, 73
Shabbat Hagadol, 73
Shabbat Shuva, 73
Shaftesbury, Lord, 142, 162, 202
shechita, 230
Short History of the English People,
141
siddur, 65
Sidgwick, Henry, 118–20
Simon, Sir John, 90
Simon, Sir Leon, 244–5
Simon, Oswald, 211
Simonson, Michael Hart, 77, 178
Sinai and Palestine (Stanley), 206
Singer, Simeon, 73, 168, 229, 235
Sketches of Anglo-Jewish History
(Picciotto), 178, 226
slavery, 192
Smith, Goldwin, 89, 116–17, 228–30
Smith, James Edward, 104
society, secular, 200
Society for the Cultivation of the
Hebrew Language and Literature,
170
Society for Hebrew Literature, 132
Sola, Aaron de, 8, 10–11, 46 (n. 6)
Sola, D.A. de, 12, 59, 170–5
Solomon, Henry, 28
Solomon, Samuel, 28–9
Southampton Synagogue, 24, 186
Spanish and Portuguese Congregation,
95, 171
Spinoza, Baruch, 208–10
Stanley, Arthur, 116, 123, 146,
206
Stanley, Edward, 201
Status of the Jew in England, The
(Egan), 150
Stein, Leonard, 245
Stephen, Leslie, 117–18
Stern, J.F., 238–9
St John's Wood Synagogue, 218
Stirling, James, 120
Sunderland, 16, 43, 242
Sussex Hall, London, 50 (n. 29), 184
Sylvester, J.J., 110–11, 127–8, 132,
136 (n. 13)

Tait, Campbell, 116, 208
Talmud, 5, 9, 25, 75, 87, 170, 185,
204, 211, 220, 235
Tamworth Manifesto, 109
Tancred or the New Crusade
(Disraeli), 157–8
Theodores, Tobias, 5, 175
Thesiger, Sir Frederick, 148
Thirlwall, Connop, 106–8, 206
Times, The, 5, 90, 108, 112, 125,
144, 147, 179, 227, 232, 235
Tocqueville, Alexis de, 197
Tomaso, Father, 180
Touro, Judah, 162
Toynbee Hall, 225
Tract for the Times (Bradshaw), 153
Tractatus Theologico Politicus
(Spinoza), 209
tracts, 11–12
Trinity College, Cambridge, 106, 110,
117–19, 129, 131–2
Trinity College, Dublin, 105, 118
Tübingen University, 198
Turton, Thomas, 107

Unitarianism, 104
United Synagogue, 17–18, 31, 35, 73,
94–5, 219–20, 227, 232–5, 237–8,
243, 245
Universities Tests Act (1871), 115, 127
University College School, 40, 98
University of Durham, 121, 123
University of London, 71, 75, 105,
127
usury, 227
utilitarianism, 1

Van Oven, Barnard, 180
Voice of Jacob, 9–10, 19, 30, 54, 57,
62, 87, 90, 92, 127–8, 148, 154–5,
177, 182

Waghorn, Thomas, 148
Walpole, Spencer, 122
Wellington, Duke of, 109
West Ham Jewish community, 226
West London Synagogue of British
Jews, 6, 25–6, 71–3, 234
West Metropolitan Jewish School, 128
Western Jewish Free School, 32–3